# A FIERCE GLORY

As Alexander Gardner was developing this photograph, the delicate, glass-plate negative cracked. But the photographer recognized that he'd captured something extraordinary, a Lincoln portrait that revealed his essential humanity like nothing else. The cracked plate only added to the image's power, evoking the president's struggles to reunite a fractured nation.

# A FIERCE GLORY

## Antietam—
## the Desperate Battle
## That Saved Lincoln and
## Doomed Slavery

# JUSTIN MARTIN

DA CAPO PRESS

Da Capo Press
Hachette Book Group
1290 Avenue of the Americas, New York, NY 10104
dacapopress.com
@DaCapoPress, @DaCapoPR

Printed in the United States of America
First Edition: September 2018

Published by Da Capo Press, an imprint of Perseus Books, LLC,
a subsidiary of Hachette Book Group, Inc. The Da Capo Press name and logo
are trademarks of the Hachette Book Group.

The Hachette Speakers Bureau provides a wide range of authors for speaking events. To
find out more, go to www.hachettespeakersbureau.com or call (866) 376-6591.

The publisher is not responsible for websites (or their content) that are not owned
by the publisher.

Editorial production by Christine Marra, *Marra*thon Production Services.
www.marrathoneditorial.org

Book design by Jane Raese
Set in 11-point Bell

Library of Congress Cataloging-in-Publication Data has been applied for.

ISBN 978-0-306-82525-5 (hardcover); ISBN 978-0-306-82526-2 (ebook)

LSC-C

10 9 8 7 6 5 4 3 2 1

TO MY COUNTRY—

FIERY, FRACTIOUS, TRANSCENDENT

# CONTENTS

# Maps

# Author's Note

John Mead Gould spent a single day at Antietam. The battle consumed him for the rest of his life.

On September 17, 1862, Gould fought on the Union side as a lieutenant with the 10th Maine. Pandemonium reigned in the close confines of the Western Maryland valley where the battle took place. So many soldiers fired so many weapons with such urgency that the field was soon shrouded in smoke. The air swam thick with projectiles; the sheer volume of noise was overwhelming. Cannon rumbled; bullets zinged. There were the shrieks of falling men, the whinnies of falling horses.

In a matter of minutes, a quarter of Gould's regiment (71 of 277 men) went down, wounded or killed. General Joseph Mansfield stumbled past, his coat flapping open to reveal a crimson bloom spreading across his abdomen. Gould helped him from the field. The general soon slipped out of this world. As Gould would recall: "how *mighty* easy it was to get killed or wounded that day."

He felt fortunate to escape such a fate. Antietam would forever hold the distinction as his most intense, most terrifying battle, even though he would fight in many others and would remain in the army until the end of the Civil War.

Afterward, Gould went back to his hometown of Portland, Maine. Before enlisting, he'd worked as a bank teller. He returned to his old job and remained for the rest of his working life, receiving a single promotion—to cashier. Along the way, Gould got married and raised three children. He taught in Sunday school, amassed a collection of buttons. Antietam never strayed far from his thoughts.

He wrote letters to his fellow Union soldiers, seeking to plumb their memories, hoping to resolve lingering mysteries. What enemy regiments had fired on his Maine boys on that fateful day? What were the exact spots where his various comrades went down? Where did General Mansfield fall?

As the years passed, the old hostilities faded. Gould began to write to his one-time adversaries. On the subject of Antietam, he found them even more expansive than his Union comrades. "Confederates are the better correspondents," he noted. Gould made repeated visits to the battlefield, sometimes even walking the grounds in the company of graying former Rebels. On one visit, he was able to "snap a little kodak," a testament to changing times, the passage of the years. On another visit, he stayed for an entire week, ceaselessly walking the field, trying to make sense of that now-distant day.

Some mysteries he managed to solve. Gould grew confident that he had identified the precise spot (near a distinctive boulder) where General Mansfield fell. Other questions would dog him to his grave. "Those things make me lie awake at night," he once stated.

Gould passed away on January 1, 1930, aged ninety, at his house on Pearl Street, the same one he'd lived in as a boy. Although seven decades removed from Antietam, he'd ever remained in its thrall.

Gould was far from alone in his obsession. After all, he was only one among the multitude who fought at Antietam; many a man would relive this day for the rest of his years. This particular battle was simply different from others: more heated, more savage, more consequential.

At Antietam, over the course of a single day—still the most lethal in American history—the death toll for the combined Union
and Confederate forces was more than 3,500 men. This dwarfed
everything that had come before. Such landmark Revolutionary
War battles as Saratoga and Yorktown routinely resulted in fewer
than 100 deaths among the Colonials. The entire War of 1812
(which, belying its name, stretched over nearly three years) produced 2,200 US fatalities, a lower number than occurred during a
mere twelve hours at Antietam. Even such days of infamy as Pearl
Harbor and September 11 saw fewer Americans killed.

But Antietam was a desperate contest; that's why the death
toll wound up so high. The battle occurred during an especially
demoralizing stretch for the Union, filled with military losses, one
coming fast on another. The Confederacy had grown increasingly
bold, to the point of marauding into Maryland. This was the war's
first Southern incursion into Northern territory. Achieve victory
here, and the Rebel army could storm across the Union, striking
who-knows-where—Philadelphia, Baltimore, even Washington,
DC. No place would be safe. "Jeff Davis will proclaim himself
Pres't of the U.S.," panicked a New Yorker. "The last days of the
Republic are near."

Even if an attack on a major city didn't immediately follow, a
Confederate victory promised to create havoc in the North, polit-
ically and otherwise. The Rebel plan was to sow chaos and more
chaos, though some of the ploys were remarkably subtle. For example, a Union loss at Antietam might prompt skittish Northerners to vote Lincoln's Republican Party out of Congress. In would
sweep the Democrats, a conservative party circa 1862, and one that
might be more amenable to a negotiated settlement of the war.
Perhaps a Democrat-controlled Congress would bypass Lincoln,
inviting the Confederacy to rejoin the Union, slavery intact. It's
no accident that Antietam happened in September: a primary goal
was to disrupt the Union's midterm elections, only weeks away.

But this represented only one in a range of possible bad out-
comes envisioned by the Rebels. By invading Maryland, the

Confederacy had cooked up a diabolically clever scheme. Victory at Antietam promised to open up a number of different routes to the same outcome: an end to the war, substantially on Southern terms.

While the North may have been down, it could not be counted out. In the event that the Union won the battle, Lincoln was standing by with a sly secret plan of his own, what he referred to as his "last card."

The stage was set for an epic showdown.

---

I've chosen to tell this story in a different way, avoiding minutely detailed descriptions of troop movements (a standard feature of so many battle accounts) in favor of rendering a larger picture.

As such, I've also chosen to weave Lincoln more deeply into the narrative. Existing Antietam titles tend to go light on Lincoln. After all, the president was in Washington during the fighting—offstage, as it were. Nevertheless, he anxiously awaited news, any news, out of Western Maryland. If the Union somehow eked out a victory, managed to break its losing streak, Lincoln was prepared to play that final card, issuing his Emancipation Proclamation. Declaring enslaved people free in the regions still in rebellion could be expected to shake the Confederacy. It might invest the Union war effort with a new and nobler purpose.

September 17, 1862, was a day of high drama both on the battlefield and in Washington. Thus, I've elected to cut back and forth between the two locales. While my account covers the fighting in full, attending to Antietam's legendary (and horrific) sites of conflict, including the Cornfield, Bloody Lane, and Burnside Bridge, the story also circles back to the president.

Threading Lincoln more thoroughly into the tale also sets up revealing contrasts between the president and the commanders of the respective armies: the Union's George McClellan and Robert E. Lee for the Confederacy. Together, these three men form a dramatic triangle. Naturally, the rival generals felt an antipathy for one another. But Lincoln also stood in opposition to *both*. Ironically, for a victory at Antietam, Lincoln was dependent on McClellan, a Democrat who held him in withering contempt. Only a few months earlier, the impertinent general had gone so far as to demand that the president keep his "radical views" on slavery out of the war effort.

As for Lee, the contrast with Lincoln is stark. The Virginia-born general and Indiana-bred president make for perfect foils. Nevertheless, standard Antietam books attend to Lee almost exclusively as a military leader. The focus tends to be on Lee as brilliant battlefield tactician (oh, was he ever!), while the thorny issue of Lee-as-slaveholder gets conveniently ignored. Lee's views on the so-called peculiar institution as well as his treatment of his own slaves belongs in any modern take on this nineteenth-century event.

Clearly, Antietam's outcome resonated far beyond the field. The battle was even a proving ground for some world-changing ideas in such areas as medicine and photography. Antietam was the first genuine test for Union doctor-in-chief Jonathan Letterman and his notions about how to deliver faster, better care to wounded soldiers. Yes, the death toll was staggering; were it not for Letterman's innovations, it would have been even higher. Likewise, this was the first engagement in which Clara Barton realized her ambition of going directly to the treacherous front lines and rendering aid to soldiers in need. For her heroism at Antietam, she earned the sobriquet that would stick with her for the rest of her life: "Angel of the Battlefield." Meanwhile, Alexander Gardner took a series of photographs that was nothing short of revolutionary, expanding the art form, forever changing the way the public perceived warfare.

Indeed: as America's bloodiest day, as a battle with enormous military and political stakes, as a crucible for bold new ideas, as a watershed event involving such towering figures of the age as Lincoln and Lee, as the occasion for the Emancipation Proclamation—for all these good reasons—Antietam was a more critical battle than Gettysburg. Yes, Gettysburg receives more glory. Lee's second incursion into the North precipitated a marathon three-day contest that broke the Confederacy. After Gettysburg, the Rebels never again posed a substantial offensive threat, never really recovered, although the Civil War would slog along for another two years.

However, the case for Antietam is simple and irrefutable. Had its outcome been different, there would have been no Gettysburg.

Lastly, a note on sources: More than 100,000 soldiers were present at Antietam and sometimes it seems that every last one of them provided a written account. The result is an embarrassment of research riches: letters, diaries, articles, books, regimental histories, and official battlefield reports written by officers. I drew on these sources generously. Some of them furnished details and information that is published here for the very first time. In the story that follows, whenever you encounter a quotation, or a description of a regiment charging up a hillside, or even a seemingly picayune detail, such as the manner in which a soldier fell after being struck by a musket ball—it comes from this vast trove of sources.

I'm especially indebted to Colonel Ezra Ayers Carman, who fought at Antietam with the 13th New Jersey. As an obsessive battle chronicler, he outranks even John Mead Gould. Carman also spent his entire postwar life corresponding with former soldiers, both Union and Confederate. He drew on these exchanges to create a series of fourteen maps, invaluable to anyone seeking to understand the way the battle unfolded. He also wrote an 1,800-page account of the day's fighting, only recently published after sitting for decades in the Library of Congress. Carman's pioneering work is the point of departure for any student of the battle.

I also made numerous trips to Antietam National Battlefield, considered one of the most meticulously preserved Civil War sites. So much of what was there that September day in 1862 remains intact today: farmhouses and cornfields, bridges and country lanes, even so-called witness trees (trees that were alive during the battle). Walking the field in the company of a series of supremely knowledgeable guides brought history vividly to life for me. It proved essential to the task of recreating this harrowing and momentous battle.

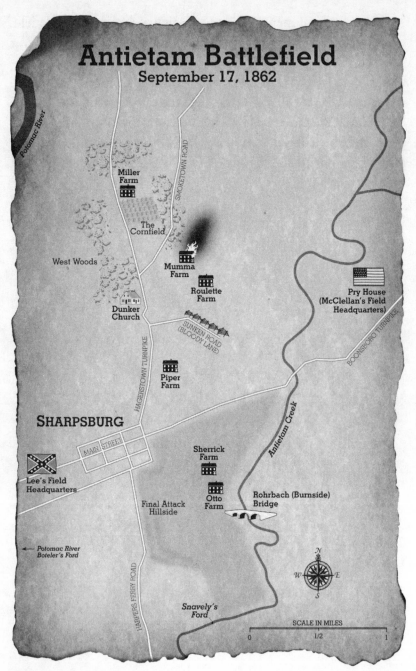

# Antietam Battlefield
## September 17, 1862

Potomac River

SMOKETOWN ROAD

Miller Farm

The Cornfield

West Woods

Mumma Farm

Roulette Farm

Pry House (McClellan's Field Headquarters)

Dunker Church

SUNKEN ROAD (BLOODY LANE)

HAGERSTOWN TURNPIKE

BOONSBORO TURNPIKE

Piper Farm

Antietam Creek

SHARPSBURG

MAIN STREET

Sherrick Farm

Lee's Field Headquarters

Otto Farm

Rohrbach (Burnside) Bridge

Final Attack Hillside

← Potomac River Boteler's Ford

HARPERS FERRY ROAD

N
W E
S

Snavely's Ford

SCALE IN MILES

0        1/2        1

© JIM MCMAHON

# CHAPTER 1

---

# HELL COMES TO
# SHARPSBURG

*It was the small hours* of a late-summer night. Light drizzle was falling. Cloud cover blotted out the moon and stars. Facing each other, separated only by a short stretch of utter darkness, were two hushed armies.

Soldiers from both sides lay upon the hard ground, out in the open, without tents. Already, they were arranged in tight battle formation. That's how they slept—those who managed sleep—shoes off, uniform on, or at least partially so, loaded muskets tucked at easy reach beside them, prepared to spring into action at daybreak. Some were lucky enough to have bedrolls, providing modest cover against the elements. Others stretched out on the damp earth.

Because a campfire is a deadly giveaway, none burned. A scattered few had been lit at nightfall by Confederate soldiers in fortunate positions, on the lee side of little knolls, shielded from the enemy. By this late hour, though, the last embers of these fires had died out. The world had been whittled down, leaving only this: a pair of fearful and recumbent armies in a night so black that, as one soldier marveled, "you could make a hole in the darkness with your finger."

Hunger was a given. Earlier in the evening, many of the troops had eaten modest uncooked dinners—apples and corn the standard Rebel fare, and for Federals, salted beef and hardtack, a biscuit as stale as it was bland. One Union regiment had been reduced to a meal of dry coffee grounds and sugar, taken in small pinches like chewing tobacco. Some Rebels had eaten less than that.

The damp air conveyed the smell of clover trampled underfoot—a home scent that should have brought comfort. But the sense of foreboding hung too heavy. Earlier, there had been none of the usual camp jollity, no antics or sing-alongs or stories spun out in leisure. Soldiers had used the final glimmerings of daylight to write letters to parents and sweethearts. With nightfall, the men clung to their last sightings of the enemy—much too close. In the darkness, crouched officers moved from soldier to soldier, seeking out green recruits and those they'd identified as potential problems. The officers whispered reassurance, but also, through clenched teeth, hissed stern commands: *Do not bolt from the ranks tomorrow! Don't you dare let down your fellow soldiers!*

An entire Union division marched to the ammo wagons in the middle of the night to pick up eighty rounds. That was twice the normal allotment, doled out with a telling somberness. This was no ordinary night of campaigning. For the veterans, it bore little relation to previous eves of battle. Some soldiers had fallen into fitful sleep, while others lay awake, minds racing. "When was the fight to begin? How long would it last? Who would win?" wondered Thomas Livermore of the 5th New Hampshire. "Was I to be killed, to be torn with a shell, or pierced with a bullet? What was death? How quickly should I be in the other world if I were killed?"

The night was filled with odd sounds and unexplained happenings—portents maybe. A Union soldier tripped over a pet dog sleeping beside its owner, then lurched into a stand of muskets. The stand collapsed with a clatter. It was like a stone hitting the calm surface of a pond, as ripples of anxiety traveled outward then outward. For both sides, there was such a palpable sense of presence, as if untold thousands of enemy soldiers had merged in the darkness into a single hulking entity, breathing, watchful, and horrifyingly aware.

In the small hours, a dreamy sense of unreality set in. Entire combat corps arrived from god-knows-where and tromped in columns among the reclining soldiers, searching out their spots in the next day's battle scheme. These late arrivals had been instructed to muffle their canteens and other metal objects to avoid making noise. No matter: amid the quiet, thousands of marching footfalls sufficed, creating the din of a rolling avalanche. Yet the uneasy stillness always returned. Soon the pickets, standing watch in forward positions, could once again hear the enemy's whispers, even make out the words. Sometimes the tension grew too great. A picket would open fire, muzzle flashing. A shot might be fired in return. But these little exchanges quickly died out. There was no sense shooting into pitch blackness.

Deep into the night—so deep that no one could even place the hour with certainty—some Rebel horses grew spooked and broke free from their ropes. The animals stomped and whinnied, then ran in maddened circles as soldiers tried to corral them, before breaking for the rear and galloping off across the darkened countryside.

And then—all too soon—the first faint hint of daylight appeared. It was roughly 5:45 A.M. A Rebel artillery team at Nicodemus Heights used the paltry glow to home in on a Federal position, then sent a cannon shell arcing across the dawn sky.

———

The two opposing armies, it turns out, were arrayed against each other in a broad and beautiful valley. The location was Western Maryland: incredibly, Confederates had undertaken an invasion of the North. The valley was about twenty miles in width, its western border formed by Appalachian peaks, obscure in the distance. Nearer loomed the valley's other border, South Mountain, a purplish hump in the hazy dawn. From here, the land sloped gradually down, moving through gentle undulations, forming little hollows and hillocks, as if South Mountain was melting across the valley floor. The morning was cool, about 65 degrees, although the temperature would rise by about 10 degrees as the day drew on. The air was moist and close, thanks to the previous night's drizzle. Little wisps of fog gathered in the low-lying areas.

Meandering through the landscape was the Antietam, still anonymous for another few hours, just a simple creek blessedly free of any larger significance or associations. Its water assumed a deep green hue in the overcast dawn; its movement seemed languid, though this could be deceptive. "Antietam" means "swift flowing water" in the language of the Delaware Indians. Its banks, rising in some spots at a severe pitch, were thickly grown with silver maple, sycamore, and witch hazel. The Antietam wended across the valley floor, spanned by a series of stone bridges, before emptying into the Potomac, which formed the border between Maryland and Virginia.

This was farm country, some of the finest on the continent. In geological terms, the valley is what's known as a karst, a stretch of land undergirded by eroding limestone and shot through with subterranean springs. In practical terms, this meant a ready water supply, nutrient-rich soil, and crops growing in near-biblical abundance. Large stone houses, home to prosperous farmers, dotted the countryside, their spreads staked out by wooden zigzag fences. On this September morning, the wheat had been harvested and the fields lay in stubble. Some of the corn had been harvested, too, while select fields stood man-high and nearly ripe. Most farmers set aside an acre or so as orchards, furnishing peaches for preserves and apples for cider. These fruits were plump and ready to pick. Crisscrossing the countryside were turnpikes and farm lanes, including the remnants of the Great Wagon Road, which had stretched during the early 1700s from Philadelphia to Augusta, Georgia. The presence of good roads, necessary in peacetime to transport the region's agricultural bounty to market, was one of the reasons that in wartime, two armies had converged in the area.

Situated on a plateau about halfway between Antietam Creek and the Potomac was Sharpsburg, also enjoying its final moments of being unknown to a larger world. The town was ninety-nine years old, founded before the Revolution, and named after Horatio Sharpe, a governor of colonial Maryland. During its earliest days, Sharpsburg had entertained dreams of grandeur. In 1790, the town fathers wrote a couple letters to President Washington, touting the six good springs and twenty-one wells, making it ideally suited to serve as capital of the fledgling nation. More recently, the biggest diversion was a public examination of Sunday school students, held each winter. Sharpsburg was laid out in a simple grid, consisting of eight streets, including Main Street, High Street, and one with no name at all. Its 1,300 residents included masons, millers, potters, broom makers, and glassblowers.

The citizens of this section of Western Maryland (both the Sharpsburg townfolk and the farmers in the surrounding countryside) were of varied heritages, with ancestors hailing from England, Scotland, France, and Switzerland. Irish workers had built a stretch of the C&O Canal near Sharpsburg, and many had decided to settle in the area after the job was done. A number of the farmers were of German stock. Among them were some belonging to a religious sect called the German Baptist Brethren, also known as Dunkers. The name stemmed from their belief in total-immersion baptism, a practice that had invited persecution in the Old Country, driving them to emigrate in search of religious freedom. The Dunkers were modest in dress, abstemious in habits; they refused all alcohol, opposed slavery, and were unwavering pacifists. In the New World, they conducted their full-on baptisms in Antietam Creek without incident.

For all the diversity, however, the citizens shared one thing in common. Almost none were present on this Wednesday morning. The previous Sunday, there had been fighting in the passes that run through South Mountain. During services, the boom of cannon had rattled church walls and shaken the congregations. Then, over the past few days, residents had looked on fearfully as the two huge armies staked out positions in their valley. This had served as fair warning. As the countryside had filled up with soldiers, it had emptied of civilians. Almost everyone had fled to safer spots.

Samuel Poffenberger, owner of eight horses, had wrapped feed sacks around their hoofs, the better to muffle their footfalls, then hidden them away in his cellar. Joseph and Sarah Sherrick had hidden $3,000 worth of gold in a stone wall on their land. Then, these and other farmers had made arrangements to wait out the battle in other locations. The Mumma family, husband Samuel, wife Elizabeth, and ten children, sought refuge in a church about five miles north of Sharpsburg. Left behind, their chickens, hogs, and sheep had free run of their 186-acre farm. A number of residents were hiding out in the Killiansburg Cave near the C&O Canal.

Still, a handful of people, for whatever reason, decided to stay put. An old couple who had lived in Sharpsburg all their lives concluded they had no place else to go. If they were to die here, so be it. The morning found the Kretzer family, with five children, huddled in the basement of their large house on Main Street, along with a number of their neighbors.

Even as that inaugural Rebel shell continued on its path, a Union artillery team sent its opening salvo arcing through the dawn sky.

From high in the air, from a shell's-eye view, it would have been possible to get a fuller picture of the two opposing armies. As a consequence of having a larger force, about 55,000 men, the Union front was longer, arrayed north to south over the countryside for about three miles. (By midday, an additional 16,000 Federals would arrive on the battlefield.) The Confederate force was considerably smaller, roughly 35,000, and these men were arranged along a front that also stretched north to south, for about two miles. Because the Union force was larger, it curved around the Rebel front, pressing down on it, threatening.

From the air, the two armies would have looked a bit like a pair of upside-down *J*'s, the smaller one representing the Rebels.

The troop placement represented the strategic cerebrations of the opposing commanding generals, the Union's George McClellan, and for the Confederates, Robert Lee. Newspapers had only just started using his middle initial, a practice he never much cared for. It was still early in the war, and the two men hadn't yet hardened in the public imagination into the myth-bound figures that they would become.

Over the preceding days and hours, McClellan and Lee had arranged their combat units with obsessive care. Although the reality of battle was about to shatter their every plan and assumption, here at the outset a kind of balance had been achieved. The Rebels were the invaders, yet they were in a defensive position. They possessed the smaller force, yet it was more experienced; more than half of Lee's men had been in at least three major battles, while McClellan's army brimmed with green recruits. Lee, drawing on his engineering experience, had also staked out the superior higher ground, along the ridges running to the east of Sharpsburg. Over much of the field, winding Antietam Creek lay before the Confederates, providing a barrier to Yankee attack. Several miles to the rear was a spot for fording across the Potomac, an exit route back into Virginia if needed.

Two huge armies required considerable support. Behind the front lines could be found surgeons, blacksmiths, farriers, saddlers, weapon-repair specialists, commissary sergeants, couriers, and clerks. The Confederate support apparatus consisted of a set of wagons gathered mostly on the outskirts of Sharpsburg, though some were on the near-bank of the Potomac. The supply train for the better-provisioned Federal army stretched back for a few miles toward South Mountain, culminating in a wagon-jam on the streets of Keedysville.

Behind the lines, there were thousands of draft animals, a mix of horses and mules. In a predictable ratio, the Union had two for every one employed by the Confederates. The draft animals were hitched to wagons: ambulance wagons, caissons filled with ammunition, commissary wagons with food for the men, and forage wagons piled high with hay—to feed the animals themselves.

Yet down on the ground, from the soldier's-eye view, none of this colossal design was evident. Look to one's left: a comrade. Look to the right: another comrade. Down here, the quirks and idiosyncrasies of the field loomed large. In the battle ahead, every feature of this landscape would come into play: the gently rolling topography, the farms and farmhouses, the country lanes, the wooded stands of oak and hickory, the steepness of the Antietam's banks, the width of its bridges, the outcroppings of limestone, everything. Even something of seemingly no matter, such as the fact that select cornfields remained unharvested, was about to assume extraordinary import.

From a soldier's-eye view, it would also have been evident that the participants in this clash weren't merely men in blue versus men in gray. For this battle, as with others in the war, the uniforms had a distinctly individual, often local flavor. After all, soldiers served in companies that had originally formed in their communities. They mustered into service together, drilled together, and ultimately fought and died together. This reality was often reflected in their manner of dress.

This was certainly the case for the Bucktails, country boys and seasoned hunters mostly drawn from north central Pennsylvania, representing such counties as Cameron, McKean, and Tioga. As a reminder of home, each attached the tail of a deer he had shot to his kepi cap. The 14th Brooklyn eschewed Federal blue altogether, opting instead for flamboyant uniforms featuring scarlet pants tucked into white gaiters each adorned with seven gold stars. That added up to fourteen stars—*the fighting 14th Brooklyn.* Then there was the 1st United States Sharpshooters, an elite regiment outfitted in green, the better to blend into the foliage as they plied their deadly skill. The regiment had been organized by Hiram Berdan, who had unyielding requirements. To be selected for his regiment, a man had to be able to shoot with accuracy, consistently, over a great distance. Berdan himself was considered the finest shot in the land. During a marksmanship exhibition, in an episode that had become legendary, he'd put a bullet through the right eye of a Jeff Davis effigy at 600 yards.

The Rebels sported an even greater variety of un-uniform uniforms, though in their case, one of the primary reasons, per usual, was scarcity. The war had severely dampened trade between Europe and the South. That, coupled with the region's paltry manufacturing base, meant that gray cloth was hard to come by in quantity. Uniforms were often handmade, resulting in a huge variety of grays. But this also meant that many a Rebel went into battle wearing the handiwork of his wife or mother—literally dressed in a reminder of home. Sometimes, homespun cloths (or captured Yankee uniforms) were dyed using a mixture of walnut hulls, acorns, and lye, resulting in a light tan color known as butternut. This morning found the Confederates in a mix of gray and butternut, donning a bewildering variety of hats, and very often lacking shoes. "My costume consisted of a ragged pair of trousers, a stained, dirty jacket; an old slouch hat, the brim pinned up with a thorn," a Rebel soldier who fought in the battle would recall, adding "I was barefooted and had a stonebruise on each foot."

Shabby though they were, the Rebels took fierce pride in their appearances. To be tattered and shoeless was, in its own strange way, a badge of individuality—fitting, too, given that the Confederate cause was states' rights, and resisting the demands of those outside their region. Anyone could don the standard-issue Union blue, went a common Southern sentiment, but it was a sign of genuine commitment to cobble together the uniform a Rebel needed to take the field. All of this was reminiscent of the poorly outfitted colonists fighting and winning against the smartly appointed British Lobsterbacks. "We are a dirty, ragged set mother," wrote a Rebel private, "but courage & heroism find many a true disciple among us, our Revolutionary forefathers never suffered nor fought as the 'Rebels' of '61 & '62 have fought & suffered."

Easily the most intense expression of localism, however, far more pronounced than the uniforms even, were the color guards. Every regiment on the field this day, North and South, had one. A typical color guard consisted of eight soldiers, drawn from the most reliable men in the ranks. One sergeant carried a pole that flew the nation's battle flag, either the Stars and Stripes for the Union or the St. Andrew's Cross for the Confederacy. Another sergeant bore the regimental flag.

While the national flags were standardized, the regimental flags were handcrafted, lovingly decorated with local symbols and slogans. They were folk art. Yet again, they were often the creations of the women back home. The 12th Massachusetts took the field this day, for example, proudly flying a white silk flag received in an elaborate ceremony filled with pomp and oratory from the ladies of Boston and featuring the state coat of arms as well as renderings of an oak leaf (symbolizing strength) and a palm leaf (victory). The two flags a regiment carried represented one's nation and one's home.

To serve in a color guard was considered the noblest assignment on the field. It was perilous, too, often bearing out a saying popular with Civil War soldiers, "The post of danger is the post of honor." Only two men in a detail were flag bearers, after all, meaning the others were there to protect them. The enemy was always keen to shoot the standard bearers and capture the flags if possible—there was major glory in that. In the battle ahead, some of the most desperate fighting would be in defense of the colors.

Looking around, another thing was striking about this gathering of troops: it wasn't exclusively white men pitted against white men. A census of the soldiers on the field this morning would have found some very notable exceptions. Several South Carolina regiments included American Indians from the Catawba tribe. There were also some Hispanics present, particularly among Florida and Louisiana regiments. The 14th Connecticut, meanwhile, included a soldier of Chinese descent named Joseph Pierce. The details of Pierce's early life are sketchy, but he was born in Canton and adopted by an American ship captain, who brought him back to Connecticut and raised him. His adoptive family had the last name of Peck. Pierce, it seems, was a name the young boy selected for himself, after President Franklin Pierce.

Significantly, at least three light-skinned African Americans who had managed to "pass" were also on the field this day. They represented both sides. Two were serving the Union as members of Wisconsin regiments and the Confederate was with the 8th Louisiana. The presence of black soldiers was remarkable.

In the North, going back to 1792, military service had been restricted to "free able-bodied white male" citizens. While an act had recently passed Congress, ostensibly breaking that barrier and allowing African Americans to serve in the army, its impact had been blunted. The new act—rife with the prejudices of the era—contained assorted qualifiers, limiting service to those blacks "found competent" and suggesting that even they were probably best suited to "constructing intrenchments" or "performing camp service." To truly open up the army to blacks would require bolstering this act with a more forceful statement of intent. At this point in the war, those who joined up served almost exclusively as laborers, not soldiers.

As for the South: blacks couldn't be soldiers and soldiers couldn't be black, simple as that. Of course, the region had no qualms about black labor, so long as it remained uncompensated, but when it came to the military, a strong exception was made. The prospect of armed slaves terrified Southerners—no doubt with good reason.

As many as eight women would also fight in the battle, dressed in drag in soldiers' uniforms. Their motives varied. Rebecca Peterman, a plucky girl from Ellenboro, Wisconsin, and just sixteen years old, had enlisted with her state's 7th regiment in search of adventure.

———

Whatever the color or condition of one's uniform, regardless of race, creed, religion, or—apparently—gender, the soldiers gathered on the field this morning carried guns, lots of guns. Muskets predominated. Therefore, the majority of soldiers were using muzzle-loaders, guns where you dropped the ammo down the barrel. Some were armed with old-fashioned smoothbore muskets, which had limited range and accuracy. But most were using rifled muskets, which meant that grooves had been etched into the insides of the barrels. Rifled muskets fired so-called Minié balls, a fairly recent innovation and brainchild of Frenchman Claudé-Étienne Minié. *Ball* is a bit of a misnomer, though. The shape was more like a squat cone. At the cone's base, grooves had been etched to catch in the rifled barrel's corresponding grooves, which, in turn, caused the projectile to spin like a tiny football. In flight, this new-style projectile achieved greatly improved stability, allowing it to travel farther and with greater accuracy.

Loading was labor intensive with either kind of musket, though. It required one to tear open a prepackaged paper cartridge, roughly the size and shape of a small cigar, containing black powder and a bullet (either old-style round shot or innovative minie ball). You would pour the contents down the barrel. Then, you used a ramrod to seat the bullet and pack the powder. As a final step, it was necessary to prime the gun. Many models featured a little nipple onto which one affixed a percussion cap made of brass or copper and containing a drop or two of highly volatile mercury fulminate.

Squeeze trigger, hammer strikes cap, spark is generated, black powder ignites, little lead projectile—in a fraction of a fraction of an instant—is guided down the length of the barrel and streaks out across the open air.

Repeat. Repeat again. Even in the best conditions, a soldier could usually get off maybe three shots in a minute. But battle conditions meant fingers fumbling, ears ringing, eyes stung with smoke, a race of seconds as the enemy also reloaded to take a fresh shot at you. Adding to the anxiety, it's pretty much impossible to load a musket lying down. To drive the ramrod home, one has to be standing up—fully exposed.

And then, there were the cannons. They would bring a nightmarish extra dimension to the battle ahead, for even as a soldier tried to stay aware of the enemy on the ground, at any moment, anywhere, heavy iron could rain down onto him from the sky. Not for nothing would this battle come to be known as "artillery hell." The valley's rolling topography featured many little plateaus, perfect spots for these weapons, and first light found nearly five hundred present on the field.

Poor Rebels: to the battlefield they had hauled forty-five 6-pound cannons, twenty-year-old relics from the era of the Mexican War. But they also had plenty of newer models thanks to Richmond's mighty Tredegar Iron Works, an exception and showpiece for the South's otherwise limited manufacturing capabilities. At Tredegar, the Confederacy churned out knockoffs of the same cannons used by the North. Throw in the Rebel knack for capturing cannons during battles, and they would hold their own, at least, against a larger concentration of Federal artillery.

The workhorse for both sides was the Napoleon, a French design that the old U.S. Army (in its prewar incarnation) had obtained a license to manufacture in 1857. Napoleons were smoothbore cannon, meaning they suffered from the same problems as smoothbore muskets—limited range and accuracy. But both sides also had the newer rifled Parrott guns, named after their inventor, Robert Parrott, superintendent of the West Point Foundry. The most fearsome versions of these cannon could hurl a 20-pound projectile one mile with accuracy, a journey during which the missile would remain aloft for a seeming eternity: twenty seconds.

As for the types of cannon shot employed, they were truly the dark flowers of cruel imaginations. There was solid shot, simply a heavy iron ball often lobbed at the enemy with the greatest of nonchalance. It might strike its target, or it might not—no matter—for the ball was sure to bounce or ricochet or roll, causing sundry mayhem. There were also shells, projectiles with powder-filled chambers and a fuse that could be timed for explosion in flight, raining chunks of iron down on the infantrymen. Yet another, known as canister, consisted of a tin can stuffed to the breaking point with sawdust plus twenty-seven plum-size iron balls. On firing, the engorged can couldn't clear the end of the cannon muzzle, but sufficient momentum was achieved to send the balls tearing through the flimsy tin, whereupon they'd spray out in all directions. Canister, used at close range, turned a cannon into a giant shotgun.

Perhaps the most diabolical projectile of all was case, a kind of hybrid of the others. For this one, a shell's chamber contained both powder and a load of small iron balls. Firing case demanded the careful coordination of an artillery team, usually consisting of eight men. Using a pendulum hausse (an aiming device) and calculation tables, they would endeavor to sync up flight and fuse so the case would burst near the end of its trajectory when it was nearing the ground and had built up horrific momentum. Upon explosion, a swarm of balls and sharp iron shell fragments would hurtle forward, pelting soldiers on the ground. Case was the invention of a Brit whose last name would live on well beyond any specific memory of the man himself: Henry Shrapnel. His invention would prompt the British government to grant him a pension of £1,200.

Those first two cannon shots, the opening salvos from each side, completed their journeys. A raw-edged fragment of shell casing whirled through the air, slashing the throats of side-by-side horses in a New Hampshire unit. A shell exploded amid an Alabama regiment, sending a piece of a soldier's skull flying through the air to land in the middle of a Mississippi regiment. It was just a few ticks past 5:45 A.M. The battle was under way.

During the hours ahead, the action would unfold in distinct stages, with fighting concentrated in three different portions of the field. McClellan intended to use his army, bent around the Confederate force as it was, to simultaneously press from the top and bottom, squeezing the Rebels as though in a vise. He could finish the battle with a decisive blow to the middle of their line. Or, viewed another way, McClellan intended to deliver a combination of punches, striking the enemy's left eye, then right eye, and then maybe a pop to the nose. It was a plan, to be sure, but deceptively *un*simple. Still, execute properly, and the war might end this very day, a knockout for the Union.

But it wasn't as if the Rebels didn't have a plan of their own, albeit one that was looser and more improvisational. Although Lee didn't actually know the precise number of McClellan's men, obviously he was outnumbered. That had prompted his Army of Northern Virginia to settle into a defensive posture, although in war defense should never be mistaken for a disadvantage—far from it. If the Union overcommitted on some portion of the field, the Rebels might launch a focused attack elsewhere. Defense, with stunning rapidity, could shift to offense. Given the right opportunity, the Confederates were fully capable of routing their Union adversaries.

The "ball had opened," to use a bit of Civil War slang that equates the beginning of a battle with the thing in the world that it is most *unlike*—a formal dance.

# CHAPTER 2

## STAKES

*At first light,* Abraham Lincoln would also have been wide awake. As a dedicated early riser, he tended to be up at dawn, if not considerably earlier. He was also a long-suffering insomniac. Even so, the president would have been unaware of the current activities of his army.

This isn't to say that Lincoln wasn't eager for information—he was, in fact, desperate for it. But news traveled differently in this era. So, he was forced to be content with a series of telegrams from General McClellan, the last one received nearly twenty-four hours earlier. The dispatches provided a record of the Union army's progress through Maryland, mentioning such places as Frederick, Middletown, and ultimately Sharpsburg. The names would have meant little to Lincoln. While he'd been keenly aware that action was imminent—maybe tomorrow, perhaps it already happened the day before—he had no way of knowing that a great battle was actually under way.

Lincoln was fifty-five miles away from Sharpsburg at the Soldiers' Home, site of his family's retreat just outside the Washington City limits. Here, spread out over 250 acres, was an entire community, consisting of barracks for 150 retired and disabled veterans. There were also several stone guest cottages on the grounds, Gothic style with gingerbread trim, one of which was occupied by the Lincolns. The cottage was casual and cozy; Lincoln liked padding

16

PENNSYLVANIA

Gettysburg

Hagerstown

Sharpsburg
Antietam

Shepherdstown

Frederick

Potomac River

MARYLAND

Winchester

VIRGINIA

**Antietam and area, 1862**

Washington

0   10   20
MILES

about in his slippers. It featured a library stocked for pleasure reading, with volumes of Shakespeare and Aesop, and a broad, inviting
veranda where Lincoln enjoyed lounging at the close of a long day.

For the First Family, this spot offered a refuge from Washington in every sense. It was a refuge from the sweltering heat of
the capital in summertime. It was also a refuge from the endless
official duties placed on both the president and First Lady. Longtime acquaintances of Lincoln couldn't help but notice a drastic
change in his appearance: how careworn he now looked. His long,
peculiar face seemed longer, the rosiness drained from his cheeks.
He was slower to mirth, not as ready with a story. An old friend
found Lincoln "grievously altered from the happy-faced Springfield lawyer" who he'd known before.

The friend continued: "His hair is grizzled, his gait more
stooping, his countenance sallow, and there is a sunken, deathly

look about the large, cavernous eyes, which is saddening to those who see there the marks of care and anxiety . . ."

This wasn't only the stress of a wartime presidency, either. It was personal, shared with wife, Mary, who could keep it together just barely, if that. And so the Soldiers' Home was also a refuge from excruciating personal grief, the recent loss of their son, Willie.

Each day, during the summer months, Lincoln made a three-mile commute to the White House. Each night, he returned. The cottage sat on a hillside and received a cool, comforting breeze. In the distance, the Capitol's new cast-iron dome was visible, still under construction and surrounded by scaffolding. On this morning, the only thing the president knew with certainty was that the war was going very badly.

Then again, most everyone, Northerners and Southerners, had seen the war go through an unexpected and harrowing transition. It was September 17, 1862, well into the second year of the conflict, and everything had changed.

By this point, the incident that had opened the war must have seemed like a gauzy relic from a bygone age. The seizure of Fort Sumter had been so courtly, like something out of an Arthurian legend. The fort, situated on a small man-made island in Charleston Harbor, was US government property that the recently seceded South Carolina wished to claim. To do so required driving out Major Robert Anderson and his small Federal force of 127 men. They had been holding the fort for more than three months, but provisions were running low, down to pork and water.

On April 12, 1861, at 4:30 A.M., Confederate batteries opened fire. The citizens of Charleston began to gather in the streets to watch; some stood on their rooftops, cheering. Through that day and all throughout the night, the little Federal band held on. But on April 13, the American flag came down and a white flag was raised above the ramparts of Sumter. Citizens then tumbled into rowboats and paddled out to the fort to witness the surrender. Roughly four thousand shots and shells had been exchanged during a thirty-four-hour standoff, yet not one person had been killed in the fighting. The headline that ran in the *Charleston Mercury* kind of sums it up: "Bombardment of Fort Sumter! Splendid Pyrotechnic Exhibition."

The victory was celebrated all across the South. In St. Augustine, church bells pealed and cannons were fired. In Goldsboro, North Carolina, a rowdy crowd gathered, chanting Jeff Davis's name. Assorted buglers and drummers came together spontaneously in Richmond, then wended their way through the streets, stopping at one point in front of the governor's mansion, where they struck up "Dixie." This song, infernally catchy, only two years old and penned by a Yankee, at that, was about to sweep the South, would soon become the unofficial Confederate national anthem.

But the North was also overcome with celebration—even in defeat. Major Anderson, hard-luck hero of Sumter, led a rally in Manhattan's Union Square attended by an estimated 100,000 people. Blue Union neckties became a brisk seller. Currier & Ives rushed into production with a lovely, albeit wildly romanticized, twenty-five-cent print of the battle in Charleston Harbor. And the flags—they were everywhere. During the rally, Anderson attached the tattered Sumter flag to an equestrian statue of George Washington, provoking a rousing hurrah. A flag was hoisted to the very tip of Trinity Church's spire, at 281 feet, the highest point in New York City. Throughout the South, the Stars and Stripes were lowered, replaced by the Confederate Stars and Bars.

There's a French term, *rage militaire*. Like most French, it defies exact translation, but it means roughly "martial glee." During the opening months of the war, this sentiment had very much prevailed. Simmering regional tensions that existed since the nation's very inception had broken at last, and it was thrilling. Both sides were certain they were on the side of truth, justice, and the Constitution, with the North intent on upholding a sacred bond among the states, and the South relieved to be shaking off tyranny at last.

Young men enlisted in droves. In the North, the fresh recruits descended on Washington, where they bivouacked on the White House grounds. Lincoln met many of these inaugural soldiers personally, walking along their inspection lines and shaking hands. In the South, soldiers reported for duty armed with 1818 flintlocks, sometimes carrying no weapons at all, yet brimming with enthusiasm. One onlooker described these fresh Rebels as "jubilant as if they were going to a frolic instead of to fight."

If an anxiety existed among the soldiers, it was that they wouldn't get a chance to see any action. The prevailing wisdom was that this would be a very short war, lasting two months perhaps. Neither side thought the other had the courage of its convictions. A saying popular in the South held that "a lady's thimble will hold all the blood that will be shed."

During the first months of 1861, even as he dealt with the weighty matters of a secession crisis followed by the outbreak of a war, Lincoln also had experienced a kind of jubilance, at least in his personal life. That's because he was living under the same roof as his two young sons, Willie and Tad. (Robert, the eldest, was away at Harvard.) During the preceding years in Springfield, Lincoln had been something of an absentee father. His professional obligations as a lawyer had required him to put in long hours and frequently be away on business. The Lincolns' new home became an oasis of familial happiness. Mary would describe those first months in Washington as a period of "so much bliss." Across the North, people shared in their joy.

As it happened, the White House had been a childless residence for a number of years. James Buchanan, Lincoln's immediate predecessor, had been a bachelor president. Before that, Franklin Pierce, having already twice suffered the death of young sons, lost his only remaining child in a tragic accident just prior to taking office: While traveling by train, Pierce's car derailed and rolled down an embankment. As the president-elect and his wife looked on in horror, Benjamin, their eleven-year-old son, expired. Two months later, Pierce was sworn in on a gray, chilly day that would set the tone for his presidency. What a welcome change: with the Lincolns now occupying the White House, the papers fairly brimmed with stories about the exploits of the two young boys from faraway Illinois.

Willie, who arrived in Washington shortly after his tenth birthday, was very much his father's son. Although the boy didn't resemble Lincoln physically (he was small of stature with blue eyes and light brown hair), the two had many mannerisms in common. Willie had a certain way of tilting his head while thinking hard, the spitting image of his father. There was a soberness to his pursuits. When he grew up, he said, he wanted to be a preacher, though locomotive driver was just fine, too. He had a toy train set while in the White House, and also showed an aptitude for memorizing railroad timetables. Willie could convey an imaginary train from Chicago to New York without making a single mistake, an achievement that made his father very proud.

Tad, who turned eight soon after arriving in Washington, had been named Thomas Lincoln III at birth. But Lincoln thought the boy's large head and squirmy little body gave him the look of a tadpole—so Tad he became. Emotional, risible, talkative: this son shared more of Mary's nature. He spoke in rapid bursts, but due to a cleft lip and palate, often had trouble making himself understood. He threw frequent temper tantrums. During Tad's toddler years, Lincoln had enjoyed holding him at arm's length, watching him kick and flail. Tad may also have had a learning disability. At age eight, he was not yet able to dress himself and lacked even rudimentary reading skills. Whereas Tad proved immune to the White House tutor, Willie was a joy. He was an avid reader and good at math, too, like his father.

Lincoln could be notoriously lenient with his sons. *Spare the rod* was very much his style. Perhaps this was a reaction to his hardscrabble upbringing; his own father sometimes beat him. Or maybe it reflected a surprisingly modern view of parenting, certainly well ahead of his peers. Then again, given all the time Lincoln had spent away on business, it could simply be that he was keen to enjoy his children, without undue discipline.

At the White House, the boys took full advantage. Even though he was younger, Tad was the instigator, his dark eyes flashing mischief. The boys had a full-scale menagerie—dogs, goats, rabbits, ponies—the gifts of an admiring public. One never knew what manner of beast was about to come scuttering down a White House hallway, hitched to a cart. Then there was the time the boys received pocketknives, and decided to carve up the green cloth covering the desk of one of Lincoln's secretaries. They also spilled ink all over the cloth. Or the time they discovered a little attic room with wires that rang all the bells, calling staff to various locations. Willie and Tad went wild, sending the confused help running this way and that.

Whenever anyone complained, the president just smiled indulgently. Apparently, William Herndon, his law partner back in Springfield, was no stranger to this response. He once described Lincoln as "blinded to his children's faults," adding: "Had they shat in Lincoln's hat and rubbed it on his boots, he would have laughed and thought it smart."

The two boys were instantly swept up in martial glee. A favorite activity was accompanying their father during troop inspections. They also built a fort on the White House roof, featuring a log as a cannon. For soldiers, they recruited Bud and Holly Taft, the sons of a DC attorney who lived nearby, and the Lincoln boys' constant playmates. Everyone was outfitted with a musket—a real one, but also one that happened to be damaged beyond repair. Willie wrote a letter to a friend back in Springfield, explaining that he was "raising a battalion" and that it was "in a high state of efficiency and discipline."

Meanwhile, the first clashes of the Civil War were taking place: Big Bethel, Fairfax Court House, Bowman's Place, Hoke's Run, Corrick's Ford. These were the names, slashing across newspaper front pages in big, blazing headlines. Citizens in both the North and South could recite the heroes and goats, wrung their hands over botched tactics, thrilled at recounting clever maneuvers. Of course, what passed for battles at this early juncture were mostly skirmishes, and sometimes even less, little more than armed feuds between neighbors who found themselves on opposing sides. Casualty counts rarely exceeded the single digits.

One such early action was the Union raid on Alexandria, Virginia. When the Commonwealth formally ratified secession on May 23, 1861, the town became part of the Confederacy. For the North, this was simply untenable. Alexandria was situated directly across the Potomac from the District of Columbia, within cannon range of the White House. That very night, a Union force stole across the river to retake the town. Among the soldiers involved in this maneuver was Elmer Ephraim Ellsworth.

Ellsworth was a stocky little man with a big, boyish confidence. Just twenty-four years old, he had already achieved a measure of success as the onetime leader of the U.S. Zouave Cadets. This outfit was inspired by—indeed took its exotic name (Zouave) from—a legendary Algerian force that had outfought the French army. The cadets' uniforms were a fanciful take on the garb worn by the Algerian desert guerrillas, featuring billowing scarlet trousers, sky-blue blouses, and enough gold braid and tassel to hobble a camel.

Colonel Ellsworth took his crew on the road, traveling to towns large and small: Fond du Lac, Baltimore, Pittsburgh, Oshkosh, and Utica. During the late 1850s, as the tensions that would impel the Civil War began to rise, military preparedness became an issue of great public interest. Audiences were rapt as his sixty cadets worked their way through a series of precise formations: marching in a big circle before seamlessly falling into three parallel battle lines that lunged forward, bayonets at the ready, then stacking their muskets so quickly (their signature move) that it seemed like a magic trick. Sometimes, Ellsworth's Zouaves competed against local militias, such as the Salem Light Infantry or the Adrian (Michigan) Guards. These contests were like sporting events.

In Springfield, on a hot August day in 1860, Lincoln joined a crowd of five thousand and stood in the shade of a cottonwood, watching the U.S. Zouave Cadets. The little colonel impressed him mightily. Ellsworth struck Lincoln as an earnest young man who was going places. He invited Ellsworth to remain in Springfield, offered him a job studying law at his firm. The ever-ambitious Ellsworth accepted, instantly grasping the value of tying his fate to Lincoln's. Ellsworth stumped for Lincoln during the campaign that autumn. After the election, Ellsworth accompanied him to Washington, was even granted the honor of traveling to the capital aboard the new president's ceremonial train.

Throughout the spring of 1861, Ellsworth was a frequent guest at the White House. Willie and Tad were in whispering awe of this young man with the smart uniform and military swagger. In the course of these visits, however, Ellsworth also became aware of an unsettling fact. From the window of Lincoln's private office, on the second floor of the White House, a Confederate flag was visible flying atop an Alexandria hotel known as the Marshall House. To Ellsworth, this seemed like such a grievous insult toward the president.

On the night of the raid, Ellsworth traveled across the Potomac aboard a steamer. He helped destroy a stretch of railroad tracks. He was part of a detail charged with cutting the wires in the Arlington telegraph office. Then he broke away, setting off for the Marshall House, accompanied by a small group of soldiers. Ellsworth entered the hotel, climbed three flights, and got onto the roof. There, he found the offending flag and hauled it down.

As Ellsworth made for the street, folding the Rebel flag even as he rushed down the stairs, James Jackson, proprietor of the Marshall House, burst from his room, double-barreled shotgun in hand. It all happened so fast. Jackson emptied one barrel, point blank, into Ellsworth's chest. "My God," blurted the little colonel, collapsing in a heap. Before Jackson could even discharge the second barrel, a Union soldier slapped away his gun, sending a spray of buckshot into the wall. The soldier then shot Jackson at close range, delivering a bullet through the bridge of his nose. For a moment, the proprietor remained upright, swaying. The soldier ran him through with a bayonet, finishing the job.

Two men lay dead, the sole casualties of the moonlight raid on Alexandria. *Intimate*: the word doesn't seem like it could possibly be fitting for something as brutal as warfare, yet somehow it's apt.

On learning of Ellsworth's death, Lincoln was deeply saddened. Willie and Tad were crushed. The president sent a letter of condolence to Ellsworth's parents in Mechanicville, New York. Then, the little colonel's flag-draped coffin took a slow train ride home, making stops along the way to accommodate the mourners who turned out en masse. Across the North, "Remember Ellsworth" became a rallying cry. Newspapers ran fulsome tributes: "long after the rebellion shall have become a matter of history," declared the *New York Times*, "his death will be regarded as a martyrdom, and his name enrolled upon the list of our country's patriots." The South answered with its own collection of poems and songs and encomiums, celebrating James Jackson, brave and doomed proprietor of the Marshall House hotel.

---

Then, everything changed. Come 1862, the war had dragged on far longer than anyone would have predicted. That early sense of exuberance simply vanished. Wives, left behind on the home front, were becoming weary from the burden of caring for their households alone. Parents had grown sick with anxiety for their sons. Soldiers who had hoped to get just a taste of battle had achieved that modest goal, and sometimes more, and were eager to return home. The demand for action began to swell: something dramatic and decisive was needed to bring this conflict to an end.

The military machines cranked up. Both sides set to replacing those 1818 flintlocks and squat little vintage cannons with terrifying and efficient new weapons, such as rifled muskets and Parrott artillery pieces. The need for fresh soldiers was unquenchable. Lincoln called for 150,000 volunteers. Davis went further, instituting a draft. It was a highly controversial measure. The upstart Confederacy was predicated on state's rights, and here was its president *dictating* a blanket policy. But soldiers were needed, always more soldiers. Soon Lincoln upped the ante, calling for 300,000 more volunteers. Within a matter of months Davis hiked the age of eligibility for the draft to forty-five.

The year 1862 marks a bleak passage, as a rebellion turned into a war. Death tolls in battles surged, like nothing ever witnessed before. The Mexican War had dragged on nearly two years with a cost of 1,700 American lives lost in battle. The Alamo had resulted in the deaths of roughly 200 brave Texans. These represented the familiar dimensions of warfare, the apparent limits of carnage. But then came battles that produced death tallies of a whole other magnitude. A lady's thimble: how very quaint.

Shiloh was such a battle. It occurred in the spring of 1862; its barbarity astounded a fractured nation.

April 6 found a vast Union force camped along the Tennessee River, near a little town called Pittsburgh Landing. It was a Sunday morning, and the soldiers were enjoying a rare stretch of leisure: eating breakfast, cleaning their boots, reading the Bible. Birds were chirping away—that's what the soldiers would remember: the birds, their happy springtime chirps, and how those suddenly gave way to squawks of alarm. The air overhead began to fill with the beating of wings.

Other creatures soon joined in and began to flee. Frightened deer and rabbits burst from the woods, began darting among the soldiers in camp. It was puzzling. Then, the ground began to tremble—close, closer, now right at the edge of the woods. By the time the Union soldiers pieced it all together, the enemy was hot upon them. Even as men were dropping frying pans and pulling on their pants, a huge wave of Confederates emerged from the trees, muskets ablaze.

All day long, the Rebels contrived to drive the Federals into a broad and fatal swath of Tennessee swampland. The onslaught didn't wane until the final hour of daylight, when the Confederates simply grew too weary to continue their killing binge. During the night, a sizeable Union reinforcement arrived. The next morning, the Confederates were completely unprepared for the viciousness of the Federal counterattack. All day long, Yanks slaughtered Rebels, before they, too, found themselves spent in that final hour of light.

So ended the Battle of Shiloh. It was a Union victory, but the toll for both sides was unprecedented and oddly equitable: 1,754 Federal soldiers had been killed versus 1,728 for the Confederacy. According to legend, injured soldiers from both sides gathered after the battle around the same pond to wash their wounds. Sometimes a soldier was so badly injured that he was forced to crawl to the water's edge, where he'd lay down beside another—maybe from his side, maybe an enemy, it didn't matter, all that mattered was a cool, soothing drink. Everyone was thrown together in a kind of informal truce. No terms were spelled out, but then nothing need be said. The soldiers recognized their shared fate; both sides were now part of something that had grown big and terrible.

For Lincoln, too, the whole world transformed in 1862, like something out of a dark fairy tale. The year would prove devastating to him and Mary, personally. It was as if the war's malevolence became so vast and swollen that it broke free of its battlefield confines, stole out across the land in search of innocents.

January brought foul weather like Washington had rarely seen. It was drizzling and chilly, the whole town enveloped in damp and mud, such a departure from the sleigh-crisp Springfield winters to which Lincoln was accustomed. As he moved about the sprawling, drafty White House, the president kept a shawl wrapped around his shoulders.

Son Willie caught a cold. A pony ride that he and his brother had recently taken on the blustery White House grounds was a suspected culprit. As January slid into February, the weather was immutable. The illness lingered on, sapping the little boy's energy, quieting those rambunctious White House hallways. Tad was left to play alone.

Complications set in. It was so unexpected, so mysterious, and the Lincolns—always susceptible to spikes of parental anxiety—grew increasingly alarmed. Fortunately, Willie was in the care of Robert Stone, one of the best physicians in the country. Every indicator pointed to bilious fever, explained Dr. Stone, offering a catchall diagnosis then common for illnesses that featured such symptoms as nausea, high fever, and chills. He assured the Lincolns that Willie would be just fine. Their boy simply needed lots of rest.

When Willie's condition continued to deteriorate, the Lincolns considered cancelling the ball they had scheduled. It was to be a gala event, their first formal party as president and First Lady. Mary, in particular, viewed it as an opportunity to prove to official Washington that the new residents of the White House were people of culture, not Illinois backcountry rubes. As the date drew closer, Willie's health started to improve. But then he experienced another setback. It was confounding. Dr. Stone continued to give the Lincolns reassurance. In his care, Willie had the benefit of the most efficacious remedies available, including Peruvian bark (a source of quinine) and jalap and calomel, both powerful purgatives. The medications were to be taken every half hour and in rotation. To restore his strength, he was given beef tea and bland pudding.

On February 5, Lincoln stood awkwardly in the East Room of the White House, greeting the more than five hundred guests as they arrived. Mary wore a white satin dress trimmed with black lace and trailed by an ample train. Members of the cabinet and

Congress were present, along with Supreme Court justices and assorted Washington society figures. The military was well represented: McClellan in full uniform as well as Generals Irvin McDowell, Abner Doubleday, Erasmus Keyes, Louis Blenker, Silas Casey, and Samuel Heintzelman.

The Lincolns kept breaking away from the party to check on their sick son. Anxious Abe sat at the edge of Willie's bed, monitoring his labored breathing, while from down below came the strains of the Marine Band.

Dinner was served at the stylish hour of 11:00 P.M. When the time arrived, the door to the state dining room was inexplicably locked. The guests milled about. "I am in favor of a forward movement," quipped one, a sly reference to the disappointing progress of the war. Presently, the key was located, and the guests were led into the dining room. On one long table, a feast of fresh game was arrayed, catered by the celebrated Henri Maillard of New York. For dessert, there was a replica of Fort Sumter, done up in confectionary sugar. The last guests departed at 3:00 A.M., ushered out of the White House and into the night by the wistful strains of "The Girl I Left Behind Me."

Willie only grew worse. Then, Tad contracted bilious fever, too. Lincoln stayed up all night tending to his sons. All day, the official business of the presidency—the need to appoint a consul to Tangier, consideration of an economic treaty with the king of Hanover, endless decisions about the war—was conducted in a haze. The press reported every fluctuation in Willie and Tad's condition. On February 14, Valentine's Day, it must have seemed like a gift when the boys appeared to be making a recovery. But then Willie plummeted yet again.

Dr. Stone was flummoxed. Concern began to seep out around the edges of his polished, professional manner, and the Lincolns— barometers of worry—registered it fearfully and in full, could feel their hope sinking.

In a cavernous, formal bedchamber, featuring heavy purple drapes held by loops of golden braid, Willie lay, suffering terribly.

The bed was so big—its ornate headboard carved from rose-wood—his form so very small. Near the ceiling, above the boy, was a shield featuring an American eagle, olive branches gripped in one talon and in the other, arrows. Willie had been moved to this guest room across from the president's bedchamber, the better to monitor his condition. Some of his toy soldiers had been brought here as well. They stood in neat rows, unplayed with. His favorite books were carefully stacked, unread for days. The Lincoln's were helpless. All remedies had been exhausted. They sat by their boy's bedside, dabbing his fevered forehead with a wet towel.

Willie died at dusk on a frigid Thursday. Lincoln buried his face in his hands and shook. Then the president rose slowly to his feet, as if unfolding his long, sharp-angled limbs, and stumbled out of his son's room, able only to form "my boy is gone—he is actually gone."

The date was February 20, 1862. For the Lincolns, February had a history as such a cruel month. Back in Springfield, the couple had lost a child, little Eddie, on February 1, 1850. He had been only three years old. Now, they had lost Willie and still another child was in peril. Fortunately, Tad took a turn for the better and started to recover.

Willie's funeral was held in the East Room, many of the same guests from the recent gala in attendance, though Mary was conspicuous in her absence. It was simply too much to bear. She stayed upstairs shut in her room, and would remain there for six weeks, unable to rise from her bed. The mere mention of Willie's name set her to sobbing. Worse even than the grief was the guilt. In Mary's mind, the gala and Willie's death would forever be linked. She would always wonder whether trying to win the favor of Washington society, putting on worldly airs, as it were, had summoned some kind of divine punishment.

During the service, the oppressive gloom of February's weather gave way to sudden violence, as outside the winds could be heard shrieking and rain pelted the White House roof. Then pallbearers bore the small coffin to a waiting hearse, followed by a procession of children from Willie's Sunday school. Over the rain-drenched, mud-slicked streets of Washington, two white horses walked slowly, pulling the hearse. Lincoln followed behind in a carriage, looking careworn and haggard and of a sudden, old beyond his years. He was bidding farewell to his boy.

Yet still, the dark spell didn't lift, far from it. One's basic sense of order demands that a bad event be followed by a good occurrence, but that's not assured. Like the swift current of a river, 1862 kept moving, events swirling together with other events, heartache with heartache—so much heartache—and not only Lincoln's, but also that of so many others, all tumbled together. Lincoln had suffered a grievous loss, yet time couldn't pause. He was also the president, with a country at war to govern. Even after Willie's death, the grim tidings continued, as the North entered into a stretch featuring a number of disastrous setbacks.

Stonewall Jackson rampaged through the Shenandoah Valley, marching his troops hundreds of miles in the space of two and a half months, and, though often outnumbered, managed to defeat a variety of Union generals. Second Bull Run—fought about a year after the first battle, on roughly the same ground—produced another humiliating defeat. On September 15, Jackson struck again, capturing Harpers Ferry, site of a Federal arsenal that had been established by George Washington. Stonewall's men seized a cache of 13,000 small arms, 73 cannons, 200 wagons, as well as a large quantity of freshly baked bread. They also took 12,419 Union soldiers prisoner, a mark that would hold throughout the Civil War as the largest number of men captured in a single battle. The spate of losses was hugely demoralizing for the North.

And so it was that by this morning, as the first shots rang out in the countryside near Sharpsburg, there was a sense that the North couldn't afford one more defeat.

The stakes had grown huge.

For starters, the outcome of this battle would likely influence the 1862 midterm elections. This was more unnerving than it might at first seem. Throughout American history, midterms have served as a referendum, an opportunity either to affirm the policies of the president, or to vote in opposition leaders who will serve as a check on the current administration's power. Another Union loss would be a signal that change was sorely needed.

Ever canny, General Lee read the Northern papers diligently for the purpose of taking the measure of Yankee sentiment. At the outset of the current campaign, in a letter to Jefferson Davis, he had written: "The present seems to be the most propitious time, since the commencement of the war, for the Confederate Army to enter Maryland." A few days later, in another letter to Davis, Lee would cite the "coming elections" in the United States as one of main factors that prompted him to pounce when he did.

By September, public confidence in the war had dropped all across the North and the midterms were only weeks away, creating a situation, Lee well knew, that played right into the hands of the so-called Copperheads. These were Democrats committed to ending the war at once and offering the South entrée back into the Union, slavery be damned. Originally, Copperhead was an insult crafted by Republicans, who likened their rivals to a deadly and perfidious snake. But the Copperheads embraced the term and attempted to flip the connotation from a ruddy serpent to a copper penny, which then featured an image of Lady Liberty. They fashioned the coins into badges and wore them with pride. Throughout the Civil War, the Copperheads' influence would wax and wane in a perfect inverse relationship to the success of the Union war effort. Late summer of 1862 found the Copperheads on the rise, so much so that they adopted a snappy new slogan: "The Union as it was, the Constitution as it is."

Despite their growing influence, the Copperheads were still a mere subset of the larger Democratic Party. But even many moderate Democrats, as members of the congressional minority, were growing troubled by the progress of the war, becoming increasingly vocal in their criticism of Lincoln. A loss this day was likely to usher a new coalition into power, composed of Copperheads and various other stripes of Democrat, all bent on softening the Union's commitment to the war, maybe even negotiating peace on terms favorable to the South.

A Union loss also had the potential to tilt Maryland into the Confederacy, a potentially disastrous turn. Maryland, along with Kentucky, Missouri, and Delaware, was a border state; that is, a state that had stayed in the Union while continuing to allow slavery. If any of these four flipped, the others might follow, and the Confederacy would be enlarged along with its prospects of winning.

So far, keeping Maryland in the Union had proved a vexing challenge. Its inhabitants were deeply divided in their loyalties, fitting for a state that shared borders with both Union Pennsylvania and Confederate Virginia, and that featured small family farms as well as sprawling tobacco plantations worked by slaves. Sharpsburg was this in microcosm. According to the 1860 census, the population of the town and its environs included 150 enslaved blacks, but also 203 free African Americans. A notion popular in the South held that Maryland was simply on the wrong side—for now. The state was likened to a fair maiden, bound to the Union against her will.

When Lee invaded, he was well aware of—was, in fact, counting on—this pent-up Rebel sympathy. As his army began crossing the Potomac on September 4, regimental bands struck up "Maryland, My Maryland" and the soldiers belted out rollicking renditions. This was a new song, set to the tune of a classic, "O Tannenbaum," and penned at the start of the Civil War by a Maryland native living in Louisiana. It was also a work of unabashed propaganda, urging secession, and sprinkled with thinly veiled references to Lincoln (identified as a "despot" and "tyrant"). The Union was derided as "Northern scum."

So far, the Rebels had met with a surprisingly cool reception. Although there had been predictions of an uprising of Maryland citizens demanding secession, this hadn't materialized.

Confederates-on-Union-soil was a difficult proposition, even if they were promising to free a damsel in distress.

But a victory in this battle might alter matters. During those first weeks of September, as the Rebels had rolled through Maryland pursued by the Federals, it was noted with amusement that residents of little villages were in the habit of flying the flag of whatever side happened to be milling around the town square. When Confederates were in their midst, partisan townfolk proudly graced their porches with Rebel flags, only to take them down two days later when the Federals arrived—it then became the Union stalwarts' turn to raise the flag. This was self-preservation, to be sure. It was foolhardy to provoke men with muskets by flying the enemy's colors. But if the Confederates won this battle, those Rebel flags might go up and stay up.

Still another consequence of a Rebel victory is that it would almost certainly invite foreign meddling. America's grand experiment, only four score and six years old, had gone disastrously awry, and European powers such as France and England were weighing the opportunities. A civil war that permanently split the nation, resulting in two smaller countries on the North American continent, might very much serve their interests. They could play the two countries against each other, keeping them in perpetual weakness. They could pursue their own territorial interests without fear of reprisal.

As it happened, the power vacuum caused by the Civil War had already prompted France to launch an invasion of Mexico. Emperor Napoleon III was keen to establish a presence in the New World, something his country hadn't had since it sold the Louisiana Territory in 1803. Napoleon III intended to plunder Mexico's rich stores of silver and build a canal across the country, the better to link up with France's interests in the Far East. Even as the Civil War raged, the French army was pushing toward Mexico City, following the same route as Cortés. They had, in fact, suffered a recent defeat at the Battle of Puebla on May 5, 1862—forever after to be celebrated as Cinco de Mayo.

Napoleon III was partial to a separate Confederate nation, one that could act as a buffer between Mexico and the Union North. Throughout 1862, he weighed whether to formally extend recognition. In the finely nuanced language of international diplomacy, the Confederacy was currently classed as a "belligerent," implying that it was merely a region in rebellion. But recognition would confer legitimacy, suggesting that the Confederacy was a separate country. This, in turn, would strengthen the South's ability to make military and economic treaties and, crucially, bolster the overseas market for its war bonds. In 1778, France's official recognition of the thirteen colonies as a separate nation had been essential to America's victory in the Revolutionary War. The only thing holding Napoleon III back was that he did not want to act unilaterally without mighty, sun-never-sets Britain. As recently as July 19, he had sent a telegram to his foreign minister in London: "Demandez au government anglais s'il ne croit pas le moment venu reconnaître le Sud." Rough translation: "Ask the English whether it's time to recognize the South."

For its part, Britain was warming to the idea. Throughout the war, tensions had run high between England and the North, most dangerously following the Trent Affair, when the Union seized an English ship with two Confederate diplomats aboard. More recently, the Union blockade of Confederate seaports, designed to suffocate the South's economy, was taking an unintended toll on Britain's economy as well. Slowed to a trickle was the flow of raw Southern cotton to British mills, where it was spun into textiles. By July 1862, mills were shutting down by the score, and more than eighty thousand workers had lost their jobs. About the only thing holding England back was its legendary prudence. But then came the recent spate of Union losses. Among Britain's leaders there was a growing conviction that the time had finally arrived for recognition, or perhaps even some kind of mediation between the warring parties. The trigger would be another—just *one* more—Union loss. "If this should happen," Lord Palmerston, the prime minister, had written to his foreign secretary only a few days earlier, on September 14, "would it not be time for us to consider whether in such a state of things England and France might not address the contending parties and recommend an arrangement upon the basis of separation?"

Of all the possible consequences of a Confederate victory, however, the gravest one was this: the South would be emboldened to continue bringing the fight onto Northern soil, and Union cities would be vulnerable.

Apparently, Lee had his eye set on Harrisburg, Pennsylvania. Besides being the capital of the second-largest state in the Union, it provided a vital transportation link between the east and west. Four major railroads converged in Harrisburg. The Rebels could rip up track and knock down bridges, badly damaging the Union's ability to move around soldiers and supplies.

Then again, the target might be Baltimore, Philadelphia, New York—or who knows where? That's the thing, see: the Confederacy would have successfully switched from defense to offense. The pressure would shift to the North, left to guess what city was next for an attack. The capital was a prime Rebel enticement, an unnerving prospect. As it happened, the Federal soldiers concentrated near Antietam Creek represented the bulk of what was available in the Eastern Theater (other pieces of the Union army were hopelessly far away in such places as Tennessee and Louisiana). While McClellan's army pursued Lee through Maryland, Washington had been left vulnerable.

During the two weeks since the Rebel invasion, fear in the District had grown palpable. Gunboats were stationed in the Potomac. Government clerks had been ordered to pack up vital documents and records so that in the event of an attack, they could be moved to New York. "I believe it possible . . . that Washington may be taken," stated the bureau chief of the *New-York Tribune*.

As a bonus, marauding through Union territory meant that Virginia could get a sorely needed breather. So far, the war had been concentrated in this state, resulting in grave damage to the farmland that fed the Confederate army. Every day the Rebels remained in the North was a day for hard-used Virginia to recover.

There was brilliance in Lee's plan. Victory could result in half a dozen different scenarios, any single one of which had the potential to end the current hostilities on terms favorable to the South. Or perhaps the consequences would fall one into another, toppling like dominoes: sack Harrisburg, Democrats sweep into power in the midterm, Maryland flips, other border states follow, war over.

But Old Abe was crafty, too. Although racked by sorrow, he also had given ample contemplation to the state of matters, and what need be done.

It was a few minutes past dawn. He was at his cottage retreat, not certain of the location of his army, unaware even that they were currently fighting. But he had a plan, shared only with his closest advisers, regarding what to do in the event of a *Northern* victory.

It could change everything.

# CHAPTER 3

## THE CORNFIELD

*It was a little past 5:45 A.M.*, and thousands of soldiers were in motion. They were busy shedding tin cups, bedrolls, and Bibles, anything that might add unnecessary weight. They pared down to the bare essentials: musket, bayonet, cartridge belt, canteen, and haversack. As the soldiers prepared for battle, a man in each company, often a cook or someone else who wouldn't see action, was left to guard the discarded possessions from the enemy (or potential looters from one's own side). Also left for safekeeping were hastily scrawled letters, last words for loved ones to be mailed if a soldier didn't survive. Because the men didn't have dog tags, many also wrote their names and regiments on pieces of paper then pinned those to their uniforms, a crude but necessary form of identification.

The ball had opened. The first pairing of this grisly cotillion, concentrated in the northern section of the battlefield, pitted troops commanded by the Union general Joseph Hooker against Stonewall Jackson's men. Nearby, massed along a several-mile front that stretched southward, thousands of other soldiers, both Federals and Rebs, simply bided their time. These men had also awakened to the alarming sight of the enemy in too-close proximity. But they wouldn't be pulled into the fight until later. Thus, daybreak found untold legions simply waiting in the woods or on farms, some trading light gunfire meant to get a read on the enemy, useful later when their turn came. For now the action was concentrated in the top portion of the field.

Here, the Union's aim was to seize a plateau occupied by Rebel cannons and featuring what appeared to be a little white schoolhouse (a highly visible landmark). This spot could serve as a jumping-off point for a southward drive, while, in a coordinated effort, Federal forces on the other side of Antietam Creek drove northward. Union troops pressing in two directions could squeeze the enemy; a third punch could be delivered straight on, and the Army of Northern Virginia might be crushed.

Break it down, though, and even the task demanded on this portion of the field—reaching that little white schoolhouse—was daunting. It required Union troops to push southward approximately 1,500 yards across pastures, over fences, past woods where Rebel soldiers might lurk, and, most notably, through a cornfield. The stalks stood taller than a man and were ripe for harvest. It was just an ordinary cornfield, though an ample one, covering 30 acres and owned by David Miller, a prosperous farmer. But this humble cornfield was about to take on macabre dimensions, as one of the most ruthlessly contested places of the war.

For many soldiers, for those lucky enough to survive, the fight here would be the most intense experience of their lives. Boys who had worked in factories or on farms would return from the war to identical situations, only to devote their remaining decades to reliving a few hot moments. What was about to begin would not soon end.

As drummer boys beat the long roll, Federals streamed out of the woods. They began organizing themselves into one of the era's most basic formations, consisting of a broad line—picture a wall of men. Such lines were arranged two men deep, with one marching directly behind the other. This configuration allowed a mass

of soldiers to quickly get off shots. The man to the rear could even
fire over the shoulder of the one in front. Such a rigid formation,
however, combined with the fact that only right-handed muskets
were issued, necessitated firing as a righty even if a lefty.

The first Union battle line slated for action was 1,100 strong,
meaning it would have been 550 men wide, two deep. It was
composed of New York and Pennsylvania soldiers led by General Abram Duryee. Before these men could even begin marching, however, they encountered their first obstacle. A small group
of Rebel skirmishers lurked in the cornfield, having sneaked to
within a few hundred yards of the Union position. Eight cannons
were rolled forward. Duryee's men lay on the ground. The cannons
fired canister above them, seeking the skirmishers, and soon these
Rebels scurried back to their earlier positions. The way had been
cleared.

Duryee's line of men stood back up and started forward, across
open meadow to the edge of the cornfield. Here, they encountered
a wooden zigzag fence, designed in the words of local farmers to
be "cow high, hog low" (too high for a cow to step over, too low
for a hog to root under). Duryee's soldiers removed the top rungs
of the fencing. They slipped into the corn.

They set out across the field, trying to maintain as straight a
line as possible although the tall corn divided them. Pairs of men,
one in front of the other, marched down individual rows. A common feeling was fear: "trembling fingers," legs that "quaked so
they would scarcely support my weight," a "queer choking sensation about the throat"—those are some of the sensations of going
into battle as recalled by Civil War soldiers. John Mead Gould,
lieutenant with the 10th Maine, noted that "it is terrible to march
slowly into danger, and see and feel that each second your chance
for death is surer than it was the second before. The desire to break
loose, to run, to fire, to do something, no matter what, rather than
to walk, is almost irresistible."

A battle line, however, was designed to promote cohesion.
Even a soldier overcome by terror was loath to flee lest he let

down his comrades. Some might decide to bolt anyway, but they had first to contend with file closers, best described as a type of human bulldog. File closers were sergeants with menacingly thick builds who marched a few paces to the rear, grimacing and cursing. They relied on their fists and the flats of their muskets to drive deserters back into line.

Duryee's men continued through the corn. The regimental flags, bobbing above the tall stalks, were visible for all to see, making the soldiers' presence and position clear to the enemy. No matter: This type of war craft, relying on so-called linear tactics, had no place for subtlety. The goal was to overwhelm an opponent with a show of brute manpower. Soon enough, the easily spotted Union battle line fell under Rebel cannon fire. Shells exploded in the air above, raining shrapnel onto the men. Solid shot, 12-pound iron balls, struck limestone outcroppings and ricocheted with the loopy physics of some other, more ample dimension—the marbles of giants. Cannon fire punched into the oncoming line, knocking down men, opening gaps. To halt meant certain death, as the Rebel artillerists would be able to home in on stationary targets with ruthless accuracy. With shame and file closers to the rear, cannon shell falling all around, the Union line had no choice but to keep moving, uncertain of how far the cornfield extended, unsure of what would await them when they emerged.

Maybe it was best not to know. Roughly 200 yards beyond the far edge of the cornfield lay a long furrow. It had provided most modest accommodations the previous night to 1,150 Georgia soldiers (a number nearly equal to Duryee's force), and they were now awake positioned exactly as they'd slept, forming a broad and imposing battle line. Colonel Marcellus Douglass rushed to and fro, ordering his men to each take a quick peek, select his own personal cornrow, and then to crouch back down in the furrow, safely out of sight.

The Rebels waited. They could hear the crunch-crunch-crunch of marching feet on farm soil, the occasional clang of a musket stock accidentally smacking against a canteen. They could see

cannon shells, fired in high arcs over their own line by their com-
patriots to the rear, the lit fuses leaving spark trails across the dawn
sky, like meteors.

And then the Union soldiers emerged from the corn. *Rise up,*
*rise up*, commanded Colonel Douglass. From the furrow, a wall of
Rebels became suddenly visible. They loosed a terrifying unison
volley, hundreds of bullets traveling in a tight synchronized constellation streaked across 200 yards in an eye-twitch, smack into
the Union line. Hot metal ripped into the soldiers. The soft lead
of the bullets expanded on contact, shattering bones and slicing
through sinew. "The volley made them stagger and hesitate," Gordon Bradwell, a private with the 31st Georgia, would recall.

At its southern edge, the cornfield was bounded by another
zigzag fence, but here "cow high, hog low" became a conundrum.
While under fire, climbing over such a fence was doubly difficult. Hiding behind it was a more natural inclination, but through
the slats a man could easily be seen . . . and aimed at. Nevertheless, plenty of Duryee's men made the choice to seek the flimsy
cover of a wood fence. The Rebels, sheathed in bluish-gray smoke
from their first volley, were hurriedly reloading to deliver another.
Other Union soldiers scrambled over the fence, doing their best to
reform the battle line, and firing back at the Rebels.

Meanwhile, the backup the besieged Yanks had counted on was
nowhere to be found. Two entire brigades, numbering roughly
3,000 soldiers, were supposed to have marched across the cornfield
close behind Duryee's men, lending support. But they had been
delayed. Turns out, George Hartsuff, commander of one of these
brigades, had set out on horseback to conduct reconnaissance and
wound up with a shell fragment lodged in his left hip. He went
woozy from the loss of blood. The wound would contribute to his
death twelve years after the battle. But on this September morning, the more pressing matter was his brigade's shattered chain of

command. General Hartsuff had to be replaced by his senior regimental commander, that man by his second in command, and on
down the line. Crucial minutes ticked by as each officer assumed
his new post and became apprised of his new duties.

Colonel William Christian, commander of the other brigade,
struggled with a very different problem, but with the same result—an alarming delay. Christian was known for strict discipline,
such as prohibiting drinking among his soldiers. In the course
of a sixteen-year military career, however, he'd never participated
in actual combat. His conduct at Second Bull Run, only a few
weeks earlier, had provided an unnerving clue to how he might
react. Christian had spent the day in the shade of a tree, pleading
both heatstroke and a severe case of poison ivy. He emerged only
when the shooting ended, riding among the ranks, proudly waving a regimental flag. Such squirrely leadership alarmed his men.
They held a secret meeting to discuss whether to approach one of
Christian's superiors and request his removal. But they decided
against it.

Now, facing his first real test, Christian simply cracked up. As
the men waited to deploy, he started to drill them, bellowing out
maneuvers. Drilling soldiers in the moments right before battle
was not unusual, served, in fact, as a proven way to calm nerves
with familiar parade-ground routine. But Christian's men sensed
a rising hysteria in their leader's torrent of commands: "right
flank," "left oblique," "left flank." Suddenly, Christian dismounted
from his horse and scuttled to the rear, ducking and weaving with
every cannon report. A fourteen-year-old drummer boy spotted
the colonel cowering behind a tree. There the officer remained,
muttering, "forward, men, forward," according to a letter the boy
wrote to his parents. This also led to a delay as Christian's command reorganized.

And so Duryee's Federals were left without backup, exchang-
ing fire with Douglass's Rebels across the space of less than 200
yards. When the situation grew desperate, Duryee called for a
retreat.

The official battlefield reports of Civil War commanders are filled with textbook retreats, featuring soldiers who proceed with all the order and poise of a Sunday town-square inspection. Such reports ignore the chaos and fear—the reality. Upon receiving the order, Duryee's men raced back through the cornfield, and when they reached the other end, where the flag bearers had gathered to rally them, many just kept right on running. A brief turn in the cornfield had left a third of Duryee's thousand men either badly wounded or dead. Those lucky enough to have emerged unscathed were done for the day. The exhausted men staggered back into the woods and collapsed beneath the trees, where many fell into stuporous slumber.

But there were fresh soldiers available to enter the fight—always more soldiers. This topmost section of the battlefield, alone, contained a seemingly endless supply of men. Now, a legendary Federal fighting unit joined the action, 971 strong, under the command of General John Gibbon. Officially designated as the 4th Brigade, 1st Division, I Corps, this outfit was better known as the Black Hat Brigade, thanks to its distinctive Hardee hats, adorned with ostrich plumes. Its men were westerners for the most part, but in the 1862 conception of the term, meaning they hailed from the far-off states of Wisconsin and Indiana. They were battle-hardened veterans, known for fierceness as well as a kind of frontier insouciance. While the Rebs had a knack for needling the enemy, the Black Hats, during their most recent engagement at Turner's Gap in Maryland, had emerged as verbal victors. Even as they fought, the westerners had hurled a steady stream of insults in an easy, relaxed style.

The Black Hats lit out for that plateau, following a slightly different course than their predecessors. It required some of them to move through Miller's farm lot, stealing past his house and other structures. This was careful, excruciating work; Rebels could spring out at any moment. The western boys wended their way around the barn. Then they crept through Farmer Miller's peach orchard. They encountered a fence. Working in concert, the soldiers tried to knock it over, but it wouldn't budge. They had no choice but to use the gate; they filed through in a long line. Directing the men, a young captain waved his sword and shouted. "A bullet passes into his open mouth, and the voice is forever silent," Rufus Dawes, an officer with the 6th Wisconsin, would remember.

The perpetrators, a detachment of Rebel skirmishers, were spotted scampering away. The Black Hats continued to flood through the gate and into a garden, where they trampled across Farmer Miller's flowerbeds, and then into . . . the cornfield.

About halfway across, the battle line began to receive musket fire from off to one side. This was puzzling. The Black Hats had assumed that the enemy was in front of them; these bullets were flying in from the right. A group of Virginian soldiers, it turns out, had been hiding in the woods beside the cornfield. Now those Rebels had moved forward into a bed of clover, formed a wide battle line, and opened a punishing flanking fire. General Gibbon split the Black Hats, dispatching two regiments to engage the Confederates in the clover. Two other regiments lay down in the cornfield to wait until the way was clear.

The battle was getting frantic. The topmost section of the field fairly crawled with soldiers; they were in the corn, the surrounding pastures and meadows, and the woods that girded the open spaces. The sound had grown deafening. There were the pops of muskets, the peculiar whistling of bullets, the clip when they hit a cornstalk, the crack of striking wood, the thud of connecting with a body. Cannon fire poured in from all directions. The heavy shells screamed and sizzled, clattered in the treetops; shrapnel plopped in the soft earth or ricocheted with a metallic zing. "If all the stone and brick houses of Broadway should tumble at once the roar and rattle could hardly be greater," Alpheus Williams, a Union general, would recall of the cornfield fighting.

Most of the area's residents had fled before the battle. Still, a few remained. Panicked by the din, some women and children burst from the basement of a farmhouse where they'd been hiding, and set out running. They were like "a flock of birds," according to William Blackford, a Confederate cavalryman, "hair streaming in the wind and children of all ages stretched out behind, and tumbling at every step over the clods of the ploughed field." The Rebel cavalryman dashed forward on his horse. He pulled up beside the terrified civilians. The Yanks, he would later note, were decent enough to hold fire while he escorted them off the battlefield.

Even as the air hummed with projectiles, it also swam thick with a different, silent traffic: wigwag signals. Flagmen were everywhere, urgently waving, relaying observations and military intelligence. Prior to the battle, each side had staked out signal stations with elevated panoramic vantages, the Union choosing Elk Ridge, about two miles away, and the Confederates setting up in the cupola of the Lutheran church in Sharpsburg. There were also mobile teams of flagmen that would move to the centers of action as the battle unfolded. A Union team had drawn as close to the cornfield as safely possible. A Confederate team had taken up position in a stand of trees, behind their lines.

The flagmen sent messages using a simple code. (Waving the flag to the bearer's left signaled 1 and waving to the right signaled 2.) In standard wigwag code, the letter A was 11; B was 1221; C was 212; and so forth. Albert Myer, a surgeon from Buffalo, New York, who had earlier dabbled in telegraphy and had tried to create a new sign language for deaf-mutes, devised the system during the 1850s. The U.S. Department of War soon grasped its military value. To speed along development, he was assigned an assistant named Edward Porter Alexander.

When the Civil War broke out, New York–bred Myer sided with the Union. Alexander, a Georgian, joined the Confederacy. As a consequence, both sides had the benefit of this valuable new communication system, but each also had the ability to steal the other's signals. Both sides came up with the same solution, so-called cipher disks. These consisted of two concentric circles, often made out of heavy card stock. By rotating the disks, it was possible to revise the code. For example, the letter A, 11 in standard wigwag, might be changed to 12. It was a very basic form of encryption. Before battles, Union and Confederate signal teams synchronized their respective cipher disks with settings known only to their side.

For all this convolution and complication, the system worked surprisingly well. The flagmen wigwagged entire sentences that were instantly deciphered by relay men with field glasses stationed near McClellan, Lee, and other top generals. Then, horseback couriers were dispatched with bulletins for the field commanders, disseminating information down through the ranks.

After sorting out new command chains for Hartsuff and Christian's men, the two delayed brigades entered the action at last. They set off through the cornfield, following in the marching steps of the thousands who had already gone before them. Among these fresh troops was the 12th Massachusetts. They emerged from those tall stalks only to enter into an epic firefight with the Louisiana Tigers. Even by the standards of this battle, the clash was notable for its knee-quaveringly close range and its savagery. Perhaps this owed to the nature of these particular adversaries, men with unusually strong—and diametrically opposed—convictions.

As of 1862, soldiers enlisted for many good reasons: fending off homeland invaders, upholding their values, family obligation, a steady paycheck and possible career advancement, the chance to prove one's mettle or be heroic, adventure, or, in the case of the South, simply because they'd been drafted (the North wouldn't have a draft until 1863).

In stark contrast, many among the 12th Massachusetts were fighting to end slavery. This, at a time when Lincoln remained noncommittal in his public pronouncements on the subject, at a point where restoring the Union remained the North's stated war aim. But these were Boston boys, born and raised in the very cradle of abolitionism. After their regiment was mustered into service in 1861, they had marched off to war singing the antislavery song "John Brown's Body." The 12th Massachusetts is credited with popularizing this folk hymn. While visiting a Union camp one evening, the poet Julia Ward Howe had heard soldiers singing it. She awoke early the next morning with the tune stuck in her head, but fitted with new lyrics ("glory, glory, hallelujah") that she hastened to write down before they slipped away. And that's how the "Battle Hymn of the Republic," that soaring Union war anthem, was born—at least according to legend.

As for the Louisiana Tigers, they were a motley unit, consisting of men from wildly varied backgrounds and social stations. Jumbled together, they formed a kind of combat jambalaya that included lawyers and ex-cons, New Orleans wharf rats and pedigreed young gents from the city's most prominent families. Among the Tiger ranks were plenty of slaveholders, some the sons of wealthy plantation owners. Not only were these men fighting for regional sovereignty, but also to preserve a long-established institution and way of life.

As the two units engaged, the bullets flew so fast and thick that "the air seems full of leaden missiles," in the recollection of one participant. Yet the lines pushed ever closer, drawing to within a mere 50 yards, a smoothbore distance better suited to Bunker Hill. It was as if these men's fervent convictions had drawn them into a lethal familiarity.

Julius Rabardy, a private with the 12th Massachusetts, was shot and wounded, a victim of this hellish close-range musket melee. To his utter shock, several Rebels—"wild beasts" is how he would remember them—wriggled forward and sought shelter behind his fallen body. The Johnnies were so close he must have been able to feel their hot breath. He just lay there in pain, helpless, reduced to a human bulwark.

During thirty fraught minutes the 12th Massachusetts lost 224 of 334 men (49 killed, 165 wounded, 10 missing) in what would be the worst casualty rate suffered by a Union regiment this day. The Tigers lost 60 percent of their 550 men, and every single officer was either wounded or killed.

All the while, the Black Hats were involved in their own desperate struggle. Half of the brigade had been ordered to remain in the cornfield, lying low, while the other half chased off the Virginians pouring fire into their flank. The horizontal soldiers drew the tougher assignment. They had to remain flat on the ground, passively waiting. Dawes of the 6th Wisconsin remembered how the bullets would "spin through the soft furrows—thick, almost, as hail. Shells burst around us, the fragments tearing up the ground, and canister whistled through the corn above us."

Presently, the Virginians were driven off. The way was clear. As the western boys got to their feet, however, it must have felt like a grisly impromptu roll call. While some stood, others didn't budge, remaining face down in the rich Maryland soil. These poor souls never stood a chance. They died where they'd lain, among the cornstalks.

The Black Hats pressed on. Soon enough, they encountered more trouble. Just beyond the southwest corner of the cornfield, they ran into a mass of Rebels, two brigades' worth, totaling 1,150 soldiers under the command of General William Starke. The westerners found themselves pitted against soldiers from Alabama, Virginia, and Louisiana. They quickly fell into even closer-range combat than the Tigers and 12th Massachusetts, distance seeming to shrink as the battle's intensity grew.

The Hagerstown Pike ran along one side of the cornfield. It was just an ordinary country road. On this morning, it became a ferociously contested demarcation, both sides struggling to keep the other from crossing. Never mind that hoary *whites of their eyes*; pupils dilated in terror must have been very nearly visible as the soldiers fired across the road, sometimes trading bullets over a space of less than 100 feet.

During the fighting, the Black Hats lost one of their most beloved officers. Captain Werner von Bachelle was a German-born immigrant to Wisconsin who had served in the French army in Algiers. He was a big-hearted man with a ready store of tales about battles in faraway lands, and a soft spot for animals. When a stray dog started hanging around camp, the soldiers presented it to von Bachelle. The black and white Newfoundland became his constant companion, even accompanying him into battle. He taught it tricks, such as how to perform a military salute with its paw. Near the Hagerstown Pike, Captain von Bachelle went down in a shower of bullets. The dog refused to leave his side.

Riding out ahead of his men, carrying the colors, Rebel general Starke was also hit—three bullets knocked him from his horse and he perished within the hour. Indeed, the Civil War wasn't deadly only for foot soldiers. While privates fell in tragically greater numbers, generals (a far smaller portion of the overall fighting force) were nonetheless 50 percent more likely to be killed in battle. It's yet another consequence of the era's blunt methods, which often found generals on horseback riding out ahead of battle lines. *Aim for the mounted man* was an eminently sensible Civil War tactic. After all, a man on a horse likely held a high rank, earning plaudits for whomever brought him down. In the tight, angry confines of this battlefield, all those factors were amplified. Starke was the first of a number of major generals who would die this day.

By now, the Black Hats, along with a number of other Union regiments had fought their way through the cornfield, and they were starting to mass in the pastures beyond its southern boundary. The Federals were making real progress, had drawn to within 500 yards of that plateau with the little schoolhouse.

Unbeknownst to the Union troops, however, a large force of Rebels had gathered in the woods beyond the plateau, out of sight, safe from enemy cannon fire. The 2,300 soldiers, commanded by General John Bell Hood, included a large contingent of Texans as well as Georgians, Alabamans, Mississippians, North and South Carolinians ("Caleenyuns" to the ears of one Yankee). As for the Lone Star regiments, they were distinguished as the only ones to fight in the Eastern Theater during the Civil War.

This convocation of Rebels was eating breakfast. As one of the most experienced units in the Confederate army (Hood's men had been in two dozen engagements in 1862, including Gaines's Mill and Second Bull Run), they weren't about to let a raging battle get in the way of a chance for grub. What's more, the men hadn't enjoyed a hot meal in three days, subsisting mostly on green corn and coffee. A much-anticipated commissary wagon had arrived shortly before daybreak, but to their disappointment it had contained only cornmeal, no meat. So, the men were making hoecakes, using their ramrods to cook them over open fires.

Hood ordered the drummer boys to beat the long roll, summoning his men into battle. They entered the fight enraged at the interrupted breakfast, many of them still carrying hoecakes, stuffing them into their mouths as they fell into formation. Then they came swarming over and around the plateau. The air rang with Rebel Yells, a yip-yip-yipping that came across as at once bestial, mentally unhinged, and mocking—guaranteed to strike terror into the staunchest Yank.

Besides surprise, the charging Confederates had another decisive advantage: fresh muskets. As any Civil War soldier could attest, the first shots of the day were the truest. One's musket was still clean and cool. Already, the Black Hats and other Federals on this part of the field had fired numerous shots, leaving their muskets hot and caked thick with powder. To force a bullet down the barrel was an ordeal. In desperation, some men were picking up rocks and trying to pound home their ramrods. Panic began to spread through the ranks. This was such a mismatch: while the

Rebels advanced, shooting relentlessly, the Federal fire seemed to have slowed . . . way . . . down, like they were waging war in molasses.

The Union lines simply melted. Then, it was every man for himself as the soldiers dashed back into the cornfield. The Rebels pursued them through the tall stalks.

One particular regiment, the 1st Texas, made unnervingly rapid progress, staying hot on the shoe heels of the retreating Federals. The Texans were supposed to remain in battle line with two other regiments. Perhaps it was exuberance, or maybe simple blood-lust, but soon the regiment had pulled way out ahead. Among the many downsides of linear tactics is the need for masses of men to move in unison. A regiment that breaks off on its own and pro-gresses too rapidly can find itself dangerously isolated. The Texans were now 150 yards in the lead.

Just beyond the northern edge of the cornfield, Union soldiers waited. While the Confederacy had just loosed an angry breakfast-deprived hoard, the Union also had reserves, plenty of them, to draw upon. These fresh troops, Pennsylvania men, formed into a fearsome battle line; arranged west to east were the state's 9th, 11th, 12th, 7th, 4th, and 8th regiments. Many of them knelt be-hind a low stone wall built by Farmer Miller. Just as Douglass's Georgians relied on a tactic in the day's opening action (*select your own personal cornrow*), so too did the Pennsylvanians. The field hung thick with gun smoke; visibility was fast diminishing. So, the Pennsylvanians were instructed to wait until they could see Rebel legs beneath the smoke, then direct fire above those legs.

The 1st Texas reached that northern edge of the cornfield— alone. There was an eerie calm as they continued forward and then, the deluge. They were hit with virtually everything available in a Civil War arsenal: rifled bullets and smoothbore balls as well as cannon shells lobbed over the Union battle line. Some of the Pennsylvanians even fired buck and ball, a diabolical combination whereby a single musket load contains a ball and three pieces of buckshot, each about the size of a BB. The buckshot was capable

only of limited damage. The idea was to fill the air with tiny stinging projectiles, a swarm of leaden gnats, overwhelming the enemy.
Soon enough the *ball*, the deadly component of mixture, was sure
to find its mark. A soldier with the 4th Texas, which was trailing
behind the 1st Texas, described the onslaught as "the hottest place
I ever saw on this earth or want to see hereafter."

The 1st Texas couldn't retreat fast enough. Now it was the
Union soldiers in pursuit. But the counterattack soon fizzled. By
this point, there were so many soldiers occupying this portion of
the field that it was difficult for either side to press advantage.

Back at the southern end of the cornfield, the 1st Texas, which
had entered the tall rows with such aplomb, exited in a tattered
trickle. Of the 226 who had gone into battle, 45 had been killed, 141
wounded. That's an 82 percent casualty rate, and would stand as the
worst toll for any regiment, Confederate or Union, during a Civil
War battle. The 1st Texas suffered other losses, too, though these
were more in the realm of pride and honor. While he accounted
for survivors, Captain John Woodward was suddenly seized by
panic. "The flags, the flags! Where are the flags?" he cried.

During the retreat, it seems, some Pennsylvanians had managed to overtake the 1st Texas color guard. A desperate fight
ensued: standard-bearer after standard-bearer went down, but
someone always stepped forward to maintain possession of the
flags. Corporal William Pritchard was the last Texan known to
hold the colors. Surrounded by Yanks, he was sprayed in the face
with buckshot. As he brought up his hands for protection, a ball
lodged in his gut. The wounded corporal looked on helplessly as
men from the 9th Pennsylvania dashed off with the captured flags.
In the spot where this epic tussle took place, legend has it that the
bodies of ten Rebels were later found, each having tried valiantly
but unsuccessfully to protect the colors.

The loss of the Confederate battle flag, featuring the familiar St. Andrew's Cross, brought shame and sorrow enough to the
Texans. But they had also surrendered their regimental flag. This
was a Texas state flag, hand sewn by Charlotte Wigfall, the wife

of their first commander, the man who had originally mustered them into service. Painted onto the flag were the names of battles in which the regiment had fought: Seven Pines, Malvern Hill, and Eltham's Landing. Even the flag's lone white star had a story, for Mrs. Wigfall had lovingly cut it from her own wedding dress. The surviving Texans made for safety of the woods, lay down, and let the remorse wash over them.

By now, the morning sun had broken through the clouds, though a soldier on the field could be forgiven for not noticing the weather change. In some spots the bluish white gun smoke hung thunderhead thick, while other places it drifted in little cirrus wisps. A single wide black column of smoke stretched to the heavens, one of the battle's most visible and ominous features. It issued from Samuel Mumma's farmhouse, set ablaze by Rebels concerned that it was a prime spot for Union sharpshooters to take up residence. A soldier from the 3rd North Carolina had started the fire by tossing a chunk of burning wood through a window and onto a bed quilt.

The day was turning out to be unseasonably warm. It was disagreeably humid, too, thanks to the previous night's drizzle. The coarse powder clung to the men's damp skin like beach sand. Because soldiers tended to favor one side of their mouth for tearing open cartridges, men with half their mouth smeared with black powder—a grotesque carnival touch—was a common sight. The smell of sulfur permeated everything.

Already there had been untold momentum shifts, each starting with a promising charge through the corn, all ending the same way. The dead were distributed generously among the stalks. The wounded hobbled or limped, some even crawled, sorting themselves by a simple and poignant logic, Confederates moving south toward their lines, Federals moving north toward theirs. Above this hellscape, cannon shells screamed, birds wheeled in confusion, and the wigwag signals maintained their noiseless chatter.

"Genl Hooker wounded severely in foot," read one. He had to be carried from the field. And then another: "Genl Mansfield is dangerously wounded." Joseph Mansfield, commander of the XII Corps, had been shot from his horse and would be dead within hours (another fatality from among the ranks of generals, this second one on the Union side).

Those lucky enough to be off the field—men from Duryee's brigade, Douglass's Georgians, the Louisiana Tigers, 12th Massachusetts, Black Hats, Hood's Texans, and countless other units—sought the safety of the surrounding woods. Both sides, the Union and Confederacy, held swaths of woodland that provided havens for now. Most of these retreating soldiers were done for the day. The injured staggered toward barns and other structures set well behind the lines.

The Rebels had held so far. The Union hadn't managed to seize that plateau. Nevertheless, a select few Federal soldiers had drawn close enough to make a surprising observation.

*It was a church!* The building atop the plateau; the landmark that had served throughout the morning as a guide the way that Napoleon had used a farmhouse called La Haye Sainte during the Battle of Waterloo; what had been taken by many for a one-room schoolhouse—*was not.* The confusion was natural enough. After all, it was such a modest structure, featuring neither a steeple, nor cross, nor stained glass. But this was to be expected in a place of worship for the Dunkers, a sect that rejected ornamentation in keeping with the biblical caution to be "not of this world."

The world had very much intruded. The walls were riddled with bullets and cannon shells. Yet the little church stood.

# CHAPTER 4

## Little Mac v. Bobby Lee

*All during the cornfield contest,* as the fighting swelled, then roared, then fizzled out, the commanding generals of the two opposing armies, George McClellan and Robert Lee, monitored the action from behind their lines.

Both had built and trained enormous armies, shaping the soldiers to their wills and ways. Both had tramped through Maryland—McClellan pursuing Lee—before facing off at this location, chosen almost as if by mutual accord. When it became clear that the Union army was closing fast, Lee had staked out advantageous ground on which to make a stand. On arriving in the valley on September 15, McClellan had proceeded with great care, preparing his army for battle. The rival commanders had been like chess players. The previous day was spent carefully placing combat units, shifting them in response to the other's movements, personally overseeing the placement of artillery, making sure every advantage was exploited, every weakness masked.

McClellan and Lee had worried the details, then worried some more. At this point, there was a limit to what either could accomplish personally. Now, it was up to the soldiers to fight. The two commanders were left mostly to watch, awaiting the battle's outcome.

McClellan was sitting outside on a plump and luxurious armchair. It looked like something from a Victorian drawing room, jarringly incongruous placed there on the grass. The commander was on the front lawn of a handsome brick house, Greek Revival style, with columns framing the porch. This was the home of Philip and Elizabeth Pry, well-to-do farmers.

A couple nights earlier, George Custer, McClellan's twenty-two-year-old aide-de-camp, had informed the Prys that the commander had selected their home for his field headquarters. The location was peerless. The house sat on a bluff above a bend in Antietam Creek, roughly two miles to the northeast of Sharpsburg. The sweeping view—one that ordinarily took in a generous swath of that lush, rolling farm country—offered on this day a panorama of battle. Yet the house was also reassuringly distant from the fighting. A headquarters guard was stationed nearby, just in case, composed of soldiers from the 93rd New York.

Along with Custer, a number of McClellan's aides were present at the field headquarters. There was his brother, Arthur, and his father-in-law, who served as chief of staff. There were also members of the press, as well as couriers and wigwag specialists. Everywhere were horses, saddled and ready, hitched to the Prys' fences and trees. Stakes had been driven into the ground to serve as stands for telescopes.

From the Miller farm, a mile and a half distant, the clatter of muskets and roar of cannons had been quite audible (loud, in fact) and it had been possible to hear the soldiers sweeping back and forth across the cornfield. Periodically, a sliver of the action became visible. McClellan would rise from his armchair and peer through a telescope.

Lee was somewhere in the hills on the other side of the Antietam. His field headquarters was a tent, rather than a well-appointed farmhouse. It was in a grove of trees on the outskirts of Sharpsburg.

Lee had awakened around 4:00 A.M. As his first act of the day, he'd dashed off an urgent message, exhorting one of his generals to employ artillery to protect a nearby Potomac fording spot at all costs. Boteler's Ford, the Potomac crossing to the rear of the Rebel army, was like an exit, the only way back into Virginia if things went desperately wrong.

Lee then mounted Traveller, his treasured gray horse. On this morning, however, getting up in the saddle proved challenging due to an accident the general had recently suffered. The day after Second Bull Run ended, while conducting reconnaissance on Federal positions, Lee was standing beside Traveller. Suddenly, there was a cry, "Yankee cavalry!" Startled, the horse lurched forward, and as Lee reached for the bridle, he stumbled and fell to the ground. The Yankee-spotting turned out to be a false alarm. But Lee's fall resulted in a broken bone in one hand and left the other badly sprained. Both hands had to be splinted and bandaged.

Throughout the invasion of Maryland, Lee had bounced along in an ambulance wagon, a situation he found painfully undignified. But he was healed enough at last to get back on his horse, although his hands were still bandaged. To climb into the saddle and to ride Traveller required the help of an orderly.

At 5:30 A.M., Lee had set off along Sharpsburg's darkened Main Street. The orderly went out ahead, holding the reins. The clomp of hooves must have filled the air as Lee rode past the houses, mostly abandoned, but a few still host to occupants who were sleeping—or cowering. Lee made his slow way out to Cemetery Hill, an eminence on the edge of town, with its own panoramic view of the valley. This is one of the spots from which the general would monitor the battle.

Three stars without an encircling wreath were affixed to the collar of Lee's uniform, suggesting that his rank was only that of a colonel. He intended to forgo a general's insignia until he'd won the war for his side. By contrast, McClellan was in full commander's regalia with sash, sword, and assorted shiny gewgaws. Lee relied on a lean headquarters staff, whereas McClellan liked to surround himself with members of the press and other hangers-on. Even though Lee was injured, he would also prove more mobile than his rival, relying on little country lanes to travel behind his lines, albeit slowly. Indeed, these two commanders couldn't be more un-alike. Their styles—borne of vastly different experiences and up-bringings—would have profound consequences on the battle as it unfolded.

George McClellan was young, only thirty-five. He was short, too, though he claimed to stand five nine. No doubt, he padded on a couple extra inches. Everything about McClellan was inflated: his broad shoulders, puffed-out chest, showy uniforms, and the alpha-rooster bearing. He fairly swelled with confidence. It's a trait he projected intensely, skirting the very edge of ridiculous before somehow, mysteriously, settling on convincing. "I can do it all," he once declared with characteristic bravado.

He'd grown up in Philadelphia, where he was raised as what might best be described as a hothouse patrician. Young McClellan received the best instruction from the city's finest private tutors. He learned to speak both French and Latin. His family kept a stable of trotting horses. At an early age, he learned to ride.

McClellan's mother was a Philadelphia society fixture. Among the family friends was Daniel Webster, the statesman and orator. McClellan's father was an acclaimed surgeon, credited as the first to remove a diseased parotid (salivary) gland and an expert at eye lens extraction. Patients traveled from overseas to obtain his ser-vices. Dr. McClellan was a haughty man, variously described as "obnoxious" and "impolitic." But he was a trailblazer, as well as a founder of Jefferson Medical College, one of the first medical schools in America. Among its distinguished graduates: Samuel Gross, immortalized in *The Gross Clinic*, a painting that depicts him overseeing an operation in a crowded teaching amphithe-ater. Thomas Mütter, for many years the chair of Jefferson Medical College's surgery department, built a huge collection of anatomi-cal oddities, eventually displayed at the Philadelphia museum that bears his name.

Naturally, the extended McClellan family was filled with people who had chosen the medical profession, following in the path of the illustrious doctor. Young George, however, was drawn to the military. Growing up, he was stirred by tales of a proud Scottish heritage filled with martial glory. Among his forebears were knights, actual knights, hailing from the lowlands of Galloway. According to lore, Clan MacLellan had presented a Scottish king with Mons Meg, a celebrated bombard (a medieval cannon) used to defend Edinburgh Castle.

At fifteen, McClellan applied to West Point. Officially, he was one year too young to enroll, but he had the benefit of an intense campaign on his behalf, including a letter of recommendation from President Tyler, no less. The academy made an exception. McClellan attended West Point alongside a whole crop of future generals, North and South, including Darius Couch, John Gibbon, David Jones, and Thomas Jackson, later to be known as "Stonewall." George Pickett, he of the notorious charge, was another fellow student, distinguished by finishing dead last in the Class of 1846.

McClellan finished second in the class. He graduated just in time to enlist for the Mexican War, where he served as the army's youngest engineering officer (always the youngest, always the prodigy). He earned promotion to second lieutenant and a superior gave him a glowing commendation for his "gallant and meritorious conduct" from the halls of Montezuma.

After the war, the opportunities just kept coming to McClellan. He was chosen for an expedition to locate the source of the Red River, led by Randolph Marcy, an explorer who had achieved a national celebrity second only to the Pathfinder himself, John Frémont. Marcy even discovered a tributary in Texas that he named McClellan Creek. The young officer was also one of three selected for another choice assignment, traveling overseas to study the strategies used by European armies during the Crimean War. McClellan visited the site of the Battle of Balaclava, immortalized in the poem "The Charge of the Light Brigade." He was present as an observer during the siege of Sevastopol. Drawing on his upbringing in a distinguished medical family, he also did an extensive tour of field hospitals to learn about European innovations in caring for the war wounded. The Crimea trip furnished the grist for a report that was written by McClellan, published by Congress, and widely circulated. Somehow, he even found time to design a saddle and to translate a manual on bayonet tactics from the original French.

Nevertheless, McClellan soon grew restless. He'd embarked on a military career during a period of relative peace. Following the Mexican War, the opportunities for battlefield heroics were limited. Even among the most talented officers, a common fate was to be shunted off to some godforsaken frontier outpost to spend years damming a river, or building a fort.

McClellan was far too ambitious for that. When the opportunity arose, he left the military to take a job as a railroad executive with the Illinois Central, earning $3,000 per year, nearly three times his army salary. His golden rise only continued: soon he moved to the rival Ohio and Mississippi railroad, and tripled his salary again, making him one of the highest paid—and youngest—executives in the country. He kept a hand in soldiering by volunteering with a militia—a true weekend warrior.

Along the way, the brash young executive also found marital success. He wed Mary Ellen Marcy, daughter of the celebrated explorer. Blue eyed and beautiful, she went by the name "Nelly." To win her hand, however, required a courtship as focused and relentless as any military campaign. Nelly was a much-pursued debutante; the rivals for her affection were legion. Fortunately for McClellan, Randolph Marcy and his wife were unimpressed by the competition. He was the only suitor they deemed worthy of their society-prize daughter. At the end of five years' courtship, after rejecting the marriage proposals of eight other men, Nelly finally accepted McClellan's bid for her hand, delivered aboard a private railcar.

Whatever else might be said of McClellan (and there would be plenty), he was a devoted husband. He showed Nelly a sentimental side lacking in his other relationships. "!!Tuesday 22!!" he mooned in his diary on their May 1860 wedding date. He even tried his hand at poetry, crafting what he described as "some *very* blank verses to Nelly" on February 14, 1857: "Let these lines be indeed my Valentine and say that I do indeed love you."

Throughout their long marriage, McClellan would make an effort to write his wife a letter every day that they were separated. He showered her with such sentiments as this: "A heart so pure as yours, a mind so bright as yours—to gain thee is better than to gain an empire. You are my empire."

When the first shots were fired on Sumter, McClellan was living with his bride in a large house in Cincinnati. Instantly, his military services were in demand. His career had been an unbroken series of accomplishments, after all, even if he was no longer in the army and had virtually no battlefield experience besides (few men did). The governors of three large states (New York, Pennsylvania, and Ohio) requested that he command their militias. In short order, he became a major general in the U.S. Army, outranked only by the august Winfield Scott.

McClellan lit off for the western portion of Virginia, then in rebellion against the rebellion. (The region was balking at joining the rest of the state in secession.) He was involved in such early actions as Rich Mountain, Corrick's Ford, and the Philippi Races, the latter being a predawn attack near the town of *Philippi* that sent the Rebs *racing*. No deaths resulted, but two Confederate soldiers sustained injuries and, notably, were forced to endure the war's first amputations.

Rage militaire was in full bloom. During those giddy early days of 1861, the press was full of accounts of McClellan's brave exploits in western Virginia. "Glorious, isn't it!" crowed the *New York Times*. "We feel very proud of our wise and brave young Major-General." McClellan became one of the North's first war heroes. He even posed for a little carte de visite portrait that became a much-coveted collector's item throughout the Union, featuring him slipping his hand inside his jacket, Napoleon style.

It reinforced an association that McClellan no doubt sought to bolster, between himself and the French military icon. (As it happens, the hidden hand was then a fad in portraits; supposedly it communicated good breeding. That certainly applied to McClellan with his Philadelphia pedigree.)

And then—fresh meteoric heights. On July 22, 1861, the day after the Union's stunning and unexpected defeat at Bull Run, Lincoln sent a telegram to McClellan, summoning him to Washington. McClellan was named commander of the Federal forces in the Eastern Theater.

Between July and November, he built his army from 50,000 to 168,000 men. McClellan put in eighteen-hour days, visiting the camps that surrounded Washington. Whenever he encountered deficiencies among the troops, he urged training. This was an area in which the young general excelled. When raw recruits began to show promise—training, training, always more training. McClellan gave this force its name: the Army of the Potomac. He built it in his image.

To stoke morale, McClellan attempted to make personal contact with every single soldier, a worthy, if impossible, goal. Still, he found ways to reach his sprawling army. He made abundant speeches, the more florid the better. He arranged frequent reviews, or rather, grand reviews (*grand* being one of McClellan's favorite words) in front of thousands of spectators. No one loved pomp more than McClellan. Win the general's favor and one might be rewarded with his patented salute: he'd raise his arm in the air while twirling his cap on one finger. The men, in turn, grew fond of their commander. They even gave him a nickname: "Little Mac."

While McClellan proved inspired at building a fighting force, he seemed less inclined to actually fight. Once the general had assembled an army, a kind of perfectionism set in, as if he couldn't bear to sully his glorious creation with the tumult of actual battle. For months, the Army of the Potomac camped in a vast ring around Washington, immobile.

Lincoln grew worried. The president feared that his general suffered from what he termed the "slows."

But McClellan was not to be rushed. He bristled at any interference on the part of Lincoln, whom he held in a kind of double-barreled contempt: dismayed by the chief executive's lack of military knowledge and likewise disgusted—with every fiber of his patrician Philadelphia being—by the man's folksy manner and hardscrabble frontier upbringing. Behind Lincoln's back, McClellan called the president an "idiot" and the "original gorrilla." Publicly, he was scarcely more respectful. When Lincoln convened a war conference at the White House, McClellan sat sullenly, refusing to participate. If sensitive battle plans were revealed, the general explained, the president was sure to thoughtlessly blab them to son Tad. They'd wind up splashed all over the newspapers. One time, Lincoln went to the general's home in Washington, planning to have a private discussion. On learning that McClellan was away, Lincoln resolved to wait in the parlor. When McClellan returned, he simply snuck past Lincoln, slipped upstairs, and went to bed. Members of Lincoln's staff were astounded by the affronts the general piled on. But Lincoln waved their concerns away, saying, "Never mind; I will hold McClellan's horse if he will only bring us success."

Lincoln, shrewd judge of human nature that he was, appears to have recognized that McClellan's immense ego was also frail as bone china. Thus, he drew on reserves of forbearance in dealing with him. Because he was eighteen years older, Lincoln treated his general a bit like an errant child, alternately cajoling, imploring, demanding, yet always careful to communicate that his support remained unconditional. This missive from Lincoln to McClellan is typical: "I beg to assure you that I have never written you, or spoken to you, in greater kindness of feeling than now, nor with a fuller purpose to sustain you, so far as in my most anxious judgment, I consistently can. *But you must act.*"

Yet still McClellan dawdled. The public demand for action grew more urgent. "Onward to Richmond" became the refrain, a call to move on the Confederate capital. The night of the Lincolns' gala ball, recall, dinner was delayed by a locked stateroom door, prompting someone to quip about favoring "forward movement." That's the subtext of the comment. Everyone laughed, but one wonders whether McClellan, a guest at the gala, secretly fumed.

During the first months of 1862, Lincoln began to think about replacing his general. Although the president was legendary for his patience, he was nearing his limit. Certainly, there existed no shortage of candidates to pick from. The White House was overwhelmed with applications for military posts, stuffed into desk drawers, stacked in teetering piles that spilled across tabletops. Finding *qualified* candidates was the challenge.

The situation grew so desperate that Lincoln began to consider taking the field himself. This, despite his scant experience, as captain of an Illinois militia that had seen limited action in the Black Hawk War a full three decades earlier. Nevertheless, he was commander in chief of the armed forces. Increasingly, Lincoln wondered whether he'd need to exercise that role. He even checked out several books on military strategy from the Library of Congress.

Finally McClellan indicated he was ready to act. During that black stretch when everything transformed, the period when Willie died and Shiloh raged, McClellan revealed a plan at last. It was a bold gambit, one that almost seemed to justify the endless delays. McClellan had settled on an aquatic expedition that would convey his army to the tip of the Virginia Peninsula. From there, they could move on Richmond from the south—not the direction from which anyone would expect an attack.

On March 17, 1862, an armada of ships, carrying 121,000 troops, sailed down the Potomac and out into Chesapeake Bay. McClellan had launched his Peninsula Campaign, the largest military mobilization in the history of the North American continent, an awesome undertaking.

Upon landing on Virginia soil, however, the commander fell prey to a fresh anxiety. He began to question whether he had too few troops to march on Richmond. "Think On" is the motto that appeared on Clan MacLellan's heraldic crest. It's a useful trait in many circumstances, but perhaps not so much in battle. McClellan was proving to be a closet Hamlet, paralyzed by secret doubts.

At times of tortured uncertainty, he turned to Allan Pinkerton. He placed great trust in the famous detective due to a shared heritage (Pinkerton was Scottish, born in Glasgow) and also because they'd successfully worked together in the past. During McClellan's tenure with the Illinois Central, he'd hired the Pinkerton agency to track down train robbers and to uncover the railroad's own internal financial shenanigans. As commander of an army, McClellan relied on Pinkerton to figure out the size of the enemy forces confronting him.

While Pinkerton was a superb private investigator, his methods weren't suited to gathering military intelligence. Mostly he drew on the anecdotal findings of his agents, which he would send behind enemy lines under outrageous covers. One agent set out in a luxuriously appointed carriage, wearing a top hat and broadcloth coat, posing as an English fop on an illicit cotton-buying junket. He doled out Cuban cigars and slugs of fine port to the persons he encountered in an effort to ply them into venturing the size of the Rebel force. Pinkerton would then take the findings of these absurd undercovers and cobble them into reports for McClellan's consumption. Predictably, the troop-count estimates were suspect. Adding to the problem, McClellan requested that Pinkerton always inflate the Rebel count by 5 percent, just to be safe.

On the Virginia Peninsula, McClellan believed he was facing a Confederate army that totaled 200,000, when the actual number was probably less than half of that.

Opposing generals took full advantage of McClellan's skittishness. One of the first that he encountered during the Peninsula Campaign was John Magruder, charged with defending Yorktown.

Magruder was an inventive and ferocious general, with a big personality. It was said that Prince John, as he was known, liked to fight all day and dance all night. But his greatest passion was theater. Before the war, while stationed in one of those remote outposts characteristic of the old army, he put on plays to keep up the men's morale during the dreary winters. For a production of *Othello*, he somehow persuaded Ulysses Grant to audition for the role of Desdemona, its tragic heroine. This required Grant to wear a dress. Apparently the future architect of the "unconditional surrender" doctrine was not exactly fetching. So, Magruder decided to go in a different direction with his casting. (Prince John appears to have been gay. Although he married, his wife remained conveniently abroad in Florence, Italy, and paid him only a single visit after 1855.)

In defense of Yorktown, Magruder put his theater craft to brilliant use. At night, he set hundreds of faux campfires that blazed away, but with no one gathered around them. Mornings he ordered his buglers to make an awful racket and asked his men to scurry about, creating a sense of commotion. Then, he organized the soldiers into columns and, quite aware that his movements were being observed, proceeded to march them out of the woods, across a road, and into the opposite woods. It created the impression that a large Rebel force was on the move, when, in reality, it was the same men marching in circles, crossing the road over and over. He even placed so-called Quaker cannons, logs painted to look like artillery pieces.

With a mere 13,600 men, Magruder flummoxed McClellan, who commanded an army ten times that size. Prince John managed to slow the Union's progress up the peninsula for an entire, crucial month.

Now, one might think that a hesitating general would quickly lose the respect of his men. In McClellan's case, however, the devotion of his soldiers remained unshakeable. To those outside the military, this would be an enduring mystery. But if there's any message that the general managed to convey, it was his personal regard for each and every soldier. On parade grounds, during grand reviews, following battles, McClellan could always be counted on to deliver one of his aureate speeches, telling his charges he would watch over them, and care for them, and that he loved them—love always love: "know that your General loves you from the depths of his heart."

There's a temptation to dismiss this as its own form of theater, as disingenuous as one of Prince John's log cannons. Only it wasn't. McClellan's own private correspondence makes this abundantly clear. As a notorious backstabber, the record of the general's jibes is voluminous and Lincoln was hardly his only victim (he called Winfield Scott "a perfect imbecile"; War Secretary Edwin Stanton "the vilest man I ever knew"; and "a meddling, officious, incompetent little puppy" were his choice words for William Seward, the secretary of state). But his behind-their-backs treatment of his own soldiers showed a marked departure from this: his daily letters to his beloved Nelly are filled with such sentiments as "every poor fellow that is killed or wounded almost haunts me!"

McClellan's concern for his men was quite genuine. It was also, at least partially, the source of his hesitation. He wanted to avoid needlessly putting them in danger. The soldiers registered this fully. And they loved Little Mac for it.

Now, to Lee, McClellan's rival. Lee looked like a general straight out of an epic poem, or a children's storybook perhaps. He stood a trim five-foot eleven, with ramrod-stiff bearing, and dark, penetrating eyes. His hair was neat and distinguished gray (Lee was twenty years older than McClellan). He'd recently grown a beard, a nod to wartime fashion. Even the insides of Lee's legs cooperated with the maintenance of his image; reputedly, they were unusually flat, a quirk that allowed him to sit more squarely in the saddle. Of course, the lofty impression must have been somewhat dimmed on this day, with both his hands bandaged.

Lee, too, had built up a mighty fighting force: the Army of Northern Virginia. He had courtly manners, enviable penmanship, and pronounced *bake* as "beck"; *walnut*, "wonnut"—the result of a proud Tidewater accent that traced its origins way, way back into history.

Lee had grown up in Alexandria, George Washington's home-town. As a boy, he walked streets that Washington had planned, drank water from wells that Washington had ordered dug. He watched the militia drill on the same village green where Colonial troops had once stood at attention before General Washington. Lee worshipped at Christ Church, where a pew once occupied by George and Martha still existed, and a Bible once owned by the first president was still used in the Sunday service.

Even though the great man passed away seven years before Lee's birth, Lee's history and ancestry were inextricably bound up with Washington, Alexandria, the Revolution, and the fate of a fledgling nation. The Lees were considered one of the first families of Virginia. Two Lees were signers of the Declaration of Independence. Three were members of the Continental Con-gress. One (Richard Henry Lee) is remembered for proposing a 10th Amendment to the Constitution, designed to uphold state's rights.

Lee's father was Henry Lee III, known as "Light Horse Harry." It was a nickname coined during the American Revolution, where he'd distinguished himself as an aggressive and ingenious cavalry commander. He fought alongside Washington, becoming a favor-ite and trusted general. The immortal line "first in war, first in peace, and first in the hearts of his countrymen"—those are the words of Lee's father, delivered in a eulogy to the great Washington.

Following the Revolution, however, Light Horse Harry had difficulty adjusting to civilian life. He became involved in all kinds of shady financial schemes, such as investing a large portion of the family savings in something called the Dismal Swamp Company. It turned out quite as disastrously as the name might suggest. He dabbled in currency speculation, too, even tried to obtain inside information from Alexander Hamilton, a Revolutionary War ac-quaintance turned United States treasury secretary. Hamilton re-fused to cooperate.

Financial insecurity was a constant in young Lee's life. Only on rare occasions was his father even home; a more common occurrence, it seemed, was for one of the army of creditors that pursued Light Horse Harry to show up at the front door. Twice he was jailed for failure to pay bills. And then, when Lee was just eleven, his father died en route home from the West Indies and another busted enrichment scheme.

Thus, along with Washington, that shining exemplar, young Lee had a model of failure hovering close as can be. It was something to rage against; something not to repeat.

At West Point, Lee graduated second in the class of 1829, achieving the same rank that McClellan would nearly two decades later. But there's McClellan *second* and then there's Lee *second*: even though demerits were given for the most modest infractions—playing cards, reading a novel, a button undone on a uniform, being late for absolutely anything—Lee managed to accumulate none, zero demerits, during his entire career at the military academy. Fellow cadets nicknamed him the "Marble Model." He was like a statue come to life, seemingly not subject to ordinary human foibles.

Upon graduation, Lee joined the army, where he continued to exert this extreme self-control. He began trimming his hair a tiny bit every single day, a practice he'd continue throughout his life. It saved him the trouble of having to visit a barber. One time, as Lee set off for a new posting, a friend gave him a bottle of whiskey as a going-away present. Twenty months later, he returned and ceremoniously retrieved the bottle from his luggage, unopened. Lee wasn't a teetotaler. He enjoyed the occasional glass of wine. No, he left the whiskey bottle untapped simply because . . . he could. He was that disciplined.

As an officer in a peacetime army, however, Lee also experienced that all-too-common fate: he devoted long stretches of his career to building forts. The engineering training he'd received at West Point appeared to have more applicability than his classes on military strategy. A stretch of his early career was spent in St.

Louis clearing "snags"; that is, removing sandbars that hampered Mississippi River commerce. Periodically, Lee drew court-martial duty, something he dreaded, as it required him to spend months at far-off places, such as Fort Riley in Kansas Territory.

Lee's wife was Mary Custis, someone he'd known since childhood. She was the great-granddaughter of Daniel Parke Custis. Custis had been Martha Washington's first husband. So, that made Lee's wife the *step*-great-granddaughter of George Washington.

The couple managed a fecund union, even though military business kept Lee away from home for long stretches. Together, they had seven children. During an era of high child mortality, all lived into adulthood, making the couple far more fortunate than many of their contemporaries, such as the Lincolns. Whereas Abe was a notably lax parent, Lee was a stern disciplinarian. He was in the habit of constantly writing notes to his children, pressing the need for such qualities as "self-denial and self-control." He outfitted Robert Jr.'s room specially, purchasing the furnishings and bedding of a standard West Point cadet's room. He even subjected the boy to regular inspections.

Over his long career, Lee did manage the occasional taste of combat. Such occurrences really jolted him into life. He showed a boldness and physical bravery in battle that one can scarcely imagine in McClellan. Like his rival, Lee served in the Mexican War. One time, during a reconnaissance mission gone wrong, he was forced to hide behind a log. For hours Lee lay there, perfectly still, bitten by insects, tickled by twigs, while a steady stream of Mexican soldiers happened by, drinking from a spring, urinating in the woods. Some even sat down on the log, close enough that he could have reached up and tapped their backs. Finally, dusk fell, the enemy soldiers cleared out, and Lee made his escape. The experience left him exhilarated. It was as if the danger of warfare provided the sole opportunity for this otherwise supremely buttoned-down man to loosen up. In a telling statement, Lee once said of a battle: "It is well that this is so terrible! We should grow too fond of it!"

Another rare taste of action occurred in 1859 when Lee participated in one of the defining events of the antebellum period. He commanded a force of 88 men on a mission to recapture the United States arsenal at Harpers Ferry. John Brown—seen as an avenging abolitionist by some, a blood-mad killer to others—had seized the arsenal and planned to distribute its store of weapons to slaves, hoping to foment an armed insurrection. Brown and his band of raiders were holed up in an engine house, where they also held a group of hostages. Lee ordered his men to storm the engine house. In the space of three minutes, they rescued all the hostages and also managed to capture Brown alive. Six weeks later, Brown was hanged. His prophetic last words: "I John Brown am now quite *certain* that the crimes of this *guilty, land: will* never be purged *away;* but with Blood."

When the Civil War began, Lee's services were very much in demand—from both sides. Never mind that 300 men was the most he'd ever commanded. As with McClellan, a little experience counted for a lot at this early juncture. Only a few days after Sumter, at the urging of Lincoln, Lee was summoned to Washington and offered the rank of major general in the Union army, commanding tens of thousands of men.

The decision about whether to accept the post hinged entirely on whether Virginia remained in the Union. Indeed, Lee's highest loyalty, well above his country, was to his state, Virginia, land of Washington and those venerable family bloodlines. He felt sure that he couldn't possibly raise arms against his native state. When it became clear that Virginia planned to secede, Lee submitted his resignation from the Federal army, which he had dutifully served for thirty-two years. Soon after, he became a brigadier general for the Confederacy, the highest rank then existing in its army.

No doubt, Lee's decision was also deeply influenced by the fact that he was a slaveholder. Throughout his life, he'd had in his possession varying numbers of enslaved blacks. They'd been part of his childhood: slaves coming, slaves going—mostly *going* when they were seized by Light Horse Harry's creditors to cover the family debts. More recently, upon the death of George Washington Parke Custis (Mary's father) in 1857, the couple had inherited a mansion called Arlington along with a sprawling 1,100-acre plantation and 196 slaves.

Slaves were simply a fact of Lee's world, part of the background, property that fluctuated in quantity with the ebb and flow of one's fortunes.

Indeed, this latest bounty, 196 slaves, wasn't meant to last forever. Custis's will provided for their disposition. They were to be freed within five years of his death and once Arlington was out of debt. Of course, this left room for interpretation. So long as the plantation remained financially encumbered, one could make the argument that the enslaved people must remain. That's precisely what happened: the years passed and Lee didn't provide for their manumission. *In bondage, set free:* to him, these were mere legal considerations related to property and a will.

Slavery just wasn't a topic that particularly engaged Lee. On those rare occasions when he even discussed it, he offered such platitudes as "I think it however a greater evil to the white than to the black race." In other words, the true burden rests with the master who has to manage and care for his hapless human chattel. Lee had no compunction about selling slaves to the owners of distant plantations, breaking up families in the process.

Lee also conveniently overlooked one of the most glaring aspects of life at Arlington. His own wife, Mary, it seems, had a biracial half sister named Maria Carter. The two women grew up together, yet under vastly different circumstances. Rumor held that Mary had many other such half siblings, as well, resulting from old Custis having sex with black women he kept enslaved. There were rich Washington bloodlines to be maintained, however, so the subject was never broached. To Lee, Mary would ever and always be an "only child." It all went unacknowledged.

Lee also once described slavery as a "painful discipline" that black people must simply endure, though perhaps they could benefit from the experience.

Said discipline could take cruel form. Wesley Norris, one of Lee's slaves, would describe an episode in which he and two others were lashed repeatedly by a constable. Lee looked on, exhorting the man to "lay it on well," before ordering that the three slaves' backs be slathered in brine. (No metaphor this: salt was literally rubbed in their wounds.) A former slave would recall Lee as "the worst man I ever see."

Yes, this—along with the proud Virginia heritage and the military glory—this, too, must be part of the honest measure of Robert Lee.

Even before this battle, Lee and McClellan managed some notable encounters with one another. They had once been comrades, fighting on the same side in the old army. But they had also met as sworn enemies.

The Mexican War furnished the occasion for their first meeting. Seasoned Captain Lee was, for a time, in charge of junior officer McClellan. Their shared task was deploying howitzers, cannons designed to lob shells over walls. Sometimes, the pair labored through the night, Lee directing McClellan on the positioning of the heavy pieces. Their artful placements played a role in such successes as the siege on the fortifications at Veracruz, and the storming of the castle at Chapultepec.

But the bulk of the pair's encounters—certainly the more recent ones—were as rivals. Curiously, the first of these involved Lee's wife. During the early part of the war, Mary had continually moved from place to place in Virginia, a vagabond Southern belle. She stayed at the fine homes of various friends and relatives, always trying to remain ahead of the Union army. But she was taken by surprise by McClellan's audacious aquatic landing in Virginia. She found herself trapped behind enemy lines, a pair of daughters in tow.

Lee dispatched two aides to meet with McClellan and request that his wife and daughters be given safe passage. McClellan did one better, sending a carriage to collect them, and arranging that they be brought to his field headquarters. There, he received Mary with high ceremony, apparently spent time passing pleasantries with her. Then he sent her off in style, made sure she and the girls were conveyed on to Lee. Uxorious McClellan: he could always be counted on to hold wives in high regard, even those of rival generals.

The scene of Lee and McClellan's next encounter was the outskirts of Richmond, though encounter is an understatement, more like a drubbing. (Evidently, Mary's white-glove treatment would not be reciprocated.) After tangling with Magruder and his theater antics, McClellan had continued up the Peninsula, pushing to within five miles of the Confederate capital. Union soldiers could see the spires of the city's churches, hear the bells tolling in alarm. As the Rebels attempted to drive off the Federals, Joseph Johnston, commander of the Army of Northern Virginia, was wounded in battle, struck in the shoulder and chest by an artillery shell. Enter Lee. With the Confederacy on the brink, Jefferson Davis made an emergency promotion, elevating him from major general to commander of an army. Thereupon, Lee launched a counterattack as gutsy as McClellan was cautious.

Lee had 90,000 men at his disposal, only slightly less than what remained of McClellan's force after fighting its way up the peninsula. Rather than massing his entire army in front of Richmond, Lee took a bold gamble, splitting it into discrete pieces. A relatively small contingent (25,000) was left to defend the capital. The remainder was divided into three columns that proceeded to slam into McClellan's troops from unusual and surprising directions. During the ensuing fight, known as the Seven Days Battles, months of Northern progress was erased and McClellan's promising invasion plan was revealed to be just that, a plan, supplanted now by reality: the Union army skedaddling in retreat. The disastrous Peninsula Campaign inaugurated that rash of Federal defeats, culminating in an emboldened Confederate army invading the North.

And so it was that Maryland became the site of the most recent brushes between McClellan and Lee, among them the famous "lost order" episode. While the Union pursued the Confederates through the state, a Federal soldier found a piece of paper wrapped around three cigars. It turned out to be an order from Lee to his top generals, spelling out the disposition of the various parts of his army. Lee was in the midst of another bold gambit, the order revealed, this time dividing his army into four parts. What a stroke of luck then, that his scheme had been discovered. On receiving this extraordinary intelligence gift, an elated McClellan reportedly said: "Here is a paper with which if I cannot whip 'Bobbie Lee,' I will be willing to go home."

McClellan responded with uncharacteristic alacrity. Although it's often claimed that he failed to act on the lost order for a critical eighteen hours, the truth is that he didn't tarry. He mobilized his army quickly and set out in pursuit of the Rebels. Lee, in turn, scrambled to reconstitute his fragmented forces along the slope of a lush valley in front of a little town near a creek.

And here we are.

The two generals occupied their perches like peregrines on high, Lee at Cemetery Hill, McClellan on the bluffs surrounding the home of Farmer Pry. They restlessly scanned the battlefield spread out before them. Lee was quite aware that he faced a surpassingly cautious commander, rapid response to the lost order notwithstanding. McClellan, for his part, had received a thorough schooling in his opponent's wiles and aggression. Lee was so very comfortable risking men's lives, hurled them into battle with an almost callous indifference. He was willing to do whatever was necessary to win the war for the Confederacy. This was something his troops understood and appreciated—deeply.

McClellan's soldiers loved him. Lee's men revered him.

## CHAPTER 5

# GEORGIA BOYS AND
# GENERAL CHAOS

*It was only 9:00 A.M.*, yet already the battle had gone on for several hours. To this point the fighting had been concentrated in the topmost section of the field, while other places remained relatively calm, with entire divisions, some numbering thousands of soldiers, simply waiting to be called into action.

The bottommost section of the field had been particularly quiet. This was an unsettling development, completely at odds with McClellan's plan. While Union troops drove southward through the cornfield, then massed on the plateau around the Dunker Church, Federals at the other end of the battlefield were supposed to cross Antietam Creek and push northward. This was meant to happen simultaneously. Union troops would squeeze the Confederate army from two sides: the vise. The Rebs would be compacted and confounded, left vulnerable to a strike from straight on: the knockout blow.

Instead, Union soldiers in this bottom portion of the field were at a standstill. Some were even sitting on the ground, talking to comrades or reading. The soldiers weren't at fault. Rather, the delay was the result of a confluence of unexpected factors. For starters, this section of the field featured some of the most forbidding terrain imaginable: Crossing Antietam Creek here was no mean

77

feat. What's more, the Rebel contingent charged with preventing this action was peerless, composed of some of the most clever and able fighters in Lee's army. Because they were on defense, they were able to take advantage of this same ground—turning it to their benefit. On top of everything, a breakdown in communication had occurred between McClellan and one of his most trusted generals, likely amplified by personal tensions between the two men. Everything was a mess.

The Union force assembled on the rolling bluffs overlooking the Antietam numbered 12,500. Some men hunkered behind hillocks; others were sheltered in thick stands of trees. Such positions offered good protection so one needn't worry overmuch about being hit, even as the Confederates across the creek kept up a steady cannonade. The Federals were pretty much in the same place where they'd awoken this morning, having achieved no forward progress in the several hours since dawn. Then again, they were in no hurry to commence an attack when so many unfavorable variables lay before them, like a gauntlet.

Foremost was that terrain. The bluffs on the Union side may have looked bucolic, but only from a distance. Up close, they revealed themselves to be treacherously steep. Soldiers would need to figure out routes down the bluff sides—a challenge in its own right—and even then they would only have achieved the first step in a daunting sequence. Next, the troops would have to race—under heavy fire, guaranteed—across a broad plain that led to the Antietam.

The goal was the Rohrbach Bridge, which spanned the creek. Named after Henry Rohrbach, one of the valley's prominent Dunker settlers, it was a marvel of design and engineering: stone, built in 1836, featuring three graceful arches and a 175-foot span. It was also only 12 feet wide. This means that, at a given moment, the bridge could accommodate maybe five soldiers squeezed shoulder to shoulder, and that's being generous.

Twelve-foot-wide bridge, 12,500 Union soldiers—somewhere in those particulars lies a math problem. The potential for mayhem was incalculable. While crossing the bridge, the men would be terribly exposed. The bridge, in fact, could become a bottleneck, siphoning soldiers into a narrow chute, rendering them easy marks for the enemy to pick off.

The other option was to ford the Antietam. Its reputation very much preceded it, though, as a swift-flowing creek and possibly a deep one, too. Its banks were steep and thick grown with fox grape, Virginia creeper, and other vines. Dash across that broad plain then, and a soldier would still need to plunge down a creek bank, wade through water of unknown depth and speed, then climb the opposite bank, taking enemy fire all the while. Supposedly, there were manageable fords at other nearby spots along the Antietam. The Union would need to send out details to search for these rumored places.

This was shaping up to be quite an ordeal. But it ratcheted up to a whole other order of difficulty when one considers that many Federal officers and soldiers, having spent the morning safely behind hillocks and trees, hadn't had the opportunity to glean much about the ground that lay before them. It was akin to an obstacle course, yet few had the advantage of so much as a peek.

And then there's what waited on the opposite side of the Antietam. Here the bluffs were even steeper, may as well have been the white cliffs of Dover, and they were alive . . . with Rebels.

These soldiers had spent the previous day selecting the choicest spots. Mostly they were Georgia boys, with a substantial portion drawn from the southwestern section of the state in and around the Chattahoochee Valley. They tended to be subsistence farmers, who worked the red clay hard, growing corn and oats. Most of them were young and strapping, late teens to early twenties.

They had been busy. Using bayonets and the halves of pilfered Yankee canteens, they had dug rifle pits into the bluff sides. (A regulation Union canteen consisted of two convex pieces of tin, soldered together. Split one in half and you had a pair of very serviceable spades.) To bolster their positions, they had stacked stones and piled branches and foliage. In contrast to the conspicuous Federal blue, they were wearing dusky homespun uniforms that blended nicely into their surroundings. These Georgians were among the most shoe-deprived in Lee's raggedy army. They didn't mind so much; they valued the honesty of their bare feet on the rough earth.

If there was anything these Georgia farm boys understood, it was land. Relying on keen instincts, they had converted the steep bluffs on their side into a formidable natural stronghold.

Among their number were a couple elite teams of sharp-shooters, armed with Enfield rifles. Many had climbed elms and sycamores, stubborn trees that had managed to take root on this forbidding slant of land. They were hiding in the branches. Other sharpshooters had taken up positions atop the bluffs on the Rebel side, and were kneeling behind bales of hay, piled there by farmers. To a one, these men were unerring marksmen. They waited.

Back on the Union side of the creek, Ambrose Burnside was the general in overall command of those 12,500 soldiers. From first light, he had been on alert, instructed by McClellan to attack as soon as he received word. Shortly after 8:00 A.M., the order had arrived, delivered by an aide on horseback. But the Federals hadn't budged.

Burnside was yet another general who had enjoyed success back when the war was younger, the stakes lower. His victories at Roanoke Island, New Bern, and Fort Macon had been crucial to the Union's efforts to shut down Confederate ship traffic along the North Carolina coast. More recently, however, during the Confederate invasion of Maryland, McClellan had assessed Burnside's pursuit of the enemy as sluggish (a harsh verdict from a notoriously gingerly general). Only two days earlier, on September 15, McClellan had taken corrective action, separating the two corps that had been under Burnside. Burnside retained command of IX Corps, composed of the 12,500 soldiers on this part of the field, while command of I Corps had been transferred to General Joseph Hooker. Those soldiers wound up fighting in the cornfield, involved in the action that started the day.

For Burnside, the split of his command must have been humiliating and likely shook his confidence, as well. He was a modest man, unusual for a general, with an unprepossessing appearance: deep-set, dark-circled eyes and a bald pate. He looked kind of like a badger, an impression only heightened by the style of his facial hair. Although clean-shaven under his chin, he grew thick, bushy whiskers in front of his ears, a unique look for the time. Burnside's grooming innovation was the inspiration for the term *sideburns*, a transposition of the syllables in his last name.

Burnside was also an inventive man. Years earlier, as a young cavalry officer protecting travelers on the Santa Fe Trail, Burnside was struck in the neck by an Apache arrow. It nearly killed him, but also resulted in a eureka moment. A saber is no match for a bow and it's near impossible to load a musket on horseback—so, what about a lightweight breach-loading carbine (a short rifle) for cavalrymen? Burnside quit the army and launched a company. He managed to land a huge $100,000 contract with the Department of War to manufacture his carbine. But through some complex backroom dealings, a rival firm succeeded in getting the contract voided. Burnside, who had already ramped up production, went bankrupt and handed over his patents to satisfy creditors. During the Civil War, the Burnside carbine would be the third most popular of this class of weapon among cavalrymen, and more than fifty thousand would be manufactured. But Burnside had lost his stake in the weapon that bore his name, and didn't see a penny.

Beset by financial woes, Burnside moved in with an old friend from West Point, McClellan. This was during the years when McClellan was a railroad executive. He even helped Burnside to land a job with the Illinois Central. The two took to calling each other "Mac" and "Burn," became famous friends. "Of all men I have known, I believe I value his friendship and respect the most—and I am proud indeed to know that I possess both," McClellan once wrote to Nelly.

That relationship had now grown strained. The day before, McClellan had personally supervised the placement of troops in this challenging part of the field. He had even gone so far as to have his staff engineers mark the spots where various regiments should go. Apparently, Burnside was slow to place the troops and failed to make proper dispositions. So, McClellan sent him a message that read in part: "the commanding general cannot lightly regard such marked departure from the tenor of his instructions."

The message wasn't from "Mac" and it sure wasn't addressed to "Burn."

By 8:30 A.M., McClellan had grown impatient. "What is Burnside about?" he kept asking. "Why do we not hear from him?" He dispatched another aide on horseback to get an update on the attack. The aide returned to report that scant progress had been made. Clearly, communication between McClellan and Burnside had broken down.

But one also suspects that Burnside was simply paralyzed. McClellan had lost confidence in the general, splitting his command, chiding him for delays, yet at the same time had charged him with taking the Rohrbach Bridge, probably the most difficult assignment on the field this day.

Across the Antietam, the general in command of the Rebel soldiers on this part of the field was embattled in his own fashion. Robert Toombs was a vigorous, hulking man, who had devoted his youth to such outdoor activities as riding and hunting—and such indoor activities as drinking and brawling. Now fifty-two, he was a powerful political figure (a longtime Georgia congressman) with name recognition approaching 100 percent, and more than his share of controversies. There's the man who would be king; Toombs was the man who would be president—of the Confederacy.

Early in his political career, Toombs had been a member of the Whig Party, and sufficiently moderate to find common cause on at least one occasion with a young Illinois congressman, Abraham Lincoln. As the South dug in over states' rights and slavery, Toombs switched affiliation to the Unionist Party, then the Democrats, becoming increasingly bellicose along the way. His political prospects just kept rising. His rhetoric soared. As an orator, Toombs had extraordinary skill and power. "Defend yourselves! The enemy is at your door," he boomed on the floor of the Senate in early 1860; "wait not to meet him at your hearthstone; meet him at the doorsill, and drive him from the Temple of Liberty, or pull down its pillars and involve him in a common ruin."

His "Doorsill" speech was widely reprinted, emboldening Southerners and unsettling the North.

Toombs might even have assumed the highest office in the fledgling Confederacy, but for an embarrassing incident. In February 1861, delegates from the recently seceded states convened in Montgomery, Alabama, to select a provisional leader. Toombs's name was at the top of the list. But he got stinking drunk at a convention banquet—and at a couple of other public events, too—making a fool of himself. Toombs was no stranger to mixing politicking and drink, but maybe the high stakes and pressure caused him to lose all control. The presidential nod went instead to temperate Jefferson Davis, a man who Toombs despised. The two had once come within a hairbreadth of fighting a duel after Toombs questioned Davis's political acumen, saying that his appeal lay with "swaggering braggarts and cunning poltroons."

As a kind of consolation prize, Toombs was chosen as the Confederacy's first secretary of state. It was a job for which he was woefully unsuited. He was no foreign diplomat, having been overseas only once in his life for a quick tour of Europe, during which he'd judged each country by an unusual criterion: the quality of its cigars. After a few months, Toombs quit as secretary of state,

demanding a commission as a brigadier general in command of
soldiers from his home state. Antietam found him seething over
Georgia men who he'd lost in previous battles. He blamed their
deaths on the Yanks, to be sure, but also found ways to hold Jeff
Davis responsible.

Toombs faced Burnside; the soldiers either side of Antietam
Creek were at a standstill. On this part of the field, it had been
impossible to ignore the sounds of the fighting in Farmer Miller's
corn, constant and clamorous, issuing from roughly two miles to
the north. The wait to be called into action must have been excruciating. Nevertheless, the soldiers did their best to achieve some
kind of normalcy. Union soldiers would report that they passed
the time reading and making nervous conversation. The 21st Massachusetts even had a morning mail call. From the relative safety
of the far side of some foothills overlooking Antietam Creek, the
men pored over letters from home.

All the while, Lee directed a steady stream of Confederate
soldiers to be shifted to the top of the field, where they were urgently needed. Remember, Lee's army was considerably smaller
than McClellan's (even if McClellan didn't know it). Expediency
was Lee's only option. So far this morning, a number of brigades
had been called away and the Confederate position was thinning
out. Although the Union didn't realize it, at some spots along
those bluffs, gaps of 40 or 50 yards had opened up between Rebel
soldiers.

For Lee, the situation was growing worrisome. He awaited
General Ambrose Powell Hill, expected to deliver more than
2,000 sorely needed men to the Rebels' dwindling ranks. Earlier
in the invasion, when Lee divided his army (the subject of that infamous lost order), A. P. Hill had joined Stonewall Jackson in capturing the arsenal at Harpers Ferry. Hill and his men then stayed
behind to secure the loot and process the prisoners. Harpers Ferry

was seventeen miles away. Before going to bed the previous night, Lee had dispatched a courier with an urgent message, summoning Hill, fresh troops in tow, to the battlefield.

Hill was one of Lee's most trusted generals. He had reddish hair, a thick reddish beard, favored a red calico shirt on battle days, and carried a hambone in his pocket, a good-luck charm from his mother. It's fitting that Hill had overseen the Rebel weapons grab at Harpers Ferry, because he was like a human arsenal. He typically carried two revolvers, two horse pistols, and assorted blades, variously tucked into holsters or slipped through his rawhide belt. Hill marched his men hard, and was in the habit of riding up beside stragglers and urging them along with a thwack from the flat of his sword. On his deathbed, among Lee's last words would be a cryptic "Tell A. P. Hill he must come up." On this day, the only question was whether Hill would arrive in time.

As it happens, there was also a subplot of sorts involving Hill and McClellan. Both the Confederate general and Union commander were products of West Point, where they had been roommates and friends. Postgraduation, however, the pair entered into a heated rivalry when Hill joined the bevy of suitors pursuing Mary Ellen Marcy, a.k.a. Nelly. To win Nelly, of course, one had to also earn the blessings of her status-obsessed parents. Unfortunately for Hill, even though he was a dashing young officer from a distinguished Virginia family, the Marcys identified McClellan as the preferable match. Recall that Randolph Marcy, the eminent explorer and Nelly's father, had even named a creek after McClellan when the young man accompanied him on an expedition.

The Marcys were happy to meddle. When Nelly's mother caught wind of a scandal involving Hill, she played it to full advantage. During his career at West Point, while on summer furlough, Hill had visited New York City, where apparently he contracted gonorrhea. It was such a severe case that Hill was forced to drop out of West Point for a time, and it delayed his graduation by a year. When Mrs. Marcy learned about this episode, she went on a whispering rampage, spreading the sordid tale far and wide.

In the end, McClellan won Nelly's hand, with this parental assist. But Hill supposedly held a grudge—and now he was a Confederate general. Some claimed that he reserved a special intensity for contests with McClellan. There's even a story that during the Peninsula Campaign, a Union soldier awoke to the news that Hill was bearing down and exclaimed: "My God, Nelly, why didn't you marry him!"

To recap, then: General Burnside had failed to act on the attack order from Union commander McClellan. General Toombs was bitter over lost prospects and lost men, and detested Confederate president Jeff Davis. Lee anxiously awaited the arrival of General Hill, a man who had once courted McClellan's beloved Nelly. The soldiers on either side of the Rohrbach Bridge were at an impasse. On the Union side, they numbered 12,500, while the Rebel force was far smaller, diminished further throughout the morning as Lee shifted soldiers elsewhere on the field. Granted, through an abiding appreciation for land, the Georgia boys had taken up one of the strongest positions in the Civil War. But what the Federal command couldn't know is how few of them it actually faced, dug into the sides of those bluffs. There were roughly 450. How could such a modicum of Rebels possibly hold off the Union multitude?

# CHAPTER 6

## INSTRUMENT OF
## PROVIDENCE

Lincoln set out on his daily commute from the Soldiers' Home to the White House. Until recently, he had relished this trip—stolen time for an overburdened president. There had been a change to this routine, however, and it left him displeased. Two weeks earlier, due to the Confederate invasion of the North, he had been assigned a security detail: Company A of the 11th New York cavalry. Now, rather than traveling by himself, he had to endure the fuss and formality of being surrounded by a group of men on horses. Usually Lincoln accompanied his escorts on horseback, though sometimes he traveled by carriage.

He found the clank of sabers in the early morning air particularly jarring. He would have preferred to be alone with his thoughts, which often turned to Willie these days. Adding to his annoyance, during one recent commute, Lincoln had fallen from his horse and sprained his wrist. Although not as severe as General Lee's injury, it was a source of pain and discomfort. Doubtless, too, Lincoln blamed the accident on this fresh, foolish experiment in chaperoned presidential travel.

The cavalry detail was deemed necessary, however, due to the somewhat isolated location of the Soldiers' Home, outside the Washington City limit. Furthermore, Lincoln's retreat was near the border of Maryland, a state currently overrun by Rebels. An anxious Mary could often be spotted in the window, still in a nightgown, watching her husband depart.

Each day, Lincoln followed pretty much the same route. After passing through the Eagle Gate at the entrance of the Soldiers' Home grounds, he'd get on Rock Creek Church Road. Then he'd make a left onto the Seventh Street Turnpike, where he'd remain for about a mile and a half. Lincoln and his cavalry detail would then jog right onto Rhode Island Avenue, follow the roundabout at Iowa Circle (Logan Circle today), pick up Vermont Avenue, and then continue south to Pennsylvania Avenue and his ultimate destination.

Each morning, from the first horse stride onward, Lincoln's three-mile commute was filled with reminders of the war. The grounds of the Soldiers' Home included a cemetery, already the final resting place for 5,000 Union soldiers. Freshly turned earth was always visible, mournful evidence that new graves were being dug all the time. Out on the Seventh Street Pike, Lincoln would pass ambulance wagons transporting injured soldiers to the several makeshift hospitals in the area, including the Carver Hospital. He saw men swathed in bandages and heard their moans of pain. Along his route, the president would also frequently see escaped slaves.

The District had abolished slavery in April, only five months earlier. Runaways came flooding into the Union capital, arriving from nearby Confederate states, such as Virginia and North Carolina. They came as well from Delaware and Maryland, border states that had remained in the Union while still retaining slavery (like the District itself until recently).

On his commuting route, Lincoln would pass a large encampment set aside for these runaways, or as they were often called, "contrabands." (This was the legalistic term for property—humans, in this case—that belonged to the enemy.) The contraband camp was an especially poignant sign of these troubled times. For the president, it served as a daily reminder of slavery and its painful toll.

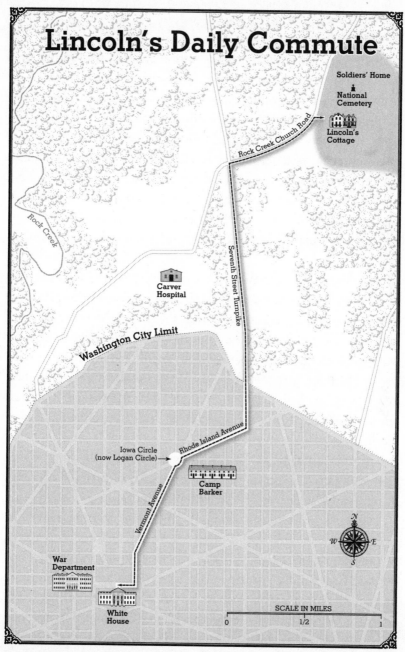

# Lincoln's Daily Commute

Soldiers' Home

National Cemetery

Lincoln's Cottage

Rock Creek Church Road

Rock Creek

Carver Hospital

Seventh Street Turnpike

Washington City Limit

Rhode Island Avenue

Iowa Circle (now Logan Circle) →

Camp Barker

Vermont Avenue

War Department

White House

SCALE IN MILES

0     1/2     1

N
W · E
S

© JIM MCMAHON

By 1862, slavery was an issue with deep roots for Lincoln, one that he had been grappling with his entire life. He had formed his own, highly personal perspective. Even though Lincoln was part of an American generation that produced such towering antislavery eminences as Harriet Beecher Stowe and William Lloyd Garrison, he was no abolitionist. He was constitutionally incapable of being so doctrinaire. He was instead a deeply moral man, also a pragmatist, with a fine-grained appreciation for nuance. Such a combination of traits guaranteed that Lincoln would have to puzzle through some contradictions. It also rendered him as someone uniquely qualified to face down perhaps the thorniest issue in American history.

Lincoln's bedrock views were formed in his earliest years. Just as slavery was an immutable fact of General Lee's upbringing, like horses or clouds, manumission was part of Lincoln's. His father strongly objected to the so-called peculiar institution, though he was also a harsh and sometimes physically abusive man. Growing up, Lincoln attended a series of separatist Baptist churches; he came of age listening to fiery preachers railing against human bondage. Slavery, Lincoln once allowed, had "the power of making me miserable." It's an interesting choice of words, and one that speaks to his unusual capacity for empathy. Unlike so many of his contemporaries, Lincoln acknowledged blacks as fellow human beings, and was deeply moved by their plight.

His viewpoint wasn't simply a noble abstraction, either. In contrast to so many abolitionists—advocates for racial equality, but from a distance, goes a standard criticism—Lincoln had opportunity to put his beliefs into practice. The Springfield where he moved as a young lawyer was unusually integrated for a US city of its time, and his home was located in close proximity to the homes of many African Americans. It was here that Lincoln befriended William de Fleurville, a Haitian immigrant who had lived in Baltimore and New Orleans upon first arriving in this country. In both cities he experienced disillusionment, then dread; though a free black man, Fleurville grew fearful that he would simply be unlawfully seized and enslaved. Springfield proved a safer and more comfortable place to settle.

When Fleurville opened a barbershop, Lincoln not only frequented it but also became a major booster, encouraging others to do so. The shop soon became a kind of community club, where Lincoln and others hung out. "This place was Lincoln's second home," according to an old account, "and if he could not be found elsewhere, he was sure to be in Fleurville's shop swapping tales with the owner and the other patrons ..."

Billy the Barber, as he was known, became a successful Springfield fixture, opening a clothes cleaning establishment and also purchasing a number of properties in town. Lincoln represented him in these transactions as a lawyer.

But practicing law also furnished young Abe with a different kind of real-world experience. Slavery took on unexpected levels of complexity when viewed through a legal prism. Lincoln's abhorrence for the institution soon began to collide with his conviction that the law was sacred. Sometimes, he found himself pulled in opposite ways. On at least two occasions he defended men accused of sheltering fugitive slaves, but he also took a case on the other side of the issue, representing a Kentuckian who was attempting to reclaim slaves who had run away while he was working in Illinois. They were the Kentuckian's rightful legal property, argued Lincoln, even in the free state of Illinois. (He lost this proslavery case, and to add insult, the client refused to pay his fee.)

As Lincoln progressed professionally, the complexity surrounding the issue of slavery seemed only to grow. During his single term in Congress, Lincoln lodged in a place that was nicknamed "Abolition House." It was the residence of choice for a number of his fellow free-soil Whigs. Lincoln recoiled at the spectacle of slave traders doing business in close proximity to the Capitol building. Yet, he voted *against* a measure designed to end slavery in the District of Columbia. It simply didn't appear workable to him. (On another occasion, he voted for such a measure.) As with the law, politics demanded its own set of considerations.

Then comes 1858, and a series of immortal debates: Beanpole Lincoln matched wits with the pugnacious five-foot four Stephen Douglas, known as the Little Giant. With his memorable statements about houses divided and the dangers of a nation part slave and part free, Lincoln offered a stark contrast to his opponent, a political conservative with a laissez-faire attitude toward slavery.

Some notes that Lincoln used to help prepare for these contests show the tenacious logic that he was capable of summoning:

> You say A is white and B is black. It is color, then; the lighter having the right to enslave the darker? Take care. By this rule you are to be slave to the first man you meet with a fairer skin than your own.
>
> You do not mean color exactly? You mean the whites are intellectually the superiors of the blacks, and therefore have the right to enslave them? Take care again. By this rule you are to be slave to the first man you meet with an intellect superior to your own.

Lincoln emerged from the debates with a national reputation. In 1860, the Republican Party—only six years old, a participant in just one previous presidential election—nominated him as their candidate. The party was a hotbed of abolitionism, but Lincoln was selected for his moderation. He represented the best hope of building a coalition, the kind capable of winning a national election by cobbling together the party's radicals with more temperate voters. In fact, the 1860 Republican platform was crafted to appeal to a broad electorate and addressed a welter of issues other than slavery, such as tariff protections, aid to homesteaders, and commitment to a transcontinental railroad.

When his presidency began with a secession crisis followed by the outbreak of civil war, Lincoln's vaunted moderation was on full display. He even took the extraordinary step of counter-manding various abolition measures, including one that sought to free slaves in Missouri, and another designed to emancipate those in Florida, Georgia, and South Carolina. It wasn't as if Lincoln disagreed with the sentiments. So early in the war, rather, he perceived a risk in hardening the South's resistance. He also had concerns about the viability of these edicts. He suspected that legal and constitutional challenges were likely to render them unworkable. Precious political capital would be squandered with nothing accomplished, save backlash.

Throughout the early days of his administration, Lincoln was exceedingly measured—*lawyerly* might be the most apt description. Restoring the Union must be the stated purpose of the war, he believed, otherwise there was a risk that valuable constituencies would be alienated. The president recognized the tenuousness of his political support.

One constituency that deeply concerned Lincoln was the military, particularly his generals. They tended to be Democrats rather than Republicans, a potential source of tension. Lincoln and McClellan, never an easy pairing, had particularly stark political differences, evident in the men's very first meetings in Illinois back in the 1850s.

McClellan, recall, was then a shiny young executive for the Illinois Central; Lincoln represented the railroad as a lawyer. The Philly patrician took an instant dislike to the prairie philosopher, put off by his rambling stories and aw-shucks aphorisms. He cared even less for Lincoln's politics. That insult he chose for Lincoln, "original gorrilla" (such a specific and curiously formed jibe) harkens back to this era. In Illinois, hostile political cartoonists enjoyed distorting Lincoln's features to make him look like a gorilla, and with that, an implication: Abe hailed from Africa same as the slaves for whom he expressed sympathy.

McClellan took a partisan interest in the famous debates, so much so that he conveyed Douglas—Lincoln's opponent—to venues throughout the state in a private railcar. In 1860, Little Mac cast his presidential ballot for the Little Giant, professing to be a "strong Democrat of the Stephen A. Douglas School." This signaled many things about McClellan, not least of which was that he lacked a strong aversion to slavery. Like Douglas, he firmly believed that one region of the country had no right to impose its values on another.

As commander of the Army of the Potomac, McClellan held fast to his political beliefs. The sole purpose of the war, as he saw it, was to quell the rebellion, forcing the seceded states back into the Union. If they returned to the fold, slavery intact, that was of no concern to him.

McClellan had little sympathy for slaves. Back in 1846, while traveling through Alabama en route to the Mexican War, he had stopped to visit a relative. He borrowed one of the relative's slaves, a man named Songo. During the campaign, Songo cooked for McClellan and groomed his horse. It seems unlikely that McClellan paid the borrowed slave for these services. It would never have occurred to him. When it came to the issue of slavery, McClellan managed about as much contemplativeness as Lee. Only on one occasion, it seems, did McClellan manage the briefest flash of insight into the plight of the enslaved. Predictably, it involved his wife. "Just think for one moment, and try to realize," he wrote Nelly, "that at the will of some brutal master you and I might be separated forever!"

Otherwise, slavery was not a matter for consideration. During the waning days of the disastrous Peninsula Campaign, Lincoln traveled to Virginia aboard the steamship *Ariel* for a meeting with McClellan. The president hoped this unusual measure (visiting a general in the field) would press McClellan into action. Lincoln chugged up the James River and docked near the general's headquarters. Upon boarding the *Ariel*, however, McClellan simply handed Lincoln a letter. It was filled with repeated formulations of the same demand, namely, that Lincoln should avoid any "declaration of radical views, especially upon slavery."

Lincoln had traveled to Virginia hoping to goad McClellan into action. Instead, he was handed this galling letter spelling out how he, the president, *should not* act. As an added impertinence, the letter closed with the suggestion that Lincoln relinquish his constitutionally prescribed role as commander in chief of the armed forces, ceding it to McClellan.

Examples of tense exchanges between American presidents and generals are legion. Still, McClellan's letter has to rank among the most provocative. Aboard that steamer in Virginia, Lincoln must have summoned every ounce of self-control. Apparently, he read the letter as McClellan looked on, then folded it and placed it back in the envelope without uttering so much as a word.

Here's the worst part of it, though: Lincoln's impertinent general was but a single constituent, albeit a vital one. Amplify the uproar twenty-two-millionfold, and one gets a flavor for the restive populace that Lincoln faced. As the war dragged on, the Union cause was starting to split, just as the nation had in April of 1861. *Commit to ending slavery*, demanded one faction. *Leave the issue out of the conflict*, insisted the other. Lincoln was pulled in two opposing directions, the public policy equivalent of a medieval rack.

He began to explore various ideas that might somehow solve this knotty mess. One that he strongly considered was so-called voluntary colonization. It had great promise as a compromise measure: abolition could become an explicit war aim, while the legitimate concerns of abolition's opponents were answered. Such a plan would address, for example, widespread worries about African Americans flooding into Northern cities, taking jobs from whites. Under voluntary colonization, blacks freed by a Union victory would also be free—to leave.

The government would even cover some of the costs of travel and resettlement. As to where they'd go, Lincoln gave this matter ample consideration. Perhaps they would move to African countries, including Liberia, a nation founded expressly as a place for blacks who had been living in America to resettle. In 1862, Lincoln's administration officially recognized Liberia and Haiti, two potential voluntary colonization destinations. Lincoln directed his minister to Guatemala to inquire about potential sites in Central America and also met with a representative of a land development company in what is today Panama.

Of course, voluntary colonization was contingent on blacks wishing to leave. It naively ignored the fact that most were generations removed from Africa; cultural ties to countries such as Guatemala were nonexistent. African Americans already had a homeland. They simply desired to be free in it. As a consequence, the voluntary colonization concept was mostly received as an insult. Frederick Douglass, a fierce opponent of colonization and staunch critic of Lincoln during the early years of his presidency, once said: "Our minds are made up to live here if we can, or die here if we must."

A more viable solution the president considered was something called gradual compensated emancipation. The idea was that the US government would *pay* states to *free* their slaves *over time*. Border states, such as Kentucky and Missouri, could serve as the laboratories for the concept. If they agreed to gradual compensated emancipation, it would more firmly bond them to the Northern cause. Maybe it would also suggest a framework for the states in rebellion to cease fighting and rejoin the Union. After all, no shortage of Southern plantation owners believed that slavery was a flawed system, even a doomed one. The problem had always lain in unraveling this complex, deeply entrenched institution. Here, then, was a possible solution: end slavery gradually with the federal government assuming the cost.

Lincoln started by working quietly behind the scenes with Delaware legislators, trying to urge the border state to adopt gradual compensated emancipation. This was an ideal test case: Delaware was tiny, firmly in the Union camp, yet retained a small population of enslaved people, estimated at 1,800 when the Civil War started. To Delaware's lawmakers, Lincoln suggested that the US government would compensate the state's slaveholders $400 for each slave set free. The state would have until 1893, too—an entire generation to accomplish emancipation.

Ultimately, Delaware proved lukewarm to Lincoln's proposal. He pressed ahead anyway, arranging a series of meetings with representatives from all the border states, including Maryland, Kentucky, and Missouri. Together, these states had 432,622 enslaved people, according to the Lincoln administration's tally. At $400 per slave, emancipation would cost $173 million. The war was costing the Federal treasury $2 million per day. So, the price of freeing the slaves in the border states would be equal to eighty-seven days of a war that promised to drag on far longer. Even so, the negotiations with the border states came to nothing.

All the while, the public outcry grew increasingly fevered. Lincoln was more torn than ever between hardcore abolitionists on one side, soft-on-slavery Democrats on the other. To maintain a measured stance, to somehow balance these competing constituencies, was becoming impossible. The quick glorious war envisioned in 1861 had slid into the quagmire of 1862. Movement in some direction was needed. As to which way Lincoln would lean, one clue could be gleaned from a candid discussion the president had with Charles Sumner, a Massachusetts senator and one of the staunchest abolitionists in the US government. "Well, Mr. Sumner," Lincoln confided, "the only difference between you and me on this subject is a difference of a month or six weeks in time."

Over the summer of 1862, during that series of Union setbacks—McClellan's debacle on the Virginia Peninsula foremost among them—the president began to weigh a new option. Amid so much pain and sacrifice, something was desperately needed to kindle a fresh Northern commitment to the war effort. He'd been working out the fine points during his evenings at the Soldiers'

Home. He jotted his thoughts on pieces of paper that he carried with him to the White House.

* * *

Lincoln and his cavalry entourage continued the morning commute, rounding Iowa Circle. They rode past Camp Barker, a settlement for contrabands. It consisted of a former military barracks converted into crowded and squalid temporary quarters, home to several thousand people.

The Lincoln family had recently hired Mary Dines, a runaway slave from Maryland who had spent her first months of freedom in a contraband camp, perhaps this very one. "Aunt Mary," as the Lincolns called her, worked as a cook at the family's cottage retreat. She had likely fixed breakfast for Abe this morning, perhaps his standard toast and egg. Aunt Mary received pay for her work, as surely as Billy the Barber was paid for a shave.

Lincoln picked up Vermont Avenue, continued south to Pennsylvania Avenue, and on to the White House. He must have arrived in a state of apprehension, eager for updates about McClellan, the Union Army, and whatever might be happening somewhere in Western Maryland. Intense fighting had already occurred in the area around the cornfield. General Burnside and 12,500 soldiers were at a standstill, trying to figure out how to cross Antietam Creek. Yet Lincoln was greeted without so much as a morsel of news. Nobody in Washington had any updates about the situation.

So, the president simply settled down for a routine workday in a sprawling mansion where he never felt at ease. He would think of the White House always and only as his temporary abode. It was a place to be borne, tolerated as the wages of the presidency. Lincoln was a modest man with simple tastes in many things, tastes rooted in a hardscrabble boyhood on the American frontier. In Springfield, he and his family had lived in a comfortable wooden cottage. Here, the proportions were utterly thrown off. The Kentucky cabin in which Lincoln was born would have easily fit inside the East Room of the executive mansion. Washington: it truly was, per its nickname, the city of magnificent distances.

Mary had done her best to make the White House a home. But on certain matters she had such different notions from her husband. After first consulting a book entitled *Lives of the Queens of England*, she'd gone on a spree, busting the presidential renovation budget, spending $6,800 on fussy French wallpaper and $2,500 for just one room's abundant swath of carpet. Lurking in corners were hulking armoires, constructed of dark, severe woods, such as black walnut and mahogany. Overstuffed furniture was scattered about. This was the style du jour in all the finest salons, yet these pieces were so very stuffed, threatening to burst at their overpriced seams. There was no refuge anywhere.

Yet for all Mary had accomplished, the White House refurbishment was blunted and cheerless. It remained in an arrested state, halted when Willie died. As a consequence, Mary's touches coexisted uneasily with decor from earlier administrations that she had never gotten around to replacing. The Blue Room was filled with Japanese bric-a-brac—swords, saddles, a tea set—the loot left behind by a diplomatic mission that had visited during Buchanan's presidency. Hidden away in nooks were dusty, uncherished vases that dated back to Madison and Monroe. There were few paintings on display, save for ancient portraits of George Washington and Andrew Jackson. It had the effect of making the walls seem even larger, and looming.

The mansion had also taken a shabby turn over these sorrowful months. In Lincoln's time, the White House was very much a public space, subject to the etiquette that prevails in a tavern, say, as opposed to a private home. The mansion had virtually no security or barriers. The president's home was open to the democratic masses; all were welcome, at most any hour, and sometimes it seemed that the entire nation had decided to drop by. Visitors tracked dirt onto the floors, spit tobacco on the expensive carpeting. They also took souvenirs, carefully cutting out the flower patterns from Mary's lace curtains, snipping tassels off the drapery.

Someone had been bold enough to shear off a yard or two from the bottom of the red brocade curtains in the East Room. Mary was an oft-absent First Lady now, not that there was much she could have done. The mistake lay in the unprecedented and exorbitant refurbishing of a house the nation's people viewed as their own.

On any given day, large numbers of visitors lined up in front of Lincoln's office on the second floor. Plenty would have been waiting when Lincoln arrived this morning. They came seeking jobs, or requesting favors and referrals. Often the line extended the length of the hallway, continued down the broad staircase, then snaked through the rooms on the first floor. Lincoln found this duty onerous but necessary. He did his best to bear it patiently. Sometimes, he'd slip away to the family's private quarters only to encounter some constituent from Chillicothe poking around in a bedroom, or testing out the miracle of indoor plumbing. (It's odd, speaks to the standards of a different era, that, although Lincoln was furnished with a cavalry escort for his commute, any stranger could walk right into the White House.)

No wonder the Lincolns chose to retreat to the Soldiers' Home whenever possible. The White House was so crowded and clamorous; there was no place to be alone with one's grief. Mary found it excruciating. She refused to set foot in Willie's bedroom, nor would she venture into the Green Room, where her little boy had been prepared for burial. During her increasingly infrequent White House visits, Mary would simply retreat to her bedroom, where for hours she could be heard sobbing. She dressed exclusively in mourning now, wearing a heavy black dress over a crinoline, and a long crepe veil.

The bereft president tried to lose himself in work and in art. Again and again, he read the same passage from Shakespeare's play *King John*, one that featured a character describing the loss of a child.

Tad's grief was agonizing. Everything had changed in an instant, leaving him bewildered and lonely. He was just nine years old, fresh from his own battle with an illness that nearly killed him. Not only had he lost his brother, but also his playmates. Bud and Holly Taft had stopped coming around. Mary had barred the two boys from visiting the White House. For her, their presence was just too painful a reminder of happier times. Together with Willie, the boys had formed their own battalion. Now the little army had dwindled to one. In response, Lincoln had arranged for the secretary of war to "commission" Tad as a lieutenant, outfitted with his own uniform in Federal blue. But the boy found scant joy in conscripting adult White House staffers who gamely stood at attention while he barked commands in a small, anxious voice.

Lincoln grew more protective of Tad, as if he hadn't always been protective. He grew more indulgent, too, as if his indulgence had ever known any bounds. Father and son became constant visitors to Joseph Stuntz's toy emporium. Tad would pick out wooden soldiers and miniature cannons. "I want to give Tad all the toys I didn't have," explained his father sadly, "and all the toys I would have given to the boy who went away."

Often Tad would burst into Lincoln's office unannounced. Even if the president was in the midst of some weighty matter of state, here came Tad—a fidgety whirl—dashing across the room and hopping into his father's lap. "Papa day," he'd shout. Because of his speech impediment, Tad could be difficult to understand. "Papa dear." That's what he was saying. Lincoln would throw his arms around Tad, clinging to his boy.

Lincoln began to think of himself as a mere vessel, on this earth henceforth only for the purpose of benefiting others. After experiencing so much loss, his own life appeared to him torn beyond repair, like one of Mary's bedraggled French curtains. But he could still be an "instrument of providence." That was the phrase he used. He could still make a difference in the lives of his family and his fellow citizens. God knows, there was such grief out there.

Only five months after Willie's passing, on July 10, 1862, Secretary of War Edwin Stanton lost his infant son, James, who died from the complications surrounding a routine vaccination.

Lincoln attended the little boy's funeral, sharing a carriage with Secretary of State William Seward and Gideon Welles, the secretary of the navy. As they rode in slow procession toward the Oak Hill Cemetery, the same place where Willie was interred, Lincoln brought up the new plan he was considering on the issue of slavery. This appears to be the first time he had shared it with anyone in his cabinet. Secretary Welles noted that Lincoln raised the topic repeatedly, discussed it with marked animation, even intensity. Welles must have been puzzled. It was so inappropriate to the occasion, a child's funeral.

Maybe that was precisely what roused Lincoln on this somber day. So much loss: surely it couldn't be without purpose.

On July 22, less than two weeks later, Lincoln called a meeting of his cabinet. With all seven members assembled, he revealed his plan to issue an emancipation proclamation. This seemed such a radical step. The president proposed to entirely skirt the border states with their fragile loyalties. Instead, he intended to aim squarely at the Confederacy, freeing slaves only in the states that were currently in rebellion.

How could such an edict even work, considering that it was directed at a region outside the control of the United States? Therein lay its brilliance. With a pen stroke, Lincoln would be setting the *Confederacy's* slaves free. For anyone who viewed as illegitimate a new "nation" dedicated to the continuance of slavery, the emancipation proclamation would serve as the call of a higher authority. The mighty US government would be declaring the Rebel South's slaves free, period.

Far from being merely symbolic, the proclamation was also enforceable. As Union troops moved through the South, they could use Lincoln's order to declare enslaved people free in territory that became occupied.

Beyond the basic human decency of such an act, all kinds of advantages might accrue to the Union. For example, the Confederate war machine was utterly dependent on slave labor. The enslaved worked in factories, making munitions and other items used in battle, and worked in fields, growing the food that fed the army. An emancipation proclamation could serve as a beacon. It might prompt slaves to abandon their labors and flee to freedom. This was a formidable weapon aimed at the heart of the Confederacy.

Such a proclamation could also be expected to stave off the threat of European intervention. To this point, with union being the North's explicit goal, Britain and France were increasingly contemplating whether to sow disunion, the better to keep the two sides fractured and weak. Making the war about slavery, explicitly, would change the equation. Britain had outlawed slavery in its colonies in 1833; France, in 1848. Neither power was likely to aid the slaveholding South against a North bent on abolition.

Lincoln was also confident that his plan would be workable, a crucial consideration for a man who was a lawyer by training. He'd even discovered a legal precedent for the federal government to emancipate slaves. Back in the 1830s, John Quincy Adams, another lawyer turned president, had argued that the Constitution's war powers allowed the United States to free slaves in a hostile territory that it was fighting against—a precise and prescient description of the current situation. Lincoln had carefully studied Adams's arguments. He concluded that this approach was legally sound, and wouldn't get hung up in endless court challenges. Of course, to ensure that the abolition of slavery held over the long term, to give such a decision the necessary weight and permanence, might require a constitutional amendment. Lincoln was quite aware of this. But he had also grown certain that in the midst of an emergency, while the Union and Confederacy were locked in armed conflict, relying on the war powers was sufficient.

As a gambit, an emancipation proclamation had the potential to be the equal of Lee's bold invasion of Maryland. It also promised to topple dominoes, one into another, only this time all to the Union's favor.

Lincoln presented the proclamation to his cabinet as a decision he'd already made. After careful deliberation, he explained, he'd come to the conclusion that this was the proper course. The only thing he desired from the members was their support and any suggestions they might make.

Secretary Seward offered one. He proposed that Lincoln wait for a Union military victory before issuing the proclamation. In July 1862, when the cabinet meeting was held, the North remained in the midst of that dreadful string of losses. If the streak continued, Lincoln's edict might be viewed as an act of desperation, or as Seward termed it, "our last shriek on the retreat."

This struck Lincoln as wise counsel. So, he'd slipped a two-page handwritten draft of the emancipation proclamation into a pigeonhole in his desk on the second floor of the White House. Two months later, it was still there, waiting.

Now, if only McClellan, a cautious general who cared not a whit about ending slavery, could somehow best Lee and deliver a Union victory.

# CHAPTER 7

## MERCY FOLLOWS A MASSACRE

*McClellan puffed on a cigar.* Spread out before him was the battle-field, in some places shrouded by plump gun smoke thunderheads, lit up here and there by muzzle flashes. It was as if he was above the weather. This was a commanding spot he'd chosen, on a bluff top near his field headquarters.

Dawn's cloud cover had burned away and the sky had turned blue. The general was bathed in sunlight. Aides leaned in close and whispered in confidential tones—a hushed heaven up here. There were dozens of them, scurrying about; McClellan insisted on a large staff and he demanded that they at all times exude calm. Periodically, an aide who was manning a telescope affixed to a wooden rail would spot something of interest down on the field and exchange a few quiet words with the commander. Then, McClellan would take his turn, peering through the telescope.

For anyone watching the watcher, however—at least one member of the staff was, and closely—it was clear that beneath the studied pose of nonchalance, McClellan vibrated with tension.

A mass of crisp new Union soldiers was headed into a fresh fight. Line upon line of them streamed forward, passing within a half mile of McClellan's lofty post. It must have made for a spectacular sight. The men were in so-called column by the flank, a snakelike troop configuration four men wide and many, many long. This was a favored marching formation, one that allowed troops to move rapidly to the site of an engagement. Once there, the men could organize into a proper fighting formation. With a single shouted command ("Front!"), entire regiments would shuffle into their appointed places, like cards on a blackjack table, achieving that Civil War combat standby: the battle line. A blue wall would materialize, just like that, hundreds of soldiers wide, two deep, and fearsome to behold.

The Union force's destination was the vicinity of the Miller farm. They aimed to finish what had been started in the cornfield. Both sides had taken a drubbing there, with the survivors retreating into the woods. These Federal newcomers planned to track down any Rebel remnants, killing them or chasing them off. Then, at last, the Union could gain the ground surrounding what was now known to be a church, the Dunker Church.

In other words, the Union was rethrowing that first punch on the topmost part of the field. Yet again, it was trying to sock Lee's army in the left eye. Succeed and it would be possible to pursue McClellan's original plan. These fresh Federals could drive southward presumably in coordination with Burnside's men who must be driving northward. They *must be*, right? Surely, Burnside's men had crossed that bridge by now.

The newly deployed Union force that marched past McClellan consisted of 5,400 soldiers—an entire division's worth. The division, in turn, was part of II Corps, under the command of Edwin Vose Sumner. Born in 1797, Sumner had served for decades, mostly as a cavalry officer, fighting Indians, Mexicans, and every other enemy of the republic save for the British (he'd just barely missed the War of 1812). He was the oldest general on the field this day. The men called him "Bull," a nickname sometimes ascribed to his booming voice. Astride his horse, the snow white–haired Sumner rode up front with his lead division. He anticipated a dribble of Rebels, no match for these 5,400 troops. If, by some chance, the men ran into problems, II Corps contained a pair of additional divisions that might be able to provide backup. They lagged a ways behind (this was an immense troop movement, after all). But there was comfort in knowing that if 5,400 couldn't finish the job, 10,000 more were bringing up the rear.

Sumner's lead division arrived at a broad, open stretch of pasture. It was like a parade ground, an ideal place for the men to switch into battle formation. Because this was such a large assemblage of troops, they formed into not one, but three parallel lines, each nearly 500 yards wide. Roughly 50 yards separated each line.

This was a battle behemoth. It consisted of thirteen different Federal regiments, hailing from a variety of places, and including such distinguished combat units as the 1st Minnesota. Surprisingly, Minnesota, far to the west and fresh to statehood (admitted in 1858) was the very first state to offer soldiers to the Union cause. This was due to a quirk of history: when Fort Sumter fell, Minnesota's governor happened to be visiting Washington, DC. Immediately, he sought out the secretary of war, pledging that his state would furnish soldiers to help suppress this act of "treason" (that's the word the governor used). Holding down the far right of the first battle line—given pride of place—was that inaugural regiment, the 1st Minnesota. It was filled with soldiers of Scandinavian descent. The second battle line featured regiments from Michigan, New York, and Massachusetts. Among them was the 20th Massachusetts, better known as the Harvard Regiment because so many of its officers had attended that university. The third battle line consisted of four Pennsylvania regiments—collectively the Philadelphia Brigade. It was led by Oliver Otis Howard, a deeply pious man and zealous abolitionist known as the "Christian General." He was only just returning to active duty, after having lost his right arm in the Battle of Seven Pines, three and a half months earlier. Following the war, the general would be a founder of the historically black institution of higher learning that bears his name: Howard University.

In the distance, to the west, was a stand of woods. This was the likely lair of those Rebel holdouts.

The Union started forward. So broad were the battle lines that they extended beyond the edge of the pasture and into Farmer Miller's cornfield. Yes, a portion of the men was actually marching across the scene of earlier havoc. The troops were moving in a new direction, though, east to west, where the earlier fighting had been north and south. They stepped around the wounded and dead, blue and gray. "Our men and Secesh [secessionists] lay as they fell," Corporal Edward Walker of the 1st Minnesota would recall, "many begging us for a drink of water, others telling us not to tread on them . . ."

But it was as if this marching force had fixed on a new lodestar, and they pressed relentlessly forward. The stand of woods began to come into focus, towering oaks and hickory forming a wall of green and shadow.

Soon, the Union troops arrived at the Hagerstown Pike, bordered on both sides by stout post-and-rail fences. These were built too sturdily to come down easily. Encumbered by muskets and gear, the men clambered over these 5-foot-tall fences instead, doing their best to stay in unison, maintaining the lines. Soon, too, they began to draw their first cannon fire. From more than a thousand yards in the distance, the guns began to blare. The Federals could plainly see the missiles, streaking through the sky— curiosities, sort of; beautiful, almost—before they completed their high arcs, and plummeted earthward. Three broad battle lines made such easy marks. A shell that overshot one was guaranteed to hit the next. Holes were punched in the Union ranks. But in its own grim way it also served as confirmation: the Rebels were due west.

Onward. The Union men continued across pasture land— clomp, clomp, clomp—like farmers setting off for the back forty on a morning errand.

Presently, they arrived in a meadow. Woods were straight ahead, woods to the left. But this was a tricky piece of terrain. The very term *meadow* suggests a flat expanse, like a manicured lawn. Not this: here, the land rose and dipped, forming crests and swirls and swales—contours more akin to a stormy sea. Keeping the lines intact became challenging. The 34th New York got separated and drifted off, confused. It was like a ball bat snapping, with a piece careening off in some unexpected direction. Only this was an entire regiment, 311 men.

Meanwhile, the first battle line continued into the woods ahead. They met with remarkably little resistance. No enemy was encountered. The Rebels—and their infernal cannons—must be further ahead. There wasn't much in the way of undergrowth to hack through, either. Remember that zigzag fencing: "cow high, hog low"? Well, its purpose was to protect the crops, providing a barrier around the corn and wheat, while keeping animals out. Among local farmers, the practice was to let the livestock roam free. As a consequence, voracious hogs and sheep had gobbled up everything on the forest floor. What was left were stately oaks and hickories, some of them three hundred years old. Moving among these giants was effortless, especially with no vines or creepers to slow one's progress. What's more, this patch of woods was only about 150 yards deep.

Perhaps it was all too easy.

As the lead battle line emerged into the clearing beyond the far edge of the woods, instantly they met with a barrage. The Rebels struck from lethally close range. They were firing case, that twisted brainchild of Henry Shrapnel. The fuses had been timed so that the shells exploded while still airborne, yet momentum carried the load of iron balls and the jagged fragments of their casing (hence "case"), forward, tight packed, directly into the Federals.

Nightmarish. Yet the situation was about to get a whole lot worse. The lead battle line had become isolated, having advanced rapidly through that patch of woods. The second line was only just entering the trees, and the third, still crossing that tempest-tossed meadow. Unbeknownst to these men—at least for a few more blissfully ignorant seconds—the section of woods to their left was swarming with Rebels.

Lee, you see, was also intent on finishing what had been started in the cornfield. He'd been busy shifting his forces accordingly. With the southern reaches of the battlefield at a standstill, he had ordered General John Walker and his division of roughly 3,750 men to hasten northward. (That left only 450 Georgians to defend against a Rohrbach Bridge crossing, but the Federals were none the wiser.) Lee had also sent General Lafayette McLaws and three brigades totaling 2,300 men, who had arrived at dawn following an all-night march from Harpers Ferry, on the move toward this same spot. Walker and McLaws's soldiers were primed for combat. What the Union had expected to encounter, Rebels chewed up by the cornfield fighting, were by this time long gone. They were currently trudging in the opposite direction toward Sharpsburg—well, save for roughly 450 stalwarts commanded by Stonewall Jackson. Quite a collection of Rebels had come together here, roughly 8,200 in total, men from Virginia, Georgia, Mississippi, North and South Carolina. Even Arkansas was represented by the state's 3rd regiment.

Just as McClellan had a plan, so too did Lee. Although badly outnumbered, the Rebel commander believed he could snatch a victory through sheer audacity and guile. He was taking his chance. By concentrating his forces on this topmost section of the field, he might be able to overwhelm the Yanks. He had used this exact tactic before, against superior numbers, to win several earlier battles. Indeed, Lee was acting in accordance with McClellan's darkest fears about him, the ones that kept his Union nemesis awake at night, counting imaginary Rebels.

What was shaping up, then, wasn't exactly an ambush, though Sumner's men could be forgiven for perceiving it as one. It was more of a collision. The Confederate forces, like their Union counterparts, were pursuing what might be termed a cornfield mop-up plan. Both just happened to wind up in the same place at the same time. As so often happens with collisions, neither party saw it coming.

Rebels streamed out of the woods. They managed to slip in behind that third Union battle line. Suddenly, the Philadelphia Brigade sensed a growing commotion, began to hear what sounded like musket pops coming from the rear. Impossible! Yet the evidence said otherwise, as men in their ranks began to fall. The Federals began turning around, but the situation behind them was difficult to assess. Graycoats could be spotted, all right, but they just as quickly disappeared, sheathed in musket smoke, obscured by the choppy terrain. The enemy bobbed into view then fell away, up and down, like the grimacing wooden horses on an old steam-powered carousel.

Sumner, heeding the danger, rode toward the third line, wildly waving his hat. "Back boys, for God's sake move back," he shouted. "You are in a bad fix."

Sumner pulled up in front of Howard, who stared at him, dumbstruck. It was all happening so fast. Sumner tried to explain that the regiments needed to pivot as one so as to confront their attackers with the strength of a battle line. It was growing louder. Howard couldn't understand what Sumner wanted. He seemed to think that Sumner was calling for some kind of charge. While on horseback, the old general pantomimed, employing broad urgent gestures to describe a maneuver that might get the Philadelphia Brigade out of this mess.

Bull Sumner's celebrated booming voice was useless in such clamor. Then again, there's a second story about the origin of his nickname. During the Mexican War, legend holds, Sumner was plunked in the forehead by a musket ball. It bounced off, leaving him oddly unfazed. The episode suggested a leathery obtuseness; apparently this was what some had in mind when they called Sumner "Bull." In one of his backstabs, McClellan said it plain, calling the general a "fool."

On this day, the second nickname story was fast gaining currency. After all, the old cavalryman had hurried into battle, not even bothering to do proper reconnaissance. So certain was he that the enemy lay squarely ahead that he'd arrayed his men in broad battle lines, a formation ideally suited for straight-on combat, but highly vulnerable to an attack from any other direction. But these were issues for future military historians—and oh, would they ever get a full airing.

Right now, in real time, Sumner knew only that he had to find a way out of this. He and Howard did their best to pivot the men around to face their assailants. Unfortunately, a maneuver that would have been easy on level ground under relaxed circumstances proved impossible in this rolling meadow during the full fever of battle. Where was the enemy anyhow (to the rear? the flank?) and how many of them were there? Panic sizzled through the ranks. Some men simply lay down, overwhelmed. It started as a trickle, then a flood, as the Philadelphia Brigade poured out of the meadow, and made for safety.

The chaos, unleashed by the Rebel rabble, now infected the venerable Harvard Regiment. A soldier from the 20th Massachusetts dropped to one knee and began squeezing off shots toward the rear. Alarmed, Captain Oliver Wendell Holmes Jr. demanded that he cease firing at once. Didn't the man realize that his fellow Federal troops were back there? The soldier refused. So, Holmes slapped him with the flat of his sword. But then, in the very next instant it became horrifyingly clear. The Philadelphia Brigade had vanished. That meant the second battle line, occupied by the Harvard Regiment, had become the rear line. The enemy was behind them, beside them—everywhere!

Holmes had but a moment's time to process this. Then, a bullet passed through his neck and he crumpled to the ground, unconscious. Colonel William Raymond Lee, the regiment's leader, attempted to restore order amid the swirling confusion. Not a chance: Momentum was fast-shifting to Robert Edward Lee, the colonel's West Point classmate, and a distant relative.

Meantime, the Union vanguard was getting clobbered. Along the first battle line, the 15th Massachusetts met with especially rough treatment. Case shells burst in the air in front of the regiment, splattering the men with grapeshot and iron rind. As they fell back through the woods, they were set upon by a Confederate horde that slammed into their flank. Amid the bedlam, the 15th Massachusetts also endured the cruel turn of being mistaken for the enemy by another Union regiment: the 59th New York (frantic, confused, sandwiched in that second battle line) opened fatal fire upon them.

Only hours earlier, seized by a mood of optimism, Richard Derby, a captain with the 15th, had written a letter to his mother. It concluded: "prospects are bright with us for giving the *rebs* a good whipping at this point. With best love to all, I remain your affectionate son, Richard."

Now Captain Derby lay sprawled on the ground, knocked out cold by a musket ball to the temple. He would never regain consciousness.

This was a beating. No, this was a rout. Yet just when it was needed the most, the rest of II Corps, that pair of divisions, was nowhere to be seen. General Sumner had raced into battle, leaving them trailing behind. His 5,400 brave men—what remained of them, anyway—could mightily use the help of those 10,000 fresh fighters about now. But the backup never materialized.

The only option was retreat. Predictably, Union officers, in their post battle reports, would describe the withdrawal as if it was a Sunday stroll. Foot soldiers had a different view of the matter. It seemed more of a mad dash to Private Roland Bowen, 15th Massachusetts, who wrote to his friend: "No God Damned Southerner is a going to catch me unless he can run 29 miles an hour."

Union men sprinted for safety. Many of them just kept on going, into the cornfield (as if the day's first action was doomed to repeat endlessly), then out the other end, and still they ran, until at last, legs jelly, lungs stinging, they reached a different stand of woods—under Federal control.

Up on his sun-soaked bluff top, McClellan suspected that something was going very wrong. Smoke from the fighting below had mottled his view. Yet it was possible to catch glimpses and clues: streams of Union men in seeming disarray, Rebels moving with unsettling confidence. *Why this Rebel swagger when they should be lying still and dead?* Nevertheless, it was difficult to sort out. It seemed that something bad had happened, but from such distance one couldn't be sure. Confirmation came by way of a wig-wag message: "Things look blue."

Then just as quickly, the action took a surprising turn. Right when the Union's prospects seemed most hopeless, the Rebel attack eased up. It was as mysterious as it was relieving.

A factor often overlooked in battles is that pummeling also takes a toll on the pummeler. These Confederates were bone tired, having first marched long (all night, in the case of General Mc-Laws's troops), and then fought hard. What's more, continued pursuit promised to carry them onto a section of the field that was a Union stronghold. To punctuate this, a mixture of retreating bluecoats and holdovers from the earlier cornfield fight managed to form defensive lines. They fired at the oncoming enemy. The Rebels were further dissuaded when shells began to rain down on them, issued by an intimidating collection of Federal artillery arrayed on the Miller farm lot. The Confederates wanted no more of this. Presently, they turned heel and drifted back to the safety of their own stand of woods—the West Woods. Lee wasn't going to overwhelm the Union army and score that surprise victory—not at this point.

Still, his men had inflicted serious damage. In a mere forty-five minutes, an entire Union division had been undone. The Rebels had sawed it nearly in half: 2,200 men had been killed, wounded, were taken prisoner, or had gone missing. The 15th Massachusetts had started out with 606 men, but, upon being hit from three sides, had lost 330 in what would hold as the largest number of casualties suffered by any regiment on the field this day.

Among its wounded was Sergeant Jonathan Stowe. The thirty-year-old farmer from Grafton, Massachusetts, slumped against a tree and recorded his real-time impressions in a diary:

"Battle Oh horrid battle What sights I have seen [and] now see around me

I am wounded! . . . Am in severe pain . . . I do sincerely hope shall not be wounded again"

Stowe grimaced, overcome by a wave of agony.

"Oh I cannot write"

---

Already, the battle had produced a colossal number of casualties. Soldiers were going down, either wounded or killed, at a rate of nearly one every second (3,600 per hour), a pace that would fluctuate, while remaining appallingly high, throughout the day. Sadly, the dead were destined to lie as they fell until the battle ended. Only then could these men be buried; in cases where they could be identified, provisions might also be made for relatives to travel to the battlefield and claim their body.

For the wounded, however, there was a chance to receive treatment even as the battle was in progress. Amid all the madness, amazingly, systems were in place to provide for their care. Both the Union and Confederates had sketched out what might be called treatment circuits, starting with the most rudimentary aid, provided right on the battleground, then onward to a field hospital, where more advanced procedures could be performed, before moving along, if necessary, to a general hospital for long-term care in such a place as Philadelphia or Richmond.

The first step in this circuit was called a dressing station. These tended to be astonishingly modest spots staked out by the small, fearless medical teams that accompanied the soldiers into battle. A barn might serve as a dressing station, though such a facility was a comparative luxury; just as often it was a stand of trees, the far side of a boulder, even a ditch. There was no opportunity to be choosy. The aim was to establish first aid stations right near where the fighting had broken out. By necessity, the spots were selected on the fly.

Typically, one or two assistant surgeons along with a steward carrying a knapsack filled with basic medical supplies manned a dressing station. Wounded soldiers such as Stowe of the 15th Massachusetts did their damnedest to get to the nearest dressing station. Comrades might carry them—they'd crawl if necessary.

For a badly wounded soldier, a dressing station offered the first, best hope of surviving. They weren't the place for amputations or other complex operations. Such procedures would have to wait for a later point, when a wounded soldier could be safely transferred to the next stop, a field hospital. The goal of a dressing station, rather, was simply to stabilize a wounded patient.

Soldiers arrived with gaping wounds, their life literally draining out of them. Surgeons applied tourniquets and pressure bandages to stanch the bleeding. Soldiers showed up with limbs shattered by minie balls and shell fragments. Surgeons set the bones, though they often relied on makeshift splints fashioned from tree branches. If nothing else, an injured man would be given a stiff drink. For pain, shock, wooziness, anxiety—really anything related to a war wound—whiskey was the catchall remedy, though it was labeled according to its medicinal name, *Spiritus frumenti*. The surgeons at a dressing station also had a supply of opiates, such as morphine. At this juncture in the war, syringes were not yet in wide use. A common practice was to rub powdered morphine directly into a wound.

Unfortunately, a soldier with a serious injury to the head or torso was considered a goner. An opiate would be administered to ease his pain. If possible, a chaplain would be summoned to administer last rites. And that was that. As for soldiers skittish enough to seek treatment for a minor injury, they could expect to wait endlessly—or possibly to be shamed into rejoining the fight.

To indicate a dressing station, a red flag was raised nearby. (Because Northern and Southern medical personnel shared a common background, both relied on this same modest marker.) If a Reb stumbled into a Yankee dressing station, or vice versa, he could expect to receive medical treatment, although surgeons were inclined to fix up their own boys first.

Dressing stations were dangerous places. No international treaties yet existed defining battlefield norms toward noncombatants, such as medical personnel and wounded soldiers. Between the Union and Confederacy, all that really existed was a gentlemen's agreement, little more than a handshake. Although no honorable soldier on either side would ever intentionally target a dressing station, a red flag fluttering above a boulder or ditch could easily escape the notice of artillerymen operating long-range cannon. Because dressing stations were set up spontaneously, right on the edge of the fighting, they were also vulnerable to errant musket fire.

Edward Revere, a grandson of Paul Revere, the Midnight Rider himself, served as an assistant surgeon in the Harvard Regiment. During the West Woods massacre, while dressing a man's wounded leg, Revere was shot through the heart and died instantly.

This was medicine at its most stark. A battlefield presented the occasion for such welcome mercy, a chance to save a soldier who otherwise might be dead within minutes. Yet that noble aim collided with the ever-present risk of losing one's own life.

---

Drawn by the opportunity to lend succor, also lured by the danger, quite frankly, was an intense forty-year-old woman named Clara Barton. About the time wounded soldiers began streaming out of the West Woods, she arrived at a farmhouse in the vicinity that served as an aid station. (Victims of the cornfield fighting were pouring in, too.) She showed up in a canvas-covered wagon, drawn by six mules, and laden with such supplies as bandages, bread, wine, chloroform, and lanterns.

Barton was not present in any official military capacity. Neither was she a representative of a battlefield relief outfit, such as the United States Christian Commission, nor was she associated with Dorothea Dix and her corps of nurses. Barton had no formal medical training. She was simply a freelancer, on her own singular mission.

The harried surgeons didn't require credentials, though. Their situation was desperate: they had run out of bandages and, after using every sheet to be found in the farmhouse, they had been reduced to dressing wounds with corn leaves. Then, along came Barton with fresh supplies. She was even tapped to perform a minor surgery, despite her lack of experience. In such a state of emergency, any help was welcome, no questions asked. She removed a minie ball from a soldier's cheek. While a burly comrade held the man still, the diminutive Barton (she stood five feet tall) extracted it with her pocketknife.

This marked Barton's very first visit to the front lines of a battlefield. Yet it was also something for which she had been preparing her entire life.

Barton was the youngest of five siblings. She was raised in North Oxford, Massachusetts, though she could trace her distinguished military lineage back to England and the War of the Roses. As a little girl, she was transfixed by her father's tales of a martial youth spent Indian-fighting in the Northwest Territory under the leadership of Mad Anthony Wayne. Alongside the battling men was a legacy of strong Barton women, among them frontier midwives and a spirited Colonial-era grandmother who had flouted the hated tea tax. Barton's mother was a North Oxford gadfly, known for speaking out about women's rights decades before this became a formal cause.

Childish pursuits held little charm for Barton. Instead of learning nursery rhymes, she memorized the forgotten generals of long-ago wars. At a time when she was only just learning to talk, Barton would recall, "I lisped these often difficult names." Her family was amused to discover that she envisioned the heroes of the Revolution or French and Indian War as actual giants, not proportioned like ordinary men. She had a vivid imagination. A stick was not merely a stick. If she found a suitable one lying on the ground, she promptly fashioned it into a bayonet. A horse was not merely a horse. Barton learned to ride almost before she could walk, and one can be certain she fancied herself a dragoon, not a duchess.

Perhaps the most formative experience of Barton's youth occurred at age eleven. During a barn raising, an older brother fell from a ridgepole and hit his head. The boy sustained serious injuries that left him an invalid for two years. Barton was a near-constant presence at his bedside, monitoring his condition and doling out medicine. Under the tutelage of his doctors, she administered the cures of the day, even such not-for-the-faint procedures as bleeding a patient. "My little hands became schooled to the handling of the great, loathsome, crawling leeches ... ," she would recall.

If not a soldier, maybe she would have made a good physician. But military careers were unavailable to women in this era, and female doctors were a rarity. On reaching maturity, however, Barton was seized with an intense ("burning" is perhaps the best word) need to find a suitable career. There was a reason for this urgency. In her own home, among her closest kin, Barton had a ready-made cautionary tale about the dangers of unfulfilled potential, courtesy of her eldest sister, Dolly.

For hours at a stretch, Dolly remained in a rocking chair in her attic bedroom: glaze-eyed, mute, rocking to and fro. Once upon a time, Dolly had been a talented, vivacious girl, and full of dreams—not unlike the youngest Barton. Almost certainly, Dolly suffered from an undiagnosed mental illness. For Clara, the sight of her sister would grow to symbolize the plight of women whose ambitions were thwarted. She once described Dolly as "so bright, so scholarly, so promising, and so early blighted." (Barton would have her own lifelong mental health struggles, suffering severe bouts of melancholy.)

At seventeen, Barton obtained a teaching certificate. She taught in various locales in the Northeast, living in boardinghouses along the way. It proved an itinerant career for Barton, but she was a natural. A highlight was launching a school in Bordentown, New Jersey. She grew the enrollment from zero to six hundred students in a single year.

Thereupon, the townspeople judged that a proper principal was needed, and a man was hired for the job. Barton received the title "female assistant." For a while, she remained at the school she had founded, though her salary was $250 a year versus $600 for the new principal. Barton moved to Washington, DC, seemingly a better city for an unmarried career woman. She found a job as a Patent Office clerk that paid $1,400 per year, the same as her male counterparts. Even in cosmopolitan Washington, however, government work was a men's club; Barton was the first and only female clerk at the Patent Office. Co-workers blew tobacco smoke in her face and circulated rumors about her sexual promiscuity. During her years at the Patent Office, her prospects rose and fell with a series of different bosses. Some liked her, some did not. Her salary fluctuated accordingly.

When the Civil War broke out, Barton ached to be involved. She started gathering supplies for the soldiers: shirts, soap, salves, tobacco, and whiskey. At first, she used her own money, while also calling on friends and acquaintances to provide whatever items they could spare. Word of Barton's efforts spread and soon she was inundated: medicine, sheets, pillows, pies, pickled vegetables, and raspberry vinegar. She rented several warehouses to store all the loot. Yet despite the success of this venture, she tortured herself about what she called the "folly and wickedness of remaining quietly at home." Stockpiling supplies was noble work, no question, but Barton hungered for something more.

She longed to go to the front lines. There, she could make a difference. The 15th Massachusetts included a company of soldiers drawn from North Oxford, her hometown. Union regiments featured companies from Herkimer, Bordentown, all the towns where she had taught, each filled with boys who had been her pupils. Barton described the Army of the Potomac as "my own army." This was the same sentiment (she used the same words even) expressed by commander McClellan himself.

Barton worked her contacts in Washington, trying to discover the sites of upcoming battles. By the time she got to Second Bull Run, though, the fighting was finished, the medical emergency already over. She arrived at Cedar Mountain a full four days too late.

Then, on September 13, a messenger had delivered a slip of paper, bearing a single enticing line: "Harper's Ferry, *not a moment to be lost.*"

For the sake of secrecy, Barton burned the slip of paper in the presence of the messenger. Then, she set out in her mule-driven wagon loaded with supplies. In a way, her military intelligence was as solid as Lincoln's. Although Harpers Ferry wouldn't end up being the venue for the big clash between the Union and Confederacy, by setting it as her destination, Barton was able to reach the general area at least. As she drew closer, on learning that Sharpsburg was the anticipated battle site, she simply adjusted her course accordingly.

On the eve of the battle, Barton had camped on the southernmost part of the field near the Rohrbach Bridge. She experienced the odd sensation of being the only woman in an ocean of slumbering men. She awoke at 3:00 A.M., earlier than General Lee even. For the longest time, she scanned the darkened horizon. And then, the first faint dabs of light appeared, followed by the sounds of battle coming from the cornfield and then the West Woods. "Follow the cannon." It would become her motto. She boarded her wagon, stirred the mule team, and headed north to where she was needed.

As the battle raged, Barton faced her share of real danger. At the farmstead where she provided aid, she traveled back and forth between the house and a barn, passing over treacherous open ground, strewn with wounded soldiers. One begged her for water. While she propped the man up with one hand, she held a vessel to his lips with the other, letting him take a soothing drink. Suddenly, she felt a whoosh. A bullet clipped her sleeve before lodging in the man's chest. He fell back, dead. Barton chose to never mend the bullet hole in the sleeve of this plain brown blouse. Ever after, it would serve as a reminder of warfare's dreadful toll; the rent blouse would become part of the modest "uniform" of this extraordinary woman.

# CHAPTER 8

## THE BLOODY LANE

*The battle was drawing ever more* soldiers into its vortex, growing in size, growing desperate, inexorably bound for a bloodletting on a scale beyond reckoning or reason. It was not 1861 any longer, and this was no Cheat Mountain, no Carnifex Ferry—bantam contests by comparison. There was a heedlessness, a terrible modernity to be found in the sheer numbers involved: a regiment, three regiments, a brigade, five brigades, the population of Cleveland maybe, larger than Cleveland, must be—more men than one could reasonably expect to meet in a lifetime, gathered into units within units within units, moving, fighting, dying, here and there.

Whatever even became of those Federal backup forces that had been trailing behind Sumner? They were two entire divisions, the balance of the Union II Corps. They had been a no-show during the West Woods disaster. So, what happened? The pair of divisions, fully 10,000 soldiers, made an unexpected change in direction, it seems, and wound up on a different part of the field.

This would have a profound effect on the course of the battle.

---

To this point, the conflict had been concentrated in and around Farmer Miller's cornfield. But fighting was about to flare up along an unpaved and meandering country lane. It had been in use for generations: as a shortcut to avoid paying toll on the Hagerstown Pike, as a way to convey grain to the gristmills on Antietam Creek. Over time, wagon wheels had worn deep grooves into this dirt road; rainwater had eroded it still further. In places, it ran 4 feet below ground level. One particular stretch, covering roughly 1,000 yards, formed the border between two prosperous farms, one owned by William Roulette, the other by Henry Piper. This sunken road was tight-packed with Confederates, about 2,500 of them. They had torn up zigzag fencing and piled the rails in front of them, creating an impressive barrier.

William French, the general leading that next-in-train Federal division (roughly 5,700 strong), was about to happen into this hive of Rebels. French was known as Old Blinky due to a disconcerting trait of fluttering his eyes. As to how he and his men wound up in this nervous-making situation, it would become a source of enduring mystery.

Maybe General French simply got lost. After all, he trailed a ways behind Edwin Sumner. He had to contend with challenging terrain (the day's recurrent problem), so one can easily see how he might slip out of coordination with the lead division. Then again, French might simply have been obeying orders, at least as he understood them. Early on, before the situation in the West Woods grew dire, Sumner's own son, serving as an aide, had located French to deliver an order. Its wording was maddeningly vague, something to the effect of "make a vigorous attack." At the time, French's men were receiving light fire from Rebels ahead of them. So, attack he did, setting off in a new direction toward his assailants and that fateful sunken road.

In the end, it didn't really matter whether French was lost, following orders, or merely improvising in the face of fast-evolving battlefield conditions. The result was the same. The general was about to attempt that haymaker aimed smack at the Confederate center. Only problem: the timing was not according to plan. The Rebels hadn't yet been squeezed in that vise—not even close.

From his high-ground post, surrounded by muted aides, Mc-Clellan would also witness portions of this next phase of the fighting. The temperature was pushing an unseasonable seventy. Down on the field, smoke wafted, carrying acrid traces of saltpeter, a gunpowder ingredient. It stung one's eyes, burned one's throat. If a cornfield could be consumed by mayhem, this modest country byway was about to become the site of unspeakable carnage.

General French halted, forming his 5,700 soldiers into three massive parallel battle lines, each roughly 500 yards wide. This was a familiar configuration, making for an awesome spectacle to rival the troops that had set out for the West Woods. But there was also a significant difference. Whereas Sumner had marched his three lines in unison, French would throw his into the action in sequence: one, two, three.

The Rebels waiting in the road were under the command of Daniel Harvey Hill, Stonewall Jackson's brother-in-law. Hill was also a college math professor. In fact, he had authored an algebra textbook filled with problems featuring such scenarios as: "A man in Cincinnati purchased 10,000 pounds of bad pork, at 1 cent per pound . . ." The point, in every example, was to call out the naïveté, foolishness, and venality of Northerners. Hill was a staunch Confederate, not averse to using the word *gratifying* to describe a field strewn with Yankee dead.

French's first battle line started forward. The soldiers marched onto the Roulette farm, a ready source of wheat, rye, oats, and potatoes, worked for seeming eons, since the time of the French and Indian War. Breaks opened up in the ranks as the troops swarmed around various farm structures, such as the springhouse and corncrib. After passing each, they struggled to quickly reconstitute the battle line, as if it was formed of globules of silvery mercury, not men.

At the far edge of the Roulette property, the land rose on a gentle incline until it reached a broad, grassy hilltop. On the other side, utterly obscured from the Union soldiers, the terrain fell off, sloping down down down, until it reached the sunken road crowded with waiting Rebels.

A few Confederate officers crept to the hilltop. Staying low so as to remain unobserved, they were able, through field glasses, to see French's lead battle line moving across Roulette's farm, headed right for them. They could also discern the two other lines, formed and waiting. At this point, a couple of notions appear to have struck the officers. They were frighteningly outnumbered. But they were also facing extremely inexperienced soldiers. "The banners above them had apparently never been discolored by the smoke and dust of battle," noted John Gordon, a colonel with the 6th Alabama.

This was a canny observation. Turns out, French had cobbled ten regiments into a division on September 16. In other words, this combat unit was one day old. More than half of its soldiers had no battle experience whatsoever. The 1st Delaware, for example, had participated only in garrison duty, as in: they had enjoyed the relative comfort of guarding a fort with a roof over their heads and regular meals. By contrast, the Confederates in the road included many hardened veterans.

The Union drummer boys beat cadence. The Rebels crouching in the road could hear the footfalls drawing closer. When the Federals reached the Roulette orchard, they were ordered to fix bayonets. An unholy clanking filled the air as the soldiers in French's first line drew 16-inch blades from their scabbards and locked them into position. The bluecoats resumed marching, but now they had taken on a menacing new appearance. Remember, each broad battle line was two men deep, making it possible for one to fire while the other reloaded. The soldiers in the lead held their muskets thrust forward, blade-first. The soldiers directly behind held theirs perpendicular, stock resting against their shoulder, bayonet pointed skyward. It gave the line the appearance of a wide, millipedal, spiky beast rumbling over the fields.

The Rebels were ready. A whispered order began to travel along the road; crouching officers skittered to and fro delivering it: target the Union soldiers' belt buckles. "Aim low! Give 'em hell! Give it to the goddamned Yankee sons of bitches!"

A perennial marksmanship peeve was that soldiers tended to aim too high, trying to deliver that fatal shot to the head. In this road rutted into a ditch, the tendency was sure to be compounded, as the Rebels would be firing up at the Federals as they crested the hill. Miss a headshot, and the bullet might zip harmlessly through empty air. But aim a bullet at that belt buckle and one's margin for error expanded in every direction, like the soft lead of a minie ball. Of course, it required patience and fearlessness to let your enemy come into full view.

The Rebels waited.

Bayonet tips danced and bobbed ... the vertical musket stocks of the second filers came into view ... now kepis ... forever ... now faces ... blouses of blue with buttons and pockets and what-not ... forever, forever ... and belt buckles, at last, brass ones, stamped "US."

"Fire!" shouted the officers, up and down the sunken road.

The Rebels loosed a fearsome volley. Bullets slammed into the Federals, chewing up their line, sending the soldiers reeling back. So stunning was the onslaught that it appears few of the men even managed to get a shot off in return. As for the bayonets, useless: roughly 50 yards still separated the two sides, reducing the blades to mere shiny metal slivers. Those lucky enough to survive retreated back over the hillside and lay down flat. In little more than an instant, one quarter of the first line had gone down.

But more Union soldiers were about to enter the fight. Even as the first attackers fell back, French's second ample line was on the move, composed of soldiers from New York, Connecticut, and Pennsylvania.

As they marched past the farmhouse, William Roulette burst from the cellar. When the two vast armies began massing in the valley, he'd fled to safety along with his family. But nobody had known for certain when the fighting might start. So he'd returned alone to his farm to check on his possessions and care for his livestock. When the battle erupted, it had taken him by surprise, and he'd sought refuge in the cellar.

During the early hours of fighting, peeking through a window, the frightened farmer had spotted only gray and butternut. He was a staunch Union man; he'd name his next son Ulysses Sheridan Roulette. To his great relief, the soldiers currently passing over his property were in Federal blue. Emerging from his cellar, he shouted: "Give it to 'em! Drive 'em! Take anything on my place, only drive 'em!"

Some Confederates were hiding in the springhouse, caught offside, same as Farmer Roulette had been. A quick-thinking soldier from the 14th Connecticut locked them inside.

But this was a trifling victory, about to be swallowed up by enormity. More so even than the troops that preceded them, these were inordinately inexperienced men. Some had never even fired a musket! Add to that, they had the disadvantage of knowing what lay ahead. They could see the remnants of the first line streaming back toward them, some sprinting in goggle-eyed terror, others staggering, wounded.

Old Blinky waged battle as though he was swinging a heavy wooden mallet. He had a reputation as a blunt-force tactician, inclined to view combat as a numbers game, strictly, and willing to dispatch soldier after soldier until the enemy was pounded into submission.

The second battle line pressed on. Following close behind, as ever, were the file closers, snarling and spitting. They brandished their muskets, promising to crack down hard on anyone who dared break and run. The fresh soldiers climbed the hill, remaining in tight, anxious formation, stepping over those lying dead or in agony. The same fate awaited them as their fallen comrades. As soon as they came into view, they were met by a hail of bullets from the Rebels in the sunken road.

Hundreds slumped to the ground killed or wounded. Within moments, another pristine battle line was riddled with gaps. The survivors fell back, aghast. "Troops didn't know what they were expected to do," Lieutenant Samuel Fiske of the 14th Connecticut would recall, "and sometimes in the excitement, fired at their own men." Pandemonium took over and those who even managed to get off a shot were as likely to hit their fellow Union soldiers as they were the enemy. Others simply made for the safe side of the hill and lay down.

For Edward Spangler, a private with the 130th Pennsylvania, the anxiety was almost unbearable. The feeling had begun the previous afternoon, only to grow over the endless hours that followed. All that worry now became justified. This was real. "I hugged the ploughed ground so closely that I must have buried my nose in it," he remembered. "I thought of home and friends, and felt that I surely would be killed, and how I didn't want to be!"

Confederates spontaneously began pouring out of the road, and started up the hill. The time was nigh for a countercharge. Some even locked their bayonets in place. It must have been an excruciating sound for Private Spangler and all the other Union soldiers lying down on the other side of the hill. But the Rebel charge proved to be disorganized, and they quickly fell back to the safety of the road. Already, the third Union battle line was on the march.

Lee was monitoring the action, same as McClellan. During much of the fighting in the sunken road, he was directly across the valley from his counterpart. He sat in the saddle, hands bandaged, as the orderly led Traveller along the backroads to choice spots where the commander could overlook his men as they struggled to hold his army's center.

Even wounded, Lee proved more mobile than his counter-part, and more apt to take risks, too. Earlier in the morning, he'd stopped on a promontory where he'd been involved in a shock-ingly close call. He was joined there by generals D. H. Hill and James Longstreet. Lee and Longstreet dismounted and sent their horses to the rear. But Hill remained on horseback.

Suddenly, a distant report rang out and a puff of smoke became visible as, from across the Antietam, one of the Federal long-range guns lobbed a projectile toward the three generals. Seconds later it sheared off the front legs of Hill's horse, right at the knees. The animal pitched forward, stumps to the ground, rear in the air. A panicked Hill struggled to get off the dying horse, knowing an-other shot would surely follow. But he was leaning in such a way that it proved impossible to swing his leg back for an ordinary dismount. Finally, yielding to gravity, Hill toppled forward over the pommel. The three generals raced for cover.

The shot that killed the horse hurtled directly past Lee. If only for a moment, this must have caused the anger that he'd been carrying inside for lo these many months to swell. Lee didn't wear animus for the enemy on his sleeve like D. H. Hill—or countless others on the field this day. That wasn't his manner. Rather, he had been carefully tending his rage, stoking it like a furnace. More than many, he felt, he was fully justified in grievance. You see, during that midnight raid across the Potomac, the one in which Colonel Elmer Ellsworth was killed, Union soldiers had seized his home. His beloved Arlington had been invaded by Yankees.

The place held a near-sacred significance for Lee. As a child, while he'd moved from home to home, his family always stay-ing one step ahead of creditors, this mansion on a hill had come to represent everything to which he aspired. He'd first visited at age four before returning countless times throughout his youth. Even though his family was in straitened circumstances, George

Washington Parke Custis, the mansion's owner, had always been kind to him. He was a Lee, after all, and along with that name came all the associations of old Virginia and the Revolution.

Custis, recall, was the father of Lee's wife, Mary, and a grandson of Martha Washington. In 1802, Custis began building Arlington as a kind of shrine to the ideals of the early republic and the memory of its very first president, who had adopted him as a son. Custis filled the mansion with assorted heirlooms that had belonged to his illustrious forebears.

During Custis's lifetime, while the White House was often overrun by rabble (as Lincoln would discover), Arlington became something of a refined public destination, almost like a museum. Custis welcomed visitors, delighted in showing off priceless Washington relics or strolling the ample grounds with the unrivaled view of the capital city just across the Potomac. (That view was precisely why the Union had seized Arlington. Cannons placed on the grounds could have reached critical targets in the District with the same ease as those that killed D. H. Hill's horse.)

Arlington meant everything to Lee. As a West Point cadet, he'd courted Mary in its gardens. He asked for her hand in the dining room. They were married in the parlor.

Upon the death of Custis—a man Lee once described as having "been to me all a father Could"—the mansion's ownership passed on to Mary. Six of Lee's seven children were born at Arlington. Because he was now related to Washington through marriage, his offspring were the first US president's great-great-grandchildren.

Lately, Lee was in continual receipt of distressing news about Arlington. The slaves had been left behind to care for the property, but many had seized the opportunity to flee. A handful remained in his possession, such as Michael Meredith and Perry Parks, who he'd taken with him to the battle, it appears. Likely, these two slaves had fixed Lee's breakfast and groomed Traveller this very morning. Others had accompanied various family members—or had been hired out to plantations.

As for the Washington relics, many had been moved to the safety of Richmond and other locations in Virginia. But everything left behind fell under siege. Union soldiers lumbered about the mansion, pilfering a punchbowl and lantern once used at Mount Vernon. For firewood, they cut down the old-growth trees in what was known as the Washington Forest. Fragments of Society of Cincinnati china were scattered on the grounds, suggesting that the soldiers had either eaten off plates once belonging to the first president, then heedlessly broken them—or else used them for target practice. The blanket that had covered Washington when he died had been removed from the house and put on public display—in the *North*. And that's what Lee found truly galling.

For thirty-two years, Lee had loyally served in the *U.S.* Army. The Union occupation of Arlington, more than any other factor—and in a very short time—succeeded in radicalizing him, turned him into a Rebel. The letters he wrote to Mary and other family members around this time are telling. He began to refer to the Union in impersonal us-versus-them terms, often calling his opponents simply "the enemy." To one of his daughters, Lee wrote the following: "Your old home, if not destroyed by our enemies, has been so desecrated that I cannot bear to think of it. I should have preferred it to have been wiped from the earth, its beautiful hill sunk, and its sacred trees buried, rather than to have been degraded by the presence of those who revel in the ill they do for their own selfish purposes."

What Lee couldn't have known was that his bitter wish for Arlington's merciful destruction had very nearly come to pass. Only a month earlier, following the Confederate victory at Second Bull Run, McClellan had issued a secret order that if Rebels advanced on Washington, the mansion should be burned down in retaliation. While the Union commander had a unique respect for wives, even those of rival generals, apparently property was fair game.

Lee and McClellan were currently separated by two miles of hot, angry valley. The temperature ticked up another degree.

The third line marched across the Roulette farm. French had saved his most able fighters for last; many of these soldiers were veterans from Ohio and Indiana. However, sandwiched in the middle of the line, experienced men to either side, was perhaps the greenest of his regiments: the 132nd Pennsylvania. Over the past day, with their first battle looming, these troops had been singled out for ceaseless taunting by the veterans who called them "pretty boys" and "mamma's darlings."

The soldiers stopped to fill their canteens at a spring that ran through Roulette's property. From up ahead, they could hear muskets firing in unison. To Frederick Hitchcock, a major with the Pennsylvania regiment, it sounded like "the rapid pouring of shot upon a tinpan, or the tearing of heavy canvas, with slight pauses interspersed with single shots, or desultory shooting." This was an ominous noise, new to these men. The nervous strain was palpable. But they pressed on, marching past a series of white crates.

The fact that the greenhorn 132nd Pennsylvania, of all regiments, happened to be near these crates at this particular time, well—it was like a cruel joke.

All of a sudden, a Rebel cannonball came skipping across the ground and bowled right through the crates. Farmer Roulette was an enterprising man; along with corn, wheat, and assorted other crops, he produced honey. And those crates—they were filled with bees. Angry stinging insects swarmed the Pennsylvanians. The boys squirmed and slapped, trying to fend them off. For some, this was simply the limit. Being musket-whipped by a file closer became a chance worth taking, as many dashed for the rear.

It required several minutes and considerable effort to restore order along the battle line. Then, the soldiers continued across Roulette's fields, up that hill, and once more into the maelstrom. The rookies of the 132nd Pennsylvania received especially rough treatment. Hiram Hummel, Jacob Long, Alonzo Gregory, Daniel

Reed, and Jephtha Milligan, privates all, along with 25 other members of the regiment—every one a mother's son—were killed. Another 114 were wounded and 8 went missing. The regiment, organized in Harrisburg only one month earlier, was devastated.

———

The Union's prospects were starting to look bleak, black—a disaster. But then came another of the day's mysterious momentum shifts. By this point, French had dispatched three sweeping battle lines and, along with generating an absurd number of casualties, had also delivered a huge number of Union soldiers, unharmed, within striking distance of the Rebels (always a numbers game for Old Blinky). Understandably, plenty had slipped off to the nearest woods, done for the day. But countless others, drawn from the 5th Maryland, 108th New York, 14th Indiana, and all the regiments that so far had engaged in suicidal charges on the sunken road, remained on the field. They were all mixed up together, taking cover on the safe side of that hill. Now, these survivors adopted a new tactic.

They stayed low, took turns crawling on their belly to the crest. There, they could get a shot off. Then, they'd slither back down and, while safe from enemy fire, they could stand up and reload, before slithering back up for another shot. This was something much closer to guerrilla warfare than linear tactics—and it worked. After all, a hilltop offered a high-ground advantage. It became possible to fire down at the Rebels massed in the sunken road.

The whole frenzied pace of the fighting began to slow. The Federals took their time, aimed carefully, became opportunistic.

They found particular success picking off Confederate officers. Although officers in the sunken road weren't on horseback, they were still plenty conspicuous, waving swords, forced to be in constant motion rallying the men. Union soldiers managed to methodically kill or wound every single officer in the 4th North Carolina.

A Federal bullet also found George B. Anderson, a general in charge of an entire Rebel brigade. It lodged in his ankle, and he was helped from the field. This sparked a bizarre chain-of-command crisis, shades of the episode that had afflicted the Union at dawn when Colonel William Christian cowered behind a tree.

After General Anderson went down, leadership devolved to the brigade's ranking colonel. This was a man named Charles Tew. An adjutant scurried along the road until he found Tew, whereupon he informed the colonel that he was now in command. Protocol required that Tew acknowledge receipt of the message. As he rose ever so slightly and tipped his cap, a Federal bullet passed through Tew's left temple and dislodged both his eyeballs from their sockets, before exiting his right temple. Colonel Tew had been in command for but a single senseless instant. The shocked adjutant turned heel and set up the road the opposite way, searching out the next-in-hierarchy, Colonel Francis Parker. As soon as he delivered the message, the adjutant fell, wounded by a bullet. Moments later, a bullet grazed Colonel Parker's skull. Blood streaming down his face, he staggered out of the road and made for the rear. Command passed to Colonel R. T. Bennett. And so it went.

Shooting officers provided a lot of buck for the bang. It crushed the morale of the Rebels in the road, leaving them increasingly disorganized.

Here came the reinforcements, though. A 3,400-man Confederate division, a bounty of fresh soldiers and still-upright officers, moved across the Piper farm on the other side of the sunken road. Stray bullets from the fighting had torn through the orchard, dropping thousands of apples. The ground was covered with them. Hungry Rebels snatched up apples and ate them on the march. They began to pour into the sunken road, seeking to fill the many gaps that had opened up.

These soldiers represented the last of the Confederate reserves. But the center must be held at any cost. The only remaining source of fighting power was A. P. Hill, who (Lee desperately hoped) was currently on the march from Harpers Ferry.

Meanwhile, the Union also received a much-needed infusion. That remaining division of II Corps (4,300 men under the command of Israel Richardson) arrived to bolster Old Blinky, whose troops were battle-worn, much diminished, and running out of ammo besides.

In the vanguard of these fresh Federal soldiers was one of the most charismatic men on the field this day, Brigadier General Thomas Francis Meagher. Meagher was an Irish nationalist who had only barely escaped from the Old Country with his life. At a time when Ireland pursued a go-along-get-along stance toward British rule, Meagher had been an agitator for armed rebellion, notorious for his incendiary "Sword Speech." In 1848, he was convicted of sedition and sentenced to be hanged, drawn, and quartered. Queen Victoria provided a last-minute reprieve, reducing the punishment to banishment for life in Van Diemen's Land (modern-day Tasmania).

Eventually, Meagher escaped from the penal colony and managed to stow away on a ship. It provided passage to San Francisco and from there he made his way to New York City. Meagher experienced a dizzying rise, becoming a lawyer, political powerbroker, and founder of the *Irish News*. Come 1861, his reinvention was complete, as a bona fide Irish American hero, a stature he used to recruit members of his community into the Union cause. His pitch was twofold. Serving in the Union army would give Irish immigrants, often targets of suspicion and hostility, a chance to demonstrate fealty to their adopted land. Along the way, they could also pick up useful martial skills. Meagher had ambitions to raise an Irish American army that could liberate the Old Country from England.

The colorful general took the field, leading 1,100 men, most of whom he'd recruited. The Irish Brigade was flying its distinctive flags. Arrayed on a background of emerald silk was a golden harp, shamrocks, and a motto in Gaelic: "Riamh Nár Dhruid Ó Spairn Iann." Translation: "Who never retreated from the clash of spears." The brigade also carried distinctive firearms. Meagher outfitted his men with 1842-issue smoothbore muskets, notorious for inaccuracy. Firing one was kind of like launching a marble from a stovepipe. But the general had his mad methods: he believed such a weapon would force his men into close contact with the enemy, increasing their ferocity, unleashing their ancient Hibernian warrior instincts.

For all the patriotic zeal, however, the Irish Brigade wasn't Irish through and through. Similar to how the rookie 132nd Pennsylvania was sandwiched between French's most experienced men, Meagher's force also had an interloper regiment. The 29th Massachusetts was a study in contrast, mostly composed of soldiers from Plymouth County, many of whom were descendants of the pilgrims. Due to a War Department clerical error, Meagher had been given command of the 29th Massachusetts when it should have been the unequivocally Irish *28th* Massachusetts. Tensions simmered. Men who traced their heritage to the *Mayflower* crossing were thrown together with men fresh off the boat; Protestants were mixed with Catholics. The Puritan-stock soldiers of the 29th were particularly put off by Meagher's florid speechifying, bearing it "coldly, in a pinched and critical silence," according to an old account.

"Boys, raise the colors and follow me," shouted the general, waving his sword and dashing forward on a white steed. Whatever tensions existed in the ranks had to be temporarily set aside—they faced a common enemy. At the right of Meagher's battle line, in the place of honor, was the 69th New York. Already this regiment was legendary, having fought bravely in a series of Eastern Theater battles. It was an enemy general (Lee, in fact) who would give them a sobriquet that stuck, calling them "that Fighting 69th."

Father William Corby, a chaplain on horseback, rode along the line, offering a hasty absolution in Latin. (Corby would become president of Notre Dame after the war.) Irish Molly—her place in history preserved only by this nickname—stood in Roulette's fields waving her sunbonnet, urging on the men. Described as "a big muscular woman," she had joined her husband in the march across Maryland, and had made herself indispensable, apparently, by doing laundry for the soldiers.

Meagher's battle line approached the sunken road at an angle, a quirky move befitting the man himself. Old Blinky had delivered his three lines so as to drive straight at the sunken road. Picture three ocean waves slamming into a wall. Coming in at an angle served the Irish Brigade well; it meant they didn't crest the hill all at once, didn't present such a broad, inviting front for Rebel fire. It also proved a boon for the soldiers' outmoded muskets. Firing into the sunken road with wild inaccuracy, but also at an angle, meant a ball that missed one man hit the man beside him, or behind him, or some other unlucky Confederate.

As Meagher had hoped, his men were able to get closer to the enemy than previous Union soldiers. They started down the hill, bellowing a half-Gaelic, half-English war chant, entirely as bone chilling as a Rebel yell. Some got off as many as six shots as they drew within mere paces of the sunken road.

"Bring them colors in here," shouted a Confederate, greedy for an emerald standard.

"Come and take them you damned rebels," taunted the flag bearer.

The 29th Massachusetts joined the action. With three hearty cheers ("hurrah, hurrah, hurrah"), the stolid Plymouth men charged. On a dead run, they came up over the rise, then hurtled down the hillside and right into the road—the first to reach it.

They shot Rebels at kissing-close range. No one seems to have used a bayonet. (It was a rarity in Civil War combat. While bayonets were unrivaled at sowing psychological terror, the gore was too much for most soldiers, not to mention that withdrawing a blade from a body proved dangerously time consuming.)

Rather, the 29th Massachusetts made quick work: firing a single shot, clubbing a Confederate or two with their musket butts, then racing back up the hillside.

The Irish Brigade served as the shock troops. By getting farther than anyone had before, they managed to spook the Rebels and shake their resolve. It came at an awful cost, though. Roughly half of Meagher's men were killed or injured. Eight men fell protecting the proud green flags, which now hung in ribbons. Father Corby moved among the casualties, delivering comfort and last rites. As for Tommy Meagher, his white horse got shot out from under him and he fell to the ground, knocked unconscious. Predictably, a rumor would circulate that the leader of the Irish Brigade had been tippling.

Breakthrough at last: while the Confederates were busy fending off Meagher's men, about 400 soldiers from another Union brigade managed to slip into a devastatingly advantageous position. These soldiers hadn't approached the sunken road straight on, or at an angle even. No, they had straddled the road at a point beyond the Confederate line. This allowed them to fire straight down the lane, something they did with aplomb. The very features that had made the sunken road such a stronghold transformed it now into a deathtrap for the Rebels. "They could do us little harm, and we were shooting them like sheep in a pen," recalled Charles Fuller, a sergeant with the 61st New York.

The Federals began to roll down the road, following in the path of countless farm wagons. Ahead, Rebels scrambled up the steep banks, trying to escape. Some were unable to get out in time. These men frantically waved handkerchiefs, or turned their muskets upside down, dumping their powder and bullets, signaling surrender. The Union managed to take about 300 prisoners in the sunken road. These men were placed under armed guard and escorted to the rear behind Union lines.

James Lightfoot, twenty-three years old, had taken command of the 6th Alabama when the regiment's leader went down. As the Union soldiers ambled down the lane, steadily firing, he was ordered to turn his men to face the enemy. The 6th Alabama was to form a bulwark against further Federal progress. But the pivot was a complex maneuver for a young temporary leader under intense pressure. Instead, Lightfoot's men started to bolt, joined by the neighboring regiment, and a general panic rippled down the Confederate line. Men by the hundreds poured out of the sunken road and raced to the rear across Piper's farm. This time, no one stopped to gather apples.

McClellan, from his bluff-top aerie, watched the whole episode through a telescope. "It is the most beautiful field I ever saw, and the grandest battle," he exclaimed.

Lee left no record of his thoughts when he learned that his army's center was starting to collapse. The Marble Model must have quaked.

The Confederate defense had shattered, leaving a gaping hole in the ranks that had lined that sunken road. Federals flooded through, a mass of men from the 1st Delaware, 88th New York, and everything in between. They set out across the Piper farm on the heels of the fleeing Rebels. E. P. Alexander, the wigwag pioneer now serving as Lee's chief of ordnance, described the stakes succinctly: "the end of the Confederacy was in sight."

Rebel color guards waved standards trying to reconstitute the broken regiments. Officers struggled to rally the troops, holding their swords above their heads, a signal for the men to join them and make a stand.

The Confederates were desperate now. But their very desperation worked a strange magic. The looming and real possibility of defeat prompted the men to reach down deep to summon unexpected reserves.

D. H. Hill, the Yankee-loathing math professor and a major general, took up a musket himself and led about 200 soldiers in a counterattack. James Longstreet, commander of one of the two wings of Lee's army, no less, remained on the field holding the horses of members of his staff as they manned a pair of abandoned cannons on the Piper farm. They loaded them with double canister, a mighty charge, but called for in such an emergency. With each firing, the overstuffed cannons jumped a few inches off the ground, then rolled violently backward. Longstreet's men worked these monster shotguns furiously, spraying chestnut-size iron balls until the air fairly swam with them.

By this point, the Union soldiers were exhausted and their guns were fouling from repeated firing. General Richardson, leader of that last-to-arrive II Corps division, was struck by a fragment of shell, which lodged in his shoulder. It knocked him from his horse, and he had to be carried from the field. The pursuit grew more and more disorganized. And then it fizzled. The Federals retreated through the Piper Farm and back across the sunken road.

Lee's army had survived a close call. The Confederacy could have ended on Wednesday, September 17, 1862—in time for lunch.

The Union army wasn't in much better shape, though. Already, McClellan had struck in two places, the top and middle of the field, yet nothing had proceeded as expected. Reality had intruded in all its messiness, making a casualty of his pristine battle plan.

But oh what a haymaker: Even if it hadn't been delivered at the appointed time, or achieved a knockout blow, as intended, it still did some serious damage. In the road, the Confederate dead were so thickly strewn that it was hard to discern any of the ground beneath them. Forever after, the sunken road would be known as the Bloody Lane.

One dead Rebel, lying on his back, had his knee raised stiffly. It was as if he was trying to walk straight up out of this carnage, and into the sky.

# CHAPTER 9

───

# DOWN TO RAISINS

*In Washington,* Lincoln was growing ever more starved for news—any news—out of Western Maryland. Was a major battle under way? Maybe it had already been fought. Could the lack of ready information, perhaps, be an ominous sign that Lee had emerged victorious, was even now charting his devious course, planning to strike Harrisburg or Baltimore, or maybe Rebels would pounce on the capital.

Lincoln had a regular habit, more necessary on this day than most. When he could steal a moment, the president would slip out of the White House and set off along a tree-shaded walkway. It was a relief to get away from the endless lines of favor-seekers, what Lincoln sometimes referred to, only half-jokingly, as "my persecutors." But this was no casual stroll to clear his mind; he had an urgent destination. The War Department, a four-story brick building, adjacent to the executive mansion, provided the nearest access to a telegraph. For Lincoln, this place had become the site of an obsessive ritual, one filled with excruciating suspense. On a given day, he sometimes slipped away multiple times to take this brief, anxious walk.

The routine was necessary because the White House hadn't been outfitted with a telegraph. It was just another example of how Samuel Morse's relatively new invention had still not entirely caught on. To much of the public, telegraphic dispatches were little more than a curiosity. Electricity played zero practical role in the life of the average citizen; it was simply a force of nature, witnessed during storms.

The Federal government was no exception. During the years before the Civil War, on those rare occasions when an official saw reason to send a dispatch, a clerk set out, handwritten message in hand, to wait in line with the rest of the public at Washington's central telegraph office, one of the only available transmission sites. Then, with the outbreak of hostilities, connection was extended to several vital locations such as the Arsenal, Navy Yard, and War Department. But not the White House: it was a public building, after all, a place for formal balls and receptions for visiting dignitaries. To wit: during an 1858 event to commemorate the completion of the transatlantic cable, a telegraph had actually been set up in the White House so that President Buchanan and Queen Victoria could exchange messages. The device was strictly ceremonial, and was removed immediately after the proceedings.

However, Lincoln was kind of a tinkerer in chief, quite a departure from Buchanan, his predecessor. He was—and remains—the only president to hold a patent (number 6,469). It was granted in 1849 for a system of inflatable chambers that could be attached to the side of a boat to help buoy the vessel over shoals and other impediments. Inspiration had struck when he was a young boatman, working the Illinois, Sangamon, and Mississippi rivers. To prove his concept, Lincoln had whittled a wooden model.

Long before he aspired to the presidency, he harbored dreams of becoming an inventor. He even worked up a speech entitled "Discoveries and Inventions," where he drew a distinction between "Young America" (those comfortable with the rash of recent innovations) and the "Old Fogy."

Lincoln certainly grasped the value of "lightning messages" (his term for telegraphic dispatches) even if many who surrounded him did not. During Bull Run, the war's first major battle, both Lincoln and Winfield Scott were about twenty-five miles away in Washington. The old general simply took a nap. At age seventy-five, as a veteran of every conflict since the War of 1812, Scott was an "Old Fogy" both chronologically and attitudinally. He was content to snooze, certain that the battle's outcome would reach him in due time. But Lincoln remained awake and on edge, awaiting updates. Of course, the president had to leave the White House if he hoped for news hot off the wires.

Lincoln's practice was to go directly to the cipher room on the second floor of the War Department. Next door, the familiar clackety-clack could be heard as the telegraph tapped out Morse code. Those messages arrived encrypted, a wartime necessity. Upon receipt, dispatches were rushed to a decipherer, who worked to translate them into comprehensible English. The messages were stacked in a desk drawer, with the most recent on top. As soon as Lincoln arrived, he would open that drawer and read through until he arrived at the last message he'd viewed during his previous visit. Then he would say: "Well, boys, I am down to raisins."

At first, the comment perplexed the men in the telegraph office. So, one day, the president explained its origin by way of one of his homespun tales. He told the story of a little girl who overindulged in treats on her birthday, culminating in a raisin binge. That night, she became violently ill and began throwing up. A doctor was summoned. When he examined her vomit, he saw a sprinkling of small black objects. This was a sign, the doctor assured the worried parents, that their daughter had finished being sick. She had emptied the entire contents of her stomach—of this he was certain. How did he know? The girl was down to raisins. "So," concluded Lincoln, "when I reach the message in this pile which I saw on my last visit, I know that I need go no further."

Unfortunately, the telegraph—so indispensable to Lincoln—was yet another source of tension with McClellan. In fact, there were times when it seemed like the general was deliberately exploiting the anxiety surrounding this newfangled communication method, though he no doubt would have claimed otherwise.

McClellan was squarely in the "Young America" camp—in stark contrast to General Winfield Scott. When it came to the telegraph, he was especially savvy. As a railroad executive, he had been part of an industry that was early to rely on the telegraph, an ideal tool, after all, for keeping track of trains. As an observer in Crimea, he had also been present for the first war in which the telegraph was employed.

Thus, McClellan began the Civil War with a keen sense of the device's possibilities. In consultation with Pinkerton, he was among the first to make use of an encrypted version of Morse code. To identify himself, the general selected the vainglorious handle "Mecca" while Washington, DC, was dubbed "Nimrod." During his campaign in Western Virginia, he went so far as to bring along a new invention: a portable telegraph. He also arranged for linemen to trail his movements, laying down wire. That way, he could be connected at his field headquarters, could send a message directly from his tent rather than having to dispatch a messenger to the nearest telegraph station. Of this luxury, he took full advantage: during one stretch of the Western Virginia campaign, he sent out dispatches on three successive days, changing battle plans—typical McClellan.

He also came to realize that he often knew what Lincoln desperately hoped to learn. That was power. The general seems to have perceived an advantage in withholding information from the president.

Just such an incident had occurred on October 21, 1861, sowing discord between the two men. Lincoln was anxiously awaiting news of the Battle of Ball's Bluff, when McClellan (who was monitoring the action remotely, from the capital) happened to stop by the White House. While talking with Lincoln, McClellan was handed a telegram. It revealed that the Union had just suffered a disastrous defeat. McClellan read it and proceeded to finish his talk with the president without sharing the news.

When Lincoln learned of his general's perfidy, he grew quite exasperated. McClellan claimed he was merely being discreet. The president lacked caution when it came to information, he argued, offering his stock scenario: Lincoln would have blabbed to Tad, spilling the news of the Ball's Bluff debacle. The episode helped give rise to a new policy whereby telegrams from officers in the field were to be sent directly to the War Department.

But this was hardly a fix for what ailed Lincoln and his general. It simply meant that when McClellan was in the field, as he currently was, he could really seize control. He could send vague messages, or incomplete ones, or simply fall telegraphically silent. "I will inform you of everything of importance that occurs," he had promised Lincoln when he first set out across Maryland in pursuit of Lee. He'd proved very sparing with updates.

———

Lincoln slipped out of the White House, took a quick walk to his recurrent destination. He entered the War Department building. One imagines the lanky president taking the steps two by two. He hurried down the hall, entered the cipher room, and slid open the desk drawer.

When he went through the dispatches, there was nothing of consequence. No news was forthcoming about the situation in Western Maryland. It was more than a day since McClellan had last been heard from. Lincoln was down to raisins once more.

# CHAPTER 10

# CAN 12,500 SOLDIERS TAKE ONE STONE BRIDGE?

*At long last,* intense fighting broke out in the bottommost portion of the field. Although the battle had raged to the north throughout the morning, this locale had been locked in hours of delay. Were this not war, the setting here would be perfect for an oil painting: the green-hued Antietam swiftly flowing past banks thick-grown with honeysuckle and sycamores, steep bluffs to either side, and spanning the creek, the graceful, tri-arched Rohrbach Bridge.

Starting at first light, this idyllic spot had been the scene of a standoff, pitting the Union on the east side of the creek against the Confederates on the west. The 12,500 Federals had no idea that they faced a mere skeleton brigade, maybe 450 soldiers, mostly Georgians. They only knew that hostile batteries kept up a fusillade. The Rebels recognized the value of raising a thunderous noise. There may as well have been 4,000 Georgians dug into the bluffside; under their cannon fire it could seem like 14,000.

With the receipt of yet another attack order, Ambrose Burnside had finally set his men in motion. Burnside was a humble man and likely humiliated, too, by the split of his command. Most certainly he faced the most difficult assignment on the field. Waiting across the creek were those Georgians under overall command of the irascible Robert Toombs—despiser of Jeff Davis, serial duelist, the man who had come within a hairbreadth of the presidency of the Confederate States of America.

For hours Toombs and his Georgia boys had been ready to fight. Burnside was answering at last, though thanks to delays and missteps, here and elsewhere on the field, any pretense of McClellan pursuing a coordinated battle plan was long gone. But the Union could still redeem the day. Seizing the west bank of the Antietam in this vital locale could provide a beachhead, a place to gather troops and launch a final assault against the Confederates. What lay immediately ahead was simple, elemental: a battle for a bridge.

The Union opened with a fierce cannonade. Guns shelled the opposite bank, contriving to "soften up" the enemy, in military parlance. This was to be followed by a wild charge down the Federal-side bluffs as a diversionary tactic. Acting in concert, another unit would storm the bridge head on. This was a textbook approach, like one would study at West Point.

From the outset, however, matters went desperately wrong. The artillery attack proved virtually impotent against the Georgians, snugly dug into their bluffside redoubt, wearing dusky uniforms that blended with their surroundings. Even the time of day worked against the Union effort, as long morning shadows served to further obscure the Rebels.

So, why didn't the artillery storm work in spite of the well-concealed Georgians? After all, it wasn't necessary to precisely target them. Fire enough random shots and one is bound to take out some enemy soldiers, right? Unfortunately for the Federals, a quirk of nature mitigated against even this. Although it was mid-September, summer still lingered; autumn would be late coming to Western Maryland in 1862. As a consequence, the trees were still in their full foliage, slowing any shells and shrapnel that

tumbled through the canopy. While getting hit remained dangerous, it lacked convincing punch on this part of the field. It's still
another indication that the Confederates had picked their spot
brilliantly. The Union could have rained the annual iron output
of Pennsylvania onto yonder bluffs, and it wouldn't have made a
dent. As it stood, the number of Georgians killed by the opening
artillery salvo could probably be counted on one grubby hand.

Now, here came that diversionary action. The 11th Connecticut burst from the woods that topped the Federal-side bluffs,
streamed downhill, and fanned out across the broad plain leading
to Antietam Creek. They weren't in one of the era's tight battle
formations, it appears. Due to the difficult terrain, the Nutmeg-
gers scampered this way and that, firing at will. Nevertheless, they
were conspicuous in their blue uniforms. The Georgians picked
them off with cruel efficiency.

Captain John Griswold reached the Antietam and waded in,
urging others to follow. The water was belly high and jarringly
cold.

Enemy bullets struck the water around him: *plink, plink*. Griswold pressed on, bottom mire sucking at his feet. He had to pick
his way among underwater stones, branches, and sundry detritus,
threats all to keeping his balance in the swift current.

*Plink, plink*. Nearer now. The Rebels were closing on their
mark. When he had waded more than halfway across the Antietam, a bullet slammed into his chest. He kept going. To Griswold,
wounded, in agony, time must have gone glacial as he slogged
through the current and muck. Without taking another bullet, he
reached the west side of the Antietam at last, the first Union soldier to get there. Captain Griswold dragged himself up the bank
and lay down on the ground bleeding (he would die the next day).

Meanwhile, the primary action—the bridge storming—had
devolved into utter farce. This duty had fallen to the 28th Ohio,
though it's not as if the regiment had any opportunity to prepare.
These soldiers, like so many others in IX Corps, had simply whiled
away the morning huddled in the woods, cooking their breakfast

and cleaning their muskets. The men had no knowledge of the surrounding terrain, let alone what would ultimately be expected of them. In fact, the Ohioans had received orders only a few minutes earlier, passed down the chain of command to the leader of the regiment, Colonel George Crook.

"The General wishes you to take the bridge," Crook was told.

What bridge? he asked.

*What bridge?* Bizarre as that question seemed, it was also valid under the circumstances. Turns out, the officer who relayed the order to Crook couldn't clarify the bridge question. He didn't know its whereabouts, either. Crook asked him whether he could at least point the way toward Antietam Creek. The officer wasn't sure.

Consequently, Crook dispatched four companies of the 28th Ohio to attempt a precision maneuver, a frontal assault on a bridge whose location *they did not know.* The soldiers wandered in the woods on the Federal side. Periodically, they would emerge from cover at a bluff's edge where they'd be afforded a view of the creek below. At such moments, they were met instantly by Rebel fire. Of course, they had no idea how many Georgians were over there. Back into the woods they'd slip, hoping next time to emerge closer to that elusive bridge. And so it went. The Ohioans, bewildered, under fire, pressed on until at last they found, to their great distress, that they were back to where they had started. The Federal soldiers had traveled in a complete circle.

So, Crook sent out five fresh companies of the 28th. They also promptly got lost. Muskets ablaze, they burst from the woods some 350 yards upstream from the bridge. They wound up pinned behind a low sandy ridge near the Antietam. From there, they exchanged desultory fire with the Georgians across the creek.

All this while, sadly, the 11th Connecticut continued to create a diversion, even in the absence of the frontal bridge attack, the action from which they were supposed to divert. When their initial assault collapsed under stiff enemy fire, the Connecticut boys just kept coming, throwing a second wave into the fight, this one led by Colonel Henry Kingsbury.

Kingsbury was a freshly minted officer, West Point class of 1861. He had just gotten married, a match notable because it made him the brother-in-law of David Jones, a Confederate general present at the battle. Kingsbury's new wife was pregnant with their first child. This had prompted him to draw up a will, naming Burnside as one of the executors. Burnside was a family friend who had become Kingsbury's legal guardian after his father had died.

In a battle that mixed together a huge variety of characters—sly men, sophisticates, renegades, and rubes—young Kingsbury stands apart for his refinement. He was described as someone who "delighted to listen to and join in conversations on literary or philosophical topics." Above all, Kingsbury was brave. Waving his sword, he led his men right to the water's edge.

As he stepped into the creek, a bullet struck him in the foot. Staggering back, he was hit again, this time in the leg. Kingsbury collapsed. Several of his men tried to bear him to safety. As had occurred throughout the battle, however, enemy soldiers had spotted an officer and they smelled blood. The colonel was hit again in the shoulder. A fourth bullet pierced his stomach. The Connecticut boys retreated, carrying their gravely wounded leader to the rear.

At a field hospital, Kingsbury faded quickly. Morphine helped to quell his excruciating pain, eased his exit from this world the following day. On learning of his death, Burnside was crushed. Jones, his Rebel brother-in-law, broke down and wept. But that's casting ahead in the story.

Right about now, more Union soldiers were wandering in the woods. A Quaker-bred general, with the unlikely name of Isaac Peace Rodman, was engaged in a quixotic mission, leading 3,200 men (a quarter of IX Corps) in search of a fording spot across the Antietam. The plan: cross downstream and surprise the Confederates on their flank. This was like a two-pronged version of

McClellan's original vise plan, and in miniature. Rodman's men could attack the Rebels from one side, while a fresh frontal attack on the bridge was attempted.

As for locating a place where 3,200 men can cross a swift-moving creek in the heat of combat, well, that's as challenging as it sounds. Laxity on McClellan's part had contributed to the problem. Crossing the Antietam here was key to his battle plan, yet during the previous day only a limited effort was made to scout the surrounding area. James Duane, McClellan's chief engineer and a West Point classmate, had identified a possible fording spot about two thirds of a mile below the Rohrbach Bridge. Good enough. When Rodman's men arrived there, however, they saw that while it was a viable fording spot (as in: the creek was narrower), a sheer bluff waited on the other side, rising 150 feet. Sure, 3,200 men could cross here, but they couldn't climb *that*.

Onward pressed Rodman, leading his men over the rutted paths that wended through the woods. For generations, local farmers had used these trails to conduct livestock from place to place. Now, Union warhorses moved gingerly over the same, some of them lugging naval howitzers. That's right, *naval* howitzers. For inexplicable reasons, Rodman's unit was saddled with five heavy cannons that, per their name, were designed for use aboard ships. To compound matters, the guns weren't properly outfitted. They lacked the rigid pole, known as a trail (such a simple but essential item) that prevents a cannon from rolling forward into the horse that's hauling it. As a jerry-rig, ropes had been attached to the guns. During downhill stretches, soldiers pulled back on the ropes to prevent the howitzers from slamming against the horses' hindquarters.

Every so often, Rodman would send some soldiers to peek out of the woods, see whether a fording spot was nearby. Predictably, they were met with a burst of musketry. Only after the battle ended would it come out that Toombs had spread his paltry number along a 1,650-yard front, the line growing thinner the farther from the bridge. In some places, soldiers were positioned with huge gaps between them. No matter. By now, the Union troops must have been convinced they faced a few odd Roman legions' worth of Rebels.

With Rodman in absentia—he and his 3,200 soldiers appeared simply to have vanished in the woods—the decision was made to launch a fresh attack on the bridge. Tapped for this duty were the 2nd Maryland and 6th New Hampshire, totaling 300 men. But this time, a new tactic was necessary. The two regiments planned to march down a country road that cut through the bluffs and would deliver them downstream a ways. Then they'd follow the east bank of the Antietam until they reached the bridge. Rather than frontal, this would be a sidelong attack.

The 2nd Maryland and 6th New Hampshire fell into a so-called column of fours. To picture this formation, summon the image of a long, skinny plank, equal to four men in width and seventy-five men in length. Now, imagine it scooting along the creek bank en route to the bridge. It made for a delicious target. As this large, tight formation passed before them, the Rebs had but to squeeze their triggers, certain of hitting someone.

It only got worse. Turns out, the progress of this human plank was blocked by a sturdy chestnut fence. Dashing ahead, officers worked desperately to create an opening, pulling down rails. But the opening soon became a fatal bottleneck. Yankee after Yankee got cut down trying to squeeze through. Besides the mayhem, what the Union soldiers, those lucky enough to survive, would remember was the "peculiar-keyed voice" of one particular officer, somehow audible above it all. "What the hell you doing there," he shrieked at the men. "Forward!"

Once through the fence gap, however, the formation quickly lost its shape. It was every man for himself. The Union soldiers sprinted along the bank, seeking the shelter of boulders and logs. This latest Federal effort came apart well short of the bridge.

About this time, McClellan dispatched yet another staffer from his field headquarters to goad on IX Corps. This irked Burnside. "McClellan appears to think I am not trying my best to carry this bridge," he complained. "You are the third or fourth one who has been to me this morning with similar orders."

Also at about this time, Rodman finally caught a break. While lost in the woods, he encountered a farmer who told him about Snavely's Ford. Rather than an impromptu crossing spot, this promised to be the genuine article, an established ford. When someone from the area traveled by carriage, this was a place for crossing the Antietam. Farmer Snavely even kept the creek bottom clear of branches and other entanglements, no doubt collecting a toll from those who used his ford. Obviously, this ford was no secret; the previous day it could have been discovered by scouting, talking to locals, or merely consulting a map. The Rebels knew about it.

Rodman and his men pushed on toward Snavely's Ford.

---

Meanwhile, back at the Rohrbach Bridge. Sheer trial and error—with the loss of many men—had yielded a fuller understanding of the surroundings. It's as if the fighting so far had been a scouting exercise. At last, the Federals had identified a promising spot for that frontal assault. Facing the bridge was a pair of knolls divided by a shallow cleft. It resembled a giant peach half rising up from the ground. The plan was to assemble soldiers on the far side of this shapely eminence. On the order to *charge*, the men would come racing down that cleft, as though it were a chute, before spilling out onto level ground. They would emerge neatly centered on the bridge, though they would need to race across another 100 yards or so of open ground to reach their destination.

A pair of 51sts (the 51st New York and 51st Pennsylvania regiments) was chosen for duty at the twin knolls. Their combined strength: 670 soldiers. Edward Ferrero, a dapper and cosmopolitan general, commanded them. Born in Spain to Italian parents,

Ferrero ran a successful dance school in New York City. He was also author of *The Art of Dancing*, an 1859 best seller that provided instruction on such then-current favorites as the Cheat, Virginia Reel, Ladies' Moulinet, and Varsovienne.

However, one of Ferrero's regiments didn't care much for ballroom formality. The 51st Pennsylvania, which contained many soldiers of German descent, had a reputation for hard fighting on the battlefield, hard living off of it. While stationed near Harrisburg, the regiment had broken guard en masse to go into town for a drunken bender. Another recent transgression involved a group of 51st Pennsylvania men sneaking out at night, slaughtering a farmer's pig, then slipping past a guard and back into camp by covering the pig in a blanket and passing it off as a wounded comrade. This was a rowdy regiment.

General Ferrero moved the two 51sts into position behind the crest of the knolls. Then he delivered a rousing speech, exhorting the soldiers to seize the bridge.

"Will you give us our whiskey?" piped up one of the Pennsylvanians.

Ferrero, as a punishment, had recently stripped the regiment of its whiskey ration.

"Yes, by god," the general answered, "you shall all have as much as you want, if you take the bridge."

This was met with nods of assent all around. The two regiments moved into position.

"Charge!"

The men, concentrated in that chute like water, streamed downhill in two long lines, 51st Pennsylvania beside 51st New York. Along the way, they had the protection of tree cover. But the moment they reached the bottom and burst out into the open, the soldiers fell under Rebel fire.

As the Federals raced across that 100-yard flat, the barrage only grew in intensity. It got so hot, in fact, that before the Pennsylvanians could reach their destination, the soldiers veered off to take shelter behind a low stone wall. The New Yorkers split off in the other direction and sought the cover of a long rail fence. The Federals were tantalizingly close, yet those final yards may as well have been moon miles.

At this point, the position of the Union soldiers can be visualized using an upside-down T with the stem as the bridge they coveted. On the left, the New Yorkers were pinned down behind that fence, which ran to the bridge's entrance. On the right, the Pennsylvanians were similarly hunkered down, behind a stone wall that extended to the entrance as well. The Georgians showered musket fire onto them. Enemy artillery on the opposite bluffs charged the very atmosphere, filling the air with zipping and zinging canister balls. Yet another Union assault on the Rohrbach Bridge appeared to have stalled.

But just when it looked most hopeless, a mysterious force seemed to intervene. Unexpectedly, the Rebel fire began to slow. At first it was almost imperceptible, but then the falloff became notable. Those bluff-blending Georgians had been engaged for some time now, fending off a variety of Federal attacks. Some had fired as many as sixty shots, leaving their shoulders kicked black and blue. They were running low on ammo. Same went for the artillery. When Confederates faced a shortage of shell, they were known to improvise, firing "military curiosities," as a journalist of the era described them. At Antietam, there are reports of Rebels flinging all manner of objects out of their cannons: marbles, chunks of rail iron, even part of a door lock. This may have been one of those times.

For the Federals, the slackening fire signaled opportunity. The two 51sts entered the bridge. Legend holds that what happened next is this: standard bearers out front, regimental colors proudly flying side by side, the Pennsylvanians and New Yorkers raced in tandem across the bridge. No. The soldiers *inched* across in a state of disorder and high anxiety. The Rebs may have been low on ammo, but their opponents were drawing ever closer, rendering them easier and easier as targets. From the bluffs, the Georgians soon had the advantage of firing nearly straight down. At close range, they employed that vicious stinging combo, buck and ball. Bodies piled up, creating further impediment. The Federals edged along, returning fire as best they could.

A Rebel marksman, shot from his treetop perch, somersaulted through the limbs in slow-motion eternity (*thwack . . . thwack . . . thump*) before a low branch snagged his uniform and he dangled momentarily, before dropping into the creek, quite dead.

The crossing required twelve minutes, according to the 51st Pennsylvania's regimental historian. Only then did the first Union soldiers emerge onto the west bank of the Antietam. They could claim the Rohrbach Bridge at last.

It was roughly 1:00 P.M.

The Rebels—those who could—scrambled up the bluff side to safety. A few hurled rocks as a parting insult. But plenty couldn't get away in time. Some attached pieces of newspaper or dirty rags to the ends of their ramrods, and from their hiding spots they waved these makeshift flags, signaling surrender. These men were taken prisoner. As a last gasp, Lieutenant Colonel William Holmes, 2nd Georgia, charged all by himself, wildly waving his sword. Earlier, he had promised to "hold the bridge or die in the ditch." The Federals obliged, riddling his body with bullets.

The Union soldiers were finally free to stream across the bridge. Here came the two 51sts, among their number George Whitman, a lieutenant with the 51st New York and younger brother of the Brooklyn poet. Here came the 21st and 35th Massachusetts, regiments that had been held back in support. Now came Marylanders and New Hampshire men, survivors of that ill-conceived plank formation, emerging from their hiding places behind boulders and logs, along with Connecticut soldiers who had fought before them—all the pieces of the various abortive Federal attacks. Eventually, Burnside would cross the Rohrbach Bridge. Regardless of how one assesses his performance this day, structures get named after generals not privates, and so it would come to be known as the Burnside Bridge.

Also at roughly 1:00 P.M.—the timing is simply a lucky coincidence—Rodman and his 3,200 men found Snavely's Ford. A small Rebel contingent awaited them on the other side. Those unwieldy naval howitzers actually came in handy for dispatching them. Then, his men began to wade across the Antietam.

Snavely's Ford was well maintained as advertised, but that doesn't mean it was an easy crossing. Unlike civilians, the troops had various critical possessions that simply could not be exposed to water. A soldier who soaked his ill-fitting leather brogans, for example, faced a hell of chafing and blisters. Better to be a barefoot Rebel. Also vulnerable were those paper cartridges filled with gunpowder. As Rodman's men waded through the belly-deep Antietam, drenching their woolen trousers, they held their muskets above their heads. They tied their brogans to the barrels, which were also hung with other essentials, such as cartridge boxes. The men made their slow way across.

Whether by bridge crossing or creek fording, the goal was to get the entire IX Corps to the west side of the Antietam. There, they could get reorganized, refill their ammo, and set out after the Confederates in the heights surrounding Sharpsburg. In a way then, the bridge—hard won, at the cost of so many men—was only a ticket to a second, larger fight.

Battles don't unfold as one might imagine. They don't progress in orderly or predictable ways. Beginning at daybreak, there had been seven hours of continual, unremitting bloodshed. Now, the entire field was about to slip into a curious lull. It would require considerable effort to get the soldiers of IX Corps into position for that larger fight. During that time, nearly every other soldier on the field, both Yank and Reb, took a needed break. The battle smoke had a chance to clear. The sun shone down, the temperature climbed to 75 degrees. It was almost as if the two sides had jointly agreed to a siesta. In truth, this break in the action was organic, spontaneous, borne of exhaustion.

From the Elk Ridge wigwag station, one of the area's highest points of elevation, a panoramic view would have been possible, taking in the field as a whole. Starting at 1:00 P.M., what became notable was the relative quiet and inactivity. Certain parts of the field (the Bloody Lane, the West Woods), sites of the morning's ferocious clashes, had gone still. The soldiers were all fought out and many were done for the day. Union and Confederate had retreated back behind their respective lines, locked in wary and weary standoff. Farmer Miller's cornfield, so recently consumed in ear-thumping war din, fell into a state of hushed devastation, the stalks all trampled or clipped by bullets, nary a one standing. One could hear a fly buzz—or an injured man groan. Still, the artillerists kept to their own mysterious clocks. Every so often, a stray shell would arc above the field, passing over the strewn dead.

During the lull, soldiers seized the opportunity to eat a meal. Bayonets—disturbing to use on a man, even one's sworn enemy—proved ideal for skewering farmers' chickens. Soldiers read books, the Bible; they wrote letters home. They swapped stories, told jokes. Out came the little portable chess sets. Some men had sewed checkered patterns onto their bedrolls, creating ready-made chessboards. The soldiers engaged in chuck-a-luck, a gambling game that employs three dice, or brag, a card game similar to poker. Those who could, napped. "The whirring of the shells above us had a drowsing effect, and some of our men dozed," recalled the regimental historian of the 35th Massachusetts.

Soldiers both Yank and Reb broke out their tobacco. They smoked cigars and pipes, popped fat plugs in their mouths to chew or took pinches of "snouse," which consisted of finely minced leaves cut with herbs. The 51st Pennsylvania, basking in their new-found status as bridge-storming legends, made coffee. They would get their whiskey, all right, though they'd have to wait until later. Sensing the quiet, a pig and her litter burst from the woods and went darting among the men of the 9th New Hampshire. The big sow ran between the legs of one soldier, lifting the shocked man off the ground and carrying him backward a ways. His comrades roared with laughter.

In other places, there was nothing but pain and grief. Wounded soldiers lay on the ground near dressing stations that were too overwhelmed by the morning's mayhem to provide aid to everyone who needed it. Hundreds of prisoners waited, consumed with uncertainty. By dint of their position upon the field, held behind enemy lines, prisoners received constant clues about the progress of the battle, yet filtered through the perspective of their captors. Cheering meant something bad had just happened to *your* side.

An episode involving a Texas prisoner is especially poignant. When a Union officer walked past carrying the flag of the 1st Texas regiment, captured during the cornfield fighting, the man recognized exactly what this signaled. He knew that his fellow Texans would not have surrendered their standard easily, meaning many must have died defending it. The prisoner implored the officer to let him hold the flag, if only for a moment. As his fingers touched the tattered Texas standard, made by Mrs. Wigfall and featuring a star cut from her wedding dress, the tears streamed down his face.

The two rival commanders were busy during the lull. For the first time this day, McClellan visited the actual battlefield, making a suitably dramatic entrance. He arrived in the saddle of a large bay horse, Daniel Webster. (Yes, the animal was named after his illustrious family friend.) Near the Bloody Lane, McClellan conferred with two of his corps commanders, William Franklin and Edwin Sumner. General Franklin counseled boldness, suggesting a fresh punch to the Confederate center. With the enemy in a torpor, now was the time. Franklin could afford courage; he hadn't yet been in the fight. Bull Sumner had—he'd experienced a drubbing in the West Woods. So, he urged the opposite, arguing that throwing additional Union troops into the conflict might prove disastrous. So far the Rebels had met every attack with stiff resistance, at the price of many Federal casualties. The Union still had no reliable count of how many men it faced. What if a new attack took still more Federals out of the fight? What if Lee seized the opportunity for a counterattack?

McClellan sided with caution.

He also sent a couple of telegrams, at last. The first was addressed to Henry Halleck, general-in-chief of the Union army, back in Washington. He knew it would be routed to Lincoln. McClellan composed with care, writing but then striking through a line hinting that "great defeat" was possible. No doubt, he worried that this would raise the specter of failure. But then another line he tried seemed perhaps too presumptuous of success; he crossed it out, too. After picking over his words, he settled on a brief message, fittingly dramatic, suitably vague, and including the following: "We are in the midst of the most terrible battle of the war, perhaps of history—thus far it looks well but I have great odds against me."

The other telegram was for Nelly. He repeated the most-terrible-battle sentiment, but also added some personal words of reassurance: "I am well. None of your immediate friends killed that I hear of. Your father with me quite safe." (Remember, Randolph Marcy was McClellan's chief of staff.)

While Little Mac sputtered, Lee schemed. The Rebel commander was busily planning a counterattack, exactly as the Federals feared. What he had in mind was trademark bold: his men would slip around the Union soldiers massed at the top of the field. That would make it possible to attack from a shocking and unexpected direction. The Rebels could strike from the rear.

An order went out for available cannon to be consolidated for the effort. Among the Confederate batteries that answered the call was one that had earlier been posted near the Dunker Church, now reduced to horses and ammo enough to operate a single gun.

Lee was down off Traveller, standing, when this particularly decrepit battery dragged past.

"General, are you going to send us in again," asked a young man, his face streaked black with powder.

At first, Lee stared through the youngster. But then the briefest flash of recognition crossed his face. Why, it was his own child! It was Robert Lee Jr., the one who had grown up with a bedroom outfitted to duplicate a West Point cadet's quarters.

"Yes, my son," said Lee, "you all must do what you can to help drive these people back."

Stonewall Jackson was rounding up soldiers for the counterattack. But it was also vital to get an idea of the strength of the Federals on this part of the field. So, he ordered a North Carolina private to shimmy up a tall hickory to do some reconnaissance. Jackson asked the soldier for an estimate of how many bluecoats they faced.

"Who-e-e! There are oceans of them, General," replied the private.

"Count their flags," demanded Jackson.

The private began to count out loud. When he reached thirty-nine, Jackson asked him to climb back down the hickory. Assuming two flags to a regiment, roughly a thousand soldiers per, the general made a quick calculation and—they faced an ocean of Federals.

Lee put his sneak attack on hold for now.

---

The lull also provided a boon for journalists. For many hours, the battle had limited their investigations. With the fighting temporarily cooled, they sallied forth, moving freely over the field. Charles Coffin of the *Boston Journal* took the opportunity to visit the Bloody Lane, where he surveyed the scene with his unflinching reporter's eye. "[W]hat a ghastly spectacle," he would write. "The

Confederates had gone down as the grass falls before the scythe. They were lying in rows, like the ties of a railroad; in heaps, like cordwood, mingled with the splintered and scattered fence rails."

The *New-York Tribune*, seeking an edge in the tough newspaper racket, had dispatched a team of four reporters. They spread out, covering different parts of the field. George Smalley, the team's ace and a highly enterprising man, ranged broadly. Somehow he had managed to commandeer a horse as well as a Federal uniform, complete with sash and sword.

"Who are you?" he was repeatedly asked.

"Special correspondent of the *New-York Tribune*, sir."

The Northern press corps was present in force. Newspapers were big business, and cities such as Buffalo, Chicago, and Philadelphia had a number of dailies each. To meet a ceaseless public appetite for war news, many papers had taken to printing multiple editions. The *New York Herald*, for example, had recently introduced afternoon editions at 1:30, 3:00, and 4:30. Besides correspondent Coffin and the four-scribe *Trib* team, easily twenty-five reporters had travelled with McClellan's army through Maryland, the 1862 equivalent of being embedded. Of course, given the communication challenge of transmitting a dispatch from a battlefield back to a paper's offices, the *latest news* often took many days to reach the public.

The Confederate press was also represented, although it had already started to feel the squeeze of wartime privation. The South had begun the war with eight hundred papers. As in the North, such cities as Atlanta, Richmond, and Montgomery supported numerous competing dailies. New Orleans alone boasted six: the *Bee*, *Commercial Bulletin*, *Daily Crescent*, *Daily Picayune*, *Daily Delta*, and *True Delta*. But shortages were setting in for printing essentials, such as oil and glue. There was a growing manpower shortage, too, as editors, printers, and compositors abandoned journalism to enlist in the Confederate army. Already, in the course of the war's first year, fifty of Texas's sixty papers had gone out of business. The years ahead would find a beleaguered Southern press using shoe blacking for ink and for paper, absolutely anything: the backs of letters, pages torn from books, and unpaid bills. At this point in the war, however, the South could still claim a viable press. In fact, two of its finest correspondents were present, Peter Alexander on assignment for the *Savannah Republican*; and for the *Charleston Daily Courier*, Felix Gregory de Fontaine.

Also out in force were the "special artists." This breed of journalist sketched the action in real time, providing a unique window into warfare for the public. A young Winslow Homer had briefly worked in this capacity, documenting McClellan's army during the Peninsula Campaign. Among the established stars in the special-artist firmament were Alfred Waud of *Harper's Weekly* and Frank Schell of *Frank Leslie's Illustrated Newspaper*. Both were present, pads and pencils out, furiously sketching.

During the break in the action, Schell visited Miller's cornfield and surveyed the horrors. Walking among the broken stalks, he was alarmed to see a kneeling Confederate pointing a musket at him.

"I jumped aside," Schell would recall, "but his aim did not follow."

Turns out, the Rebel was dead, frozen in "mute fidelity," as the artist put it, to the final pose he'd struck upon this earth.

Following a battle, special artists, such as Schell, rushed their sketches by courier back to the offices of their publications where they would be converted into engravings. An entire team was involved in this process. So-called pruners added clouds and foliage. Butchers would add detail and accuracy to faces, often working off existing photographs in the case of well-known figures, such as generals. Tailors added realistic folds to flags and uniforms. As a final step, editors tweaked the engravings, maybe removing some gore in favor of a sundry touch or two designed to make the action seem all the more glorious.

Circa 1862, the techniques required to print a photograph in a newspaper had not yet been discovered. What's more, photography required long exposure times, rendering any action shot maddeningly blurry. That's why the special artists provided an invaluable service. Such publications as the *New-York Illustrated News* served as an eager public's only means of viewing live-action scenes of battle. Wartime sent their circulations skyrocketing. (Waud of *Harper's Weekly* would manage a scoop for the ages, by the way, providing the only eyewitness sketch of Pickett's infamous charge.)

Nevertheless, there was a photographer in the midst. Alexander Gardner, a business associate of the great Mathew Brady, was here on assignment, though he dared not venture too close to the battlefield, even during this period of relative calm. Most likely, Gardner had parked his What's-it Wagon near Keedysville, about three miles distant. This curious-looking wagon was a mobile darkroom, stocked with volatile chemicals and fragile glass photographic plates. The year before, Brady himself had tried to document the battle at Bull Run, but without success. While traveling in a darkroom wagon, he had gotten caught up in the panic and chaos, and as a consequence, had failed to capture any battlefield images. Lesson learned. Gardner planned a spectacular project, something the world had never before witnessed. He knew he would have to wait.

---

The residents of Sharpsburg and the surrounding countryside also couldn't afford to be as bold as the journalists. The fighting may have temporarily quieted, but they were not inclined to peek, prairie dog–like, from their hiding spots. Of course, most of the area's civilians had left before the battle even started, seeking shelter with friends and family in neighboring towns. Those who remained had spent the morning in terror. No one knew how long this impromptu ceasefire might last; it was not to be trusted. For farmers, shopkeepers, and children trying to ride out the fight, the quiet must have seemed ominous.

By now, the Killiansburg Cave had filled to capacity, absurd since this wasn't exactly a Howe Caverns–style natural wonder.

It was more like a crevice. The view must have provided a constant reminder of everything at stake. The cave is on the Maryland side of the Potomac, Union territory. Across the river lay Virginia, Confederate territory. Roughly seventy-five frightened people, including several fugitive slaves, were currently squeezed together here.

A similar situation held at the Kretzers. The Kretzers, a German American family, lived in an ample stone house on Main Street in Sharpsburg. When the fighting started, a number of neighbors had crowded into the cellar, including old people and mothers with babies. Some had brought their beloved family dogs. The refugees huddled in the empty potato bunks and apple scaffolds, which, while offering places to sit, were also uncomfortably hard surfaces—designed for produce not people. Nobody had eaten breakfast; neither would they eat lunch or dinner. Whenever shells burst nearby, the walls shook, babies cried, dogs howled, and the old folk prayed.

At some point during the morning, six Rebel soldiers had slipped into the cellar. As Union loyalists, the Kretzers were terrified. The Rebs proved equally as frightened, though. They were merely trying to get out of the fight. The Confederates staked out their own corner of the basement, away from the others. And there they remained, "like sardines in a box," as Theresa, one of the Kretzer daughters, would recall.

Fear radiated from Sharpsburg, snaking out into the hinterlands.

If only Thaddeus Sobieski Constantine Lowe had been present, then it would have been possible to get higher than the Elk Ridge wigwag station, and to really see out across the countryside. Lowe, a renowned aerialist, had designed a hydrogen-filled observation balloon that, while tethered to the ground by rope, could rise to great heights. McClellan was a major booster of

Lowe. The commander found reconnaissance balloons extremely valuable, and had employed them throughout the Peninsula Campaign. They were an excellent means of identifying enemy positions, not to mention a source of unending curiosity. After witnessing a flight, Custer, McClellan's young aide, even had an erotic dream featuring two comely women suspended in a balloon's basket. Thanks to dream logic, he was able to float upward without the aid of a balloon, closing on the objects of his desire, but when he drew level with the basket, it was empty—the women had vanished.

Lowe was supposed to have brought his celebrated balloons to this battle, too, but there had been a miscommunication. On such a clear day, it would have been possible to see almost to Washington, DC.

There, Lincoln moved through a routine day, even as an epic battle was in progress. What else could he do save to wait—and maybe pay another visit to the telegraph office? But there was no further news. Apparently, the president found time for such mundane tasks as paying $12.62 to close out a horse-harness account.

Elsewhere, too, people were simply going about their lives, utterly unaware of the battle. In New London, Connecticut, the big event involved a young girl falling into the river. She was rescued immediately. The steamer *Ida May* departed Louisville. There was a horse show in Rockville, Connecticut; a horticultural exhibition in Boston; citizens enjoyed a music convention in Brandon, Vermont. Several "fancy drunks" went before the mayor of Indianapolis, and were summarily fined. In Charleston, South Carolina, 200 pounds of bologna sausage was sold at public auction. In Wilmington, North Carolina, the weather was unusually warm (as in Maryland) and residents were harassed by late-season mosquitoes. Ephraim Huivey of Augusta County, Virginia, was surprised when a stray red and white heifer showed up on his land. Dr. Belford visited Ebensberg, Pennsylvania, providing "an excellent opportunity to persons wishing to get Dentistry done."

In Biloxi, Canandaigua, Perth Amboy, and Frankenmuth, just a normal day—the same in Muncie, Shreveport, Wilkes-Barre, Suwanee, and Arkadelphia.

Of course, the families of soldiers were in a state of anxiety. By means of letters and newspaper accounts, they had done their best to follow the progress of loved ones through Maryland. But updates were infrequent. Worry had become a constant; there could be no expectation of relief in any given hour on any given day. Fretting mothers labored in shops, periodically looking up from their tasks to think of absent sons. Uneasy wives went about chores on farms left behind by husbands off to war. Young Sarah Morgan Dawson devoted the hours of the battle to worrying about the well-being of her pet canary. She remained blissfully unaware that her brother Gibbes of the 7th Louisiana had been badly wounded during the morning action. Franklin Alford, a man who had already lost two sons to the war, had not an inkling that a third, Warren, a private with the 14th Indiana, lay dying.

"Dearest Mother,—I am wounded so as to be helpless. Good by, if so it must be," wrote Wilder Dwight, a lieutenant colonel with the 2nd Massachusetts. He penned the letter right where he'd fallen, near the Dunker Church, struck in the left hip by a musket ball. "Dearest love to father and all my dear brothers," he added.

Indeed, this would be Dwight's last letter. It would arrive in Brookline, Massachusetts, stained with his blood.

So much sadness and madness and sorrow. Into this mournful brew, add 4 million men, women, and children forced to live as slaves.

As the afternoon shadows lengthened, stretching like fingers over earth below, the phantom balloon of Thaddeus Sobieski Constantine Lowe broke free of its moorings and gained altitude quickly, soaring high, high above this broken land.

# CHAPTER 11

## A LURID SUNSET

*A mammoth Union battle line* had been formed, stretching for a full mile to the west of the Antietam. It was 3:00 P.M. Two entire hours had been devoted to crossing the creek, causing that remarkable stretch of placidity to settle over the field, right in the midst of what McClellan termed, "the most terrible battle of the war, perhaps of history."

The crossing had been a demanding feat. It was necessary to convey to the other side of the Antietam twenty-nine regiments, consisting of the roughly 11,000 Federal IX Corps soldiers still capable of fighting. (The corps was down 1,500 from its strength when the standoff began.) Thousands of soldiers marched over that narrow bridge with space enough to accommodate maybe five men abreast. Thousands more forded the creek, arduous in its own right.

On the other side, the logistical challenges only multiplied. The men had to be arranged in that wide formation. The place selected was the brow of the bluffs on the west side of the Antietam, meaning the battle line extended along the higher ground above where the dug-in Georgians had made their stand. Entire regiments had to be shuffled around to get the Federals into position. The two 51sts, for example, were all fought out, exhausted and low on ammo after their heroic effort to take the bridge. They were moved behind the battle line, to act as reserves. Cannons and caissons had also made the crossing, along with wagons filled with sundry supplies. All these had to be positioned near the troops that needed them. So many details, so many particularities, yet working through them represented nothing beyond a point of departure.

An almost unfathomable challenge lay ahead. Lee had chosen his ground brilliantly, and this part of the field was his masterstroke. Here the severe topography approximated a fortress, the natural equivalent of one of those storybook Mexican castles to which he and McClellan together had laid siege, fifteen years earlier, during their first brief meeting. Think about it. What was the Rohrbach Bridge if not a drawbridge—and the Antietam, an improvised moat. And those Georgians: they may as well have been pouring hot oil down onto the heads of their attackers. Now that the Union had crossed the creek, the full dimensions of Lee's redoubt were revealed, and it must have been sobering. The soldiers would need to climb three quarters of a mile up a hillside, negotiating rugged terrain, before reaching the broad plateau where Sharpsburg sat, its church spires doubling as towers in this castle fantasia.

Above the broad Union line waited roughly 3,000 Confederates, among them General Toombs's resolute Georgians, having retreated to this spot. Looming, too, were forty malevolent cannons. Still, if the Federals could somehow take those heights, they might be able to cut off Rebel access to Boteler's Ford, that vital route back across the Potomac to Virginia, and safety. Such a turn of events might even embolden McClellan, convince him to commit some of the thousands of Union soldiers waiting in reserve elsewhere on the field. Lee's army had hung on so far. It could still be decimated by dinnertime.

The Union planned to throw its massive mile-wide line into the fight by echelon. That means it would be a staggered attack with the various units joining the action one after another. It's a tactic familiar to anyone who has ever played chess, where a piece might be moved into a considerably forward position. The idea here was to draw the enemy down the hill and engage it. If a particular Rebel regiment ran into trouble, the situation could be exploited, with neighboring Federal forces arrayed along the slope piling on from unexpected and devastating angles.

The echelon attack would proceed right to left. Upon order to attack, this mighty Union war beast began to stir.

Spearheading the offensive was the 79th New York, also known as the Highlanders. This regiment traced its origins to before the war, though the earlier incarnation was more like a social club for men, mostly of Scottish descent, who enjoyed conducting military drills in their off-hours. It was modeled on the British 79th Queen's Own Cameron Highlanders. The members had dressed the part: kilts, glengarry hats, and sporrans, a kind of horsehair-covered pouch (there's really no better description for this last item). When the war broke out, the regiment traded the Scottish finery for standard-issue uniforms, but with one notable variation: the men wore trews (tartan-patterned trousers) at Bull Run and other early battles. Eighteen months of hard fighting had shredded their trews, however. To a man, they were now dressed in Federal blue.

But the Highlanders remained plenty distinctive. What set them apart was their ferocity. As a unit, they were quick to anger, so much so that, about a year earlier, a denied furlough had led to out-and-out mutiny. In response, McClellan had ordered that any Highlander who failed to come to order be summarily shot. For good measure, he took away their regimental colors, saying they'd have to earn them back. That proved easy: the Highlanders could always be counted on to show valor in battle. "Thank God Lincoln had only one 79th regiment," was the verdict of one Southern paper.

No sooner had the Highlanders started out than they fell under a hellish cannonade. It was their misfortune to have become the focus of those Rebel guns. The regiment advanced only a little ways before the men were forced to lie down, seeking what shelter they could find. Overhead, coming from their rear, shells streaked, fired by Union long-range Parrott guns on the other side of the Antietam that were trying to take out the enemy cannons. The Highlanders hunkered down and waited. They would need some kind of diversion, drawing the attention away from them.

The Highlanders faced an especially grueling route. As if the terrain wasn't treacherous enough, they had the additional challenge of having to navigate the grounds of a farm. Joseph Sherrick, the owner, lived in a five-level house, Greek Revival style, nestled into the sheer hillside. Sherrick was another area farmer grown prosperous from that miracle Maryland soil.

Presently, two Union batteries (12 guns in total) were dragged a short distance uphill by horses, under heavy fire all the way. The artillery pieces were positioned on a so-called cannon park, a generous term for a patch of level ground. The Federal guns commenced firing away; and the Rebel guns answered—at last, the diversion that the Highlanders needed.

The 79th resumed its advance, sending forward skirmishers. Typically, skirmishers worked in pairs, moving in a kind of herky-jerky pattern. One soldier would press forward, while the other hung back. Then, the lagging soldier would scramble to the lead position, while his partner stood musket at the ready, covering him. It was a nervous, twitchy form of locomotion. For a regiment, skirmishers served almost like the antennae of an insect: testing, probing, trying to learn what lay ahead.

Barn, smokehouse, corncrib, apple orchard—Sherrick's farm was like a maze. Rebels could be lurking anywhere. Before vacating the area, recall, Farmer Sherrick had deposited his savings into a secret place in a stone wall. Who knows? There might even be Rebs crouching inches from where that $3,000 in gold was hidden.

Soon enough, the skirmishers made contact with the enemy. An assortment of South Carolinians had taken up positions on

Sherrick's land, concealed behind just about everything that it was possible to be concealed behind. The farm erupted into a kind of free-range fighting, a departure from the tight formations of so many of the battle's earlier actions. South Carolinians popped out from behind the barn, muskets flashing; Highlanders sought the cover of the smokehouse and returned fire. Bullets zinged through apple trees, ricocheted off the stone walls.

Meanwhile, the 9th New York was encountering its own set of difficulties. This regiment had been positioned to the left of the Highlanders in that mile-long battle line. Its progress had also been halted by the ferocious artillery battle.

The 9th was a quirky collection of soldiers that included singers, writers, dancers, producers, set painters, and others drawn from various creative fields in New York City. The regiment's very first injury of the war occurred when a man juggling a cup, plate, knife, fork, and spoon cut himself with the knife.

As befit their theatrical style, the soldiers of the 9th fashioned themselves as Zouaves. For inspiration they had looked to Elmer Ellsworth, the enterprising and ill-fated young colonel who had excited a Zouave craze on the eve of the Civil War. Without question, the 9th was the splashiest regiment on the field. Its 373 members wore loose-fitting trousers, a blue jacket with magenta trim, and on their head, a red fez with a tassel. This last touch had inspired their nickname: the Red Caps. The men had paid $21.50 each for these trappings, eschewing the standard Federal uniforms. Unfortunately, the Red Caps were among the regiments that had crossed at Snavely's Ford. As a consequence, their trousers didn't billow with trademark dash; were instead sopping wet and clingy as the men stood in the midday heat.

The Red Caps waited behind a ridge, providing suitable protection as a seemingly endless duel played out between Union cannons, positioned on the hillside above of them, and Rebel guns

The battle began with a clash in a cornfield. Midday, the Federals crossed Antietam Creek via the Burnside Bridge. Twelve hours' fighting left 3,650 men dead, the highest one-day toll in American history.

On the morning of the battle, Lincoln awoke at his cottage just outside the Washington City limit, a refuge for the president and wife, Mary, following the death of their son Willie (the case preserves a lock of his hair).

During his commute to the White House, Lincoln passed daily reminders of the wounded (Carver Hospital), the war dead (National Cemetery), and the continuing blight of enslavement (Camp Barker, a settlement for escaped slaves).

Union commander George McClellan with wife, Nelly. During the battle, his field headquarters was the Pry family's farmhouse (photograph by Alexander Gardner).

Confederate commander Robert E. Lee. Early in the war, his beloved home, Arlington, had been seized by the Union.

The battle overwhelmed the little town of Sharpsburg, Maryland, and the surrounding countryside. The Dunker Church was a scene of carnage. (Photos by Gardner.)

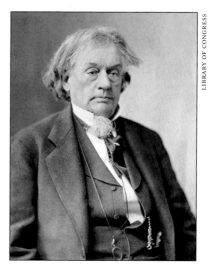

Generals (clockwise) Ambrose Burnside and Thomas Meagher of the Union and Confederates Robert Toombs and A. P. Hill.

Artists, such as Alfred Waud and Captain James Hope of the 2nd Vermont, captured the action. Hope's *A Fateful Turn* depicts fighting at the notorious Bloody Lane.

Waud's live-action sketch of the burning Mumma farm was turned into an illustration that appeared in *Harper's Weekly*.

Antietam resulted in 17,000 wounded, sparking a medical emergency answered by Clara Barton and Jonathan Letterman, the Union doctor in chief. Anson Hurd, the 14th Indiana's regimental surgeon, visits a field hospital set up on a farmstead.

553.    The "Sunken Road" at Antietam.
[FOR DESCRIPTION OF THIS VIEW SEE THE OTHER SIDE OF THIS CARD.]

Alexander Gardner (seen above in a self-portrait) documented the battle's bloody aftermath. Many of the images, such as his famous *Sunken Road*, were brisk-selling stereographs that brought the horrors of warfare into ordinary households.

Other Gardner Antietam images: a lone grave, a dead horse, and the bodies of Rebel soldiers along the Hagerstown Pike.

Shortly after Antietam, Lincoln visited the battlefield. General McClellan is facing the president; George Armstrong Custer is farthest to the right (photo by Gardner). Union victory provided the occasion for issuing the Emancipation Proclamation, a document that Lincoln had earlier shared with his cabinet per this painting by Francis Carpenter.

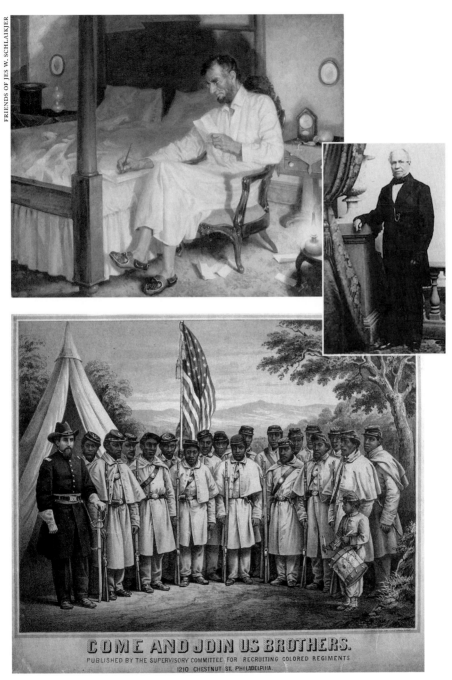

**COME AND JOIN US BROTHERS.**
PUBLISHED BY THE SUPERVISORY COMMITTEE FOR RECRUITING COLORED REGIMENTS
1210 CHESTNUT ST. PHILADELPHIA.

Evenings at his cottage, Lincoln worked on the proclamation, subject of this Jes Schlaikjer painting. The president was deeply influenced by African Americans, such as William Slade, a White House usher. The proclamation opened the Union army to black soldiers per this recruiting poster.

The Emancipation Proclamation: 719 words that changed the world.

stationed on the heights. Frequently, the enemy overshot, and the shells would hurtle overhead. "I noticed one of them coming like an india-rubber ball through the air," Private Charles Johnson would recall, describing a solid shot. "It struck the top of the hill, boring up a mass of earth, and then bounded high in the air, passing over our heads with a noise I can liken to nothing but the savage yell of some inhuman monster."

At last, the Red Caps began their advance. The portion of ground they needed to cover had its own topographical peculiarities, a striking series of dips and rises. As the Zouaves advanced, they slipped in and out of view, fire raining down on them whenever they were in the open. A bullet clipped a Red Cap near his ear and the man dropped his musket and launched into an oath-filled conniption. Another wasn't so lucky as a single canister ball grooved across the top of his head, like a fatal hair parting. "[W]e lost men at almost every step," is how Lieutenant Matthew Graham described the advance.

For the besieged Red Caps, the goal was always the next hollow. They would dash down into it, and make for the far side, which offered protection against artillery fire. At each stop, the battle line grew shorter for loss of men. Each stop also provided an opportunity to reorganize the line. But they had to remain low. The men of the 9th New York filled the gaps by crawling towards one another on their hands and knees. Then they'd climb up out of safety and face the Rebel wrath anew. For someone standing at the bottom of the incline, the Zouave battle line would have appeared then disappeared several times, going up over ridges and down into hollows, growing progressively shorter. This would *not* have been an optical illusion.

By now, Union forces were splashed across the hillside on both sides of the Red Caps. Any sense of the original plan, the echelon attack, was rapidly disintegrating. The term *echelon* is derived from *échelle*, the French word for "ladder." Whatever was happening on this slope had assumed a rather more organic shape. Then again, a tactic out of a military textbook proved no match for this daunting and idiosyncratic stretch of ground.

To the right of the Red Caps, the Highlanders were sputtering. They had gotten the best of the firefight on Sherrick's farm, clearing the outbuildings and driving the South Carolinians back up the hillside. But the Rebels withdrew only as far as a gristmill owned by Solomon Lumm. During ordinary times, when farm wagons set out on the sunken road transporting grain to be milled, this was one of the destinations. In wartime, the stout stone building may as well have been the Alamo. The Highlanders were brave, but storming Lumm's mill would be lunacy. They could progress no farther.

To the Red Caps' left, meanwhile, a set of three New England regiments (the 8th and 16th Connecticut and 4th Rhode Island) were supposed to be advancing as a single unified line. Because of variations in terrain, however, the line soon began to break apart.

The separation of the regiments was worrying. The 8th Connecticut, rapidly pulling ahead, was well drilled and well equipped, composed of soldiers drawn from such towns as Danbury, Norwich, and Stonington. It was a cohesive unit; the men attended church together and had even raised $40 for their own regimental library. By contrast, one of the two lagging regiments, the 16th Connecticut, was unusually inexperienced, even by the standards of McClellan's army. In fact, the 16th had been mustered into service only three weeks earlier. During that brief span, the regiment's strength had dropped from 1,000 to fewer than 800 men despite not seeing any battle action. The attrition was due to illness and desertion. The regiment had never drilled, barely knew how to form a battle line.

This had potentially grave implications. An inexperienced regiment occupied the far left of the hillside, without the support of the seasoned 8th Connecticut. Even more alarming: all the sites of earlier fighting, such as Miller's Cornfield, the Bloody Lane, and

Rohrbach Bridge—and all the Union soldiers still congregated near those spots—were situated at some distance up the field. The 16th Connecticut now occupied the extreme edge of the Union's forces. In other words, a greenhorn regiment represented the flank of McClellan's entire army.

The Red Caps were making progress at least. The farther up the hill they pressed, though, the more they fell into the range of enemy muskets, and they began to draw heavy fire from a pair of Confederate brigades, 600 men, including Virginians, Georgians, and South Carolinians.

Even as these Rebels unleashed a musket storm, the cannonade didn't abate. All that changed was the type of ammo being used. Increasingly, the Rebels relied on canister, showering the Zouaves with iron balls. For the Confederate artillerymen, however, it proved difficult to find the proper firing angle, with the 9th New York pushing ever closer, yet on a downhill trajectory. Some gunners introduced a devious twist. They packed double loads of canister, then tilted their gun barrels toward the ground. Firing at such a severe angle caused the fifty-four iron balls to stay low, fanning out across the ground, then skittering down toward the Zouaves like a herd of evil marbles.

The Red Caps dove into the safety of a broad furrow. They redressed their line yet again. Climbing the hillside had come at a dreadful cost. But they were drawing close to the top.

The two Rebel brigades fell back behind the safety of a long stone wall.

Everyone waited.

On the command to charge, the Zouaves surged up and out of the furrow, howling their distinctive war cry: "Zoo! Zoo! Zoo!" Sharpsburg was in sight now; its streets could be reached in a single concerted dash. A Rebel solid shot, fired from mere yards away, slammed into the line; the iron ball stared blackly into a soldier's widening eyes for the briefest instant before it tore his head from his body. This proved so unnerving that the men nearly wavered. But they kept going.

As they charged, a few of the men chanced to look back over their shoulders. All down the hill they could see their fallen comrades, strewn like red-clad rag dolls. One gravely wounded Zouave, in particular, left a haunting impression, recounted in the regimental history: "The lower portion of his jaw had been carried away, and the torn fragments that remained, together with his tongue, clotted with gore, hung down upon his breast."

This injured soldier had raised himself up on an elbow. With his other arm, he waved his red fez, urging on his fellow Zouaves. He gave off a jaunty air, like a man casually reclining at a picnic, but one need only linger on this sight for an instant and—my God!

Under withering fire, the Federal charge began to slow. The Confederates, hunkered behind that stone wall, had staked out another intimidating position. Rebs continually popped up, squeezed off a volley, and dropped to safety only to be replaced by fresh ones, like some infernal carnival game. In quick succession, they managed to pick off the 9th New York's color guard. Others stepped forward to secure the regimental flag, only to be cut down. Eight Zouaves were shot trying to defend their colors.

But the Red Cap line held firm and continued to inch forward. The distance between the enemies kept shrinking; only a low stone wall separated the sides.

When the Zouaves drew to within wave-to-your-neighbor range, they broke into a run and vaulted the wall. A melee ensued: angry, ugly, and chaotic. The regimental history describes it as a "scene of the wildest confusion," even raises the specter of bayonet use, coupled with the suggestion that only cowardly Rebs would resort to such a tactic. The men traded punches and curses. Face to sweaty, powder-streaked face, the Red Caps must have sensed the desperation of their opponents. The Graybacks, for their part, would have heeded the blind rage of the Zouaves, who had lost so many during that hillside slog. With no opportunity to reload, a musket becomes a club; soldiers must have swung them wildly, crashing the heavy stocks down on skulls. Perhaps soldiers—both sides—even resorted to those gruesome bayonets.

In this battlefield bar brawl, the Red Caps emerged victors. The Rebels began streaming back toward Sharpsburg. "Oh, how I ran!" Private John Dooley of the 1st Virginia wrote in his journal. The latest 9th New York standard bearer planted the tattered regimental flag in the ground. Union colors now waved atop that plateau. Soon, other Federal regiments, such as the 45th Pennsylvania, crested the hilltop. The Union had reached the outskirts of Sharpsburg.

In growing disorder, the Rebels retreated into the town. Soldiers became separated from their regiments. Some did so willingly, as this seemed an opportune moment to desert. Stretcher bearers were the gawkiest runners, forced to move in tandem, weighted down by their wounded charges, but run they did as fast as they could. Horses strained, pulling cannons behind. Long-range Federal artillery had succeeded in damaging many of the Rebel guns; cannons on boggety wheels clattered down the streets of Sharpsburg.

Young Theresa Kretzer took the opportunity to climb from her basement to the attic. From the window, she could see soldiers in Federal blue beginning to congregate at the edge of town. "I thought it was the prettiest sight I ever saw in my life," she would recall.

At the same time, Savilla Miller, a young woman who lived only a few houses away, stood in the street, seemingly oblivious to her own safety. She, too, was German American, but her family supported the Confederacy. Savilla, carrying a pitcher, bravely dispensed water to the retreating Rebels.

Lee was on the scene as Sharpsburg slid into chaos. The commander was inside his castle. He did his part to stem the crisis, heading off stragglers, steering men back to their regiments.

Suddenly, Lee spotted heavy columns of soldiers in the distance marching in his direction. He asked a lieutenant: "What troops are those?"

The lieutenant removed a telescope from a case, and offered it. "Can't use it," said Lee, raising his bandaged hands.

So, the lieutenant peered through the scope. "They are flying the United States flag."

No, not those soldiers, indicated Lee. The movement that had drawn his notice was farther to the south; could the lieutenant maybe shift his gaze to that spot?

"What troops are those?" repeated Lee.

Sure enough, these soldiers were flying Confederate flags.

Lee was elated. A. P. Hill's men had arrived. Recall that Hill— McClellan's red-shirted, venereal rival—had set off from Harpers Ferry at dawn. He'd driven his men relentlessly, goading them on with sword slaps, making only a few brief rest stops while covering seventeen miles in the rising heat. They had recently forded the Potomac and their trousers were soaking wet. But what exquisite timing: Just when Lee's army had been pushed to the brink of annihilation, roughly 2,500 fresh soldiers were poised to enter the fight.

At the very same time, Union signalmen on Elk Ridge also spotted the arrivals. A wigwag message went out: "Look well to your left. The enemy are moving a strong force in that direction."

The dispatch made a slow, clumsy circuit through the Union chain of command. It arrived too late.

Already, the newly arrived Rebels were streaming off the Sharpsburg plateau and down the hillside, aiming for that soft Union flank. The 16th Connecticut and 4th Rhode Island were still making glacial progress. They now lagged nearly half a mile behind the 8th Connecticut. Worse still, the two regiments had gotten hung up in a hillside cornfield. As on Farmer Miller's plot, the corn here was yet to be harvested. Unlike the site of the day's first fighting, however, this cornfield was on about a 30-degree gradient. (When the soil is this rich, it seems, steepness was no obstacle.)

As the Confederates bore down, they could see their bluecoat marks milling about in the cornfield below. Because of the tall stalks, the Federals, in turn, appear to have been oblivious to the imminent danger.

This promised to be such an unequal fight, pitting the New Englanders against some extremely seasoned South Carolinians, led by the terrifying, scimitar-wielding Maxcy Gregg. The Rebels dove into the corn. General Gregg didn't even bother to organize them, shouting, "Commence firing, men, and form the line as you fight."

First to be hit was that green Connecticut regiment, its men falling into utter disorder. Some fled, some set off in the wrong direction, others fired into the backs of comrades. "In a moment we were riddled with shot," Corporal B. F. Blakeslee would write in his diary. "Many necessary orders were given which were not understood."

The Rhode Islanders were still in the lower portion of this ample, 40-acre cornfield. The men could hear a commotion ahead of them, but they couldn't discern the cause. Some officers believed they spotted a Union flag, yet what sounded like an exchange of musket fire was also audible. Puzzling. The officers set out to investigate, only to wander into a fatal firetrap.

This particular episode would become notorious, the source of endless speculation stretching years into the future. The Rebs, some would claim, employed trickery to dispatch the two Union regiments. Remember: A. P. Hill's men had just arrived from Harpers Ferry, where they had helped process captured loot, including Federal shoes and uniforms. Among the Union survivors, there would be whisperings of Rebels dressed crisply in blue, and—more ignominiously—flying the Union flag so as to draw close, before swapping it out in favor of their own Confederate colors.

Amid the tall corn and confusion, all that can be said with certainty is that the flags of select South Carolina regiments, featuring white palmettos against fields of blue, could be mistaken for the Union stars and stripes.

Now the flag—whether Old Glory, or a Rebel standard—started downhill. Like a shark fin cutting through the sea of corn, it made directly for the Rhode Islanders.

Here came General Rodman, riding to their aid. Among the regiments in his command was this ill-starred New England trio that had fallen dangerously out of phase. From high on the hillside, he'd seen the fresh Rebel soldiers arrive. Hoping to avert disaster, Rodman set off as fast as his horse could carry him. He intended to goad the two regiments out of the cornfield, and to get them to close the gap with the 8th Connecticut. But he had to cover a considerable distance while the situation rapidly deteriorated. By the time he drew close, it had devolved into a bloodbath.

An equally cruel fate awaited the general. Isaac Peace Rodman, who started his day wandering almost biblically through wilderness in search of an elusive ford, ended it when a minie ball, fired by a South Carolina sharpshooter, pierced his left lung and exited through his back. Rodman tumbled to the ground and was carried from the field, critically wounded. He would die two weeks hence. Rodman's riderless horse gingerly picked its way down the slope.

The Union echelon attack had been launched from right to left. The collapse now rippled left to right, as Hill's men drove like a wedge across the middle of the slope. The most advanced Federal regiments, such as the 9th New York and 45th Pennsylvania, soldiers who had fought to the outskirts of Sharpsburg, were forced to yield their ground. They had to scamper back down the hill, lest they be sandwiched by Rebels to their front and rear.

As the counterattack built, General Toombs joined in the effort. His Georgia boys, who had held the Rohrbach Bridge for so many hours, were too exhausted to fight. (They were resting near Sharpsburg.) So, the general assembled a kind of spit-and-glue force with fresh soldiers from several other Georgia regiments. They came charging down the slope.

The 8th Connecticut ended up surrounded, squeezed between Toombs's and Hill's soldiers. An old history captured the mayhem: "John McCall falls bleeding. Eaton totters, wounded, down the hill. Wait, bullet-riddled, staggers a few rods, and sinks. Ripley stands with a shattered arm. Russell lies white and still. Morgan and Maine have fallen. Whitney Wilcox is dead. Men grow frantic."

Matters grew so desperate that the 8th Connecticut's chaplain snatched up the musket and cartridge box from a deceased member of the regiment, and fought for his very life.

It was now late afternoon. All of a sudden, a regiment sprang into action on a part of the battlefield that had lain dormant for hours. It was like a cuckoo clock cranking into motion: jarring, weird, and slightly grotesque. Back around noontime, the 7th Maine had participated in a brief engagement near the Bloody Lane. Afterward, they had hunkered down in a choice spot among some boulders, protected from stray shells and shots. For the past several hours, the Down Easters had been methodically picking off enemy artillerists and sniping at Rebel officers who wandered into range. They expected that their day's fighting was about to come to a close.

But now—seemingly apropos of nothing—Colonel William Irwin demanded that the 7th Maine storm the Piper Farm, the place where the Confederates had fallen back after being routed at the Bloody Lane. It was crawling with Rebels.

A heated argument ensued between Colonel Irwin and Major Thomas Hyde. Hyde was twenty-one years old, a native of Bath; the 7th Maine, his regiment—he felt a deep responsibility to his boys. The proposed mission was absurd, certain suicide. But Colonel Irwin commanded the entire brigade; he ranked above regimental leader Hyde. Irwin insisted, saying, "Are you afraid to go, sir?"

So go they did: 181 men lit off for the farm, where an assemblage of Texans, Georgians, Louisianans, and Mississippians—dwarfing the 7th Maine in numbers—waited. They soon found themselves boxed into the tight confines of the apple orchard, where they proved ripe for the picking. It was all over quickly, perhaps the one consolation.

The 7th Maine then retreated back to the same spot from which they'd set out. Only now the regiment was down many men: 12 were dead, 63 injured (13 of whom would soon die), and 20 were missing. Major Hyde and the survivors lay on the ground, sobbing like children. Why this senseless sortie? It turned out that Colonel Irwin had been driven by nothing more than the "inspiration of John Barleycorn," as Major Hyde put it. That's right: late in the day, a drunken officer had sent the Maine boys to their demise, and for nothing. (In the course of the afternoon, Lee's top-of-the-battlefield sneak attack had also been launched and had fizzled, but without the same pointless loss of life.)

Back on that broad and bloodied slope, Toombs was gaining momentum. As he surged downhill, sweeping the Federals ahead of him, he joined forces with various wayward and shattered commands, soon assembling a formidable line. To the men, he seemed nearly possessed. He leapt from his mare, Gray Alice, and ran out in front of the line. There, the mad-maned, fire-eating old secessionist strode to and fro, spitting words and gesticulating wildly. He said he wanted to drive the Federals into the Antietam. He urged the men to retake his bridge—*his* bridge, he called it. Toombs hadn't accepted the verdict; it was the Toombs Bridge née the Rohrbach Bridge, never to be the Burnside Bridge.

The sun sank toward the horizon. Daylight was slipping away. From the Pry's bluff, McClellan followed the action, his mood growing darker as he witnessed the turn in the Union's fortunes. Agitated, he climbed into Dan Webster's saddle and rode toward the action, as if being closer could somehow affect the outcome. He encountered a horse courier bearing a message from Burnside, a simple one: send more troops and more ammo. McClellan offered a message in return: "Tell General Burnside this is the battle of the war. He must hold his ground till dark at any cost."

Yet somehow this didn't seem sufficient. McClellan added: "Tell him if he *cannot* hold his ground, then the bridge, to the last man!—always the bridge! If the bridge is lost, all is lost!"

The first notes of hysteria crept into the Union commander's voice.

Onward came Toombs. Near the bottom of the hillside, the 35th Massachusetts, another alarmingly unproven regiment, had formed in battle line. They now represented the last bulwark against the Rebel hordes. Retreating Union soldiers poured through the line, making for the rear. Lawrence Branch, a general from North Carolina, raised his field glasses to get a better view of the scampering Federals. A minie ball passed through his cheek, killing him instantly. Yet another general had gone down, this one a Confederate. Still, onward came Toombs.

Bullets showered down on the men from Massachusetts.

"Meserve, I'm hit," cried Corporal Roscoe Bradley.

"So am I," replied Sergeant William Meserve, as two bullets struck his arm in rapid succession.

"Meserve, I'm killed," shrieked Corporal Bradley, collapsing onto his sergeant.

The Massachusetts men grew so panicked that they fired without aiming. Some accidently left in their ramrods, and on squeezing the trigger, sent long, metal sticks twirling through the air when only a bullet would do. Desperately low on ammo, Burnside ordered some cannons to fire blank cartridges—as if clamor alone would be sufficient to stem the Rebel onslaught.

But then, just when matters appeared most desperate—blessed Union relief. The fever of musketry and cannon began to break. At first it was undetectable, but soon it could not be ignored. A chorus of quiet began to settle over the field, akin to one of those enigmatic silences that sometimes ripple through a noisy room.

Just when a Confederate breakthrough seemed imminent, the same factor that had caused attack after attack to falter this day had appeared yet again: sheer exhaustion. It's hard to maintain such intensity. It's draining to live in a state of pure danger. Unexpectedly, Toombs's men simply pulled up. Then they began climbing back up the hillside toward Sharpsburg. The Union IX Corps gathered on the brow of the bluffs to the west of the Antietam. One of history's most intense days of battle had ended, and with a whimper not a bang. Soon, it grew "as quiet as a Quaker village on Sabbath day," a Georgia soldier recalled with evident awe.

"Both parties fought with a desperation," Private Roland Bowen of the 15th Massachusetts would write to his uncle. "Both parties wavered at times. Each party chased the other, and were chased in turn. Each side slew the other by Thousands."

Beyond that, about all that could really be said of a day's hard fighting: the Union moved a few hundred yards forward in select places, and managed to take a bridge.

---

The sun pressed on the horizon, hostile and red. Journalist Charles Coffin, spotting some Union artillerists on a knoll, noted the way the men and their gun stood out in black silhouette against the swollen disk. The feeling it gave him was one of disquiet. No comfort to be found in the fading light. Much too large and far too red: this was a lurid sunset.

With the day's fighting ended, soldiers took the opportunity to wash the grime and black powder from their bodies. Some collapsed, exhausted. Many were famished. Dinner for the 35th Massachusetts consisted of boiled beef contained in a barrel; the soldiers filed by taking large handfuls. Others just ached for coffee, one of the few genuine comforts for Civil War soldiers. Quite aware that his was a vital errand, the nineteen-year-old commissary sergeant of the 23rd Ohio drove a wagon across the Rohrbach Bridge, located his regiment among all the others, and delivered coffee—hot, heavenly coffee. The young sergeant's name was William McKinley; he had a distinguished career ahead of him.

Many soldiers had ended the day trapped behind enemy lines. There was an obvious tactic—and if it occurred to one, it must have occurred to a hundred men.

Play dead. Of course, this could be a challenge. During the final Federal push, Private Almon Reed had gotten separated from his regiment, the 89th New York, and had wound up trapped high on the hillside. He did his best to pass for a corpse, even as a succession of Rebs riffled through his pockets looking for valuables. As darkness fell, Private Reed and numerous others appeared to rise from the dead, and scampered back to the safety of their lines.

With nightfall, the field's recognizable landmarks once again receded. Over the course of the day, the soldiers had become quite familiar with the Dunker Church and Rohrbach Bridge, but now they slipped into darkness. The mood became palpably different, one of emergency. Corn cribs and store houses, set ablaze by shells during the battle, burned brightly, spitting embers into the sky. At wigwag stations, signalmen waved fiery turpentine-soaked rags, sending urgent nighttime messages. Lanterns bobbed as soldiers set out to locate wounded comrades. "Half of Lee's army were hunting the other half," is how Henry Kyd Douglas, a Confederate officer, would describe the situation.

The air teemed with the groans and howls of the wounded. The choked cries for water were most horrible. Through the slats of many a barn a warm glow issued, what might, in other circumstances, lend a homey feel. Inside, however, there was crisis, nothing but crisis, as surgeons worked feverishly by candlelight, trying to save lives.

By candlelight, too, the four journalists from the *New-York Tribune* met in a farmhouse. As ace reporter, George Smalley had been selected to cull their collective findings into a single article. Time was pressing. To beat the competition, the article would need to be transmitted to New York City headquarters as soon as possible. At roughly 9:00 P.M., Smalley set off on horseback for the twenty-five-mile ride to Frederick, the nearest telegraph station. (McClellan prohibited journalists from using the military telegraph.)

Lee met with his generals. They gathered in an open field near the tent headquarters from which he'd set out at 5:30 A.M. for that slow ride on Traveller. Since then, everything had changed. James Longstreet, David Jones, John Bell Hood, Stonewall Jackson, and both Hills (A. P. and D. H.) took turns gloomily detailing the losses sustained by their commands. Despite the pitiable state of his army, however, Lee elected not to retreat back into Virginia—not this night. More than ever, he recognized that he faced a trepidatious opponent. He decided the men should hold their ground awaiting McClellan's next move.

McClellan was also planning. First thing in the morning, according to his orders, Union troops were to seize a piece of high ground, Nicodemus Heights, and use that as a jumping-off point for a fresh attack on the Rebels. He mulled this endlessly, his mind flickering like candlelight. Then, sometime after midnight, he countermanded his attack order, deciding to wait for morning, instead, see how the situation unfolded, make his move when more certainty emerged.

Few achieved slumber this fitful night. Those who slept couldn't find peace. Private Johnson of the 9th New York would recall being "troubled by a dream in which demons, rattlesnakes, Hell, brimstone, cannon-balls and railroad iron, bayonets and pitchforks, powder and smoke were all conglomerated into one shapeless, endless whirl, with me in the midst . . ."

It was hard to distinguish nightmare from wakefulness following such a day as this.

# CHAPTER 12

## THURSDAY'S RECKONING

A pair of gray eyes fluttered open in the first light of Thursday, September 18, 1862. They were set in a craggy, deep-seamed face. To those who knew him best, this man's appearance had undergone a startling transformation of late. Sorrow and worry had left their record, finely etched. And the beard, grown upon winning high office at the cheerful suggestion of a little girl—its connotation had changed to one of fathomless shadow. The gray eyes blinked then blinked again, like ciphered code. Only Lincoln could know what thoughts churned in his restless mind. Likely, the president had suffered through another night of his constant malady, insomnia. At his cottage retreat, he did his best to accommodate the hard fact of a new day.

The same dawn that filtered through the windows of Lincoln's cottage stole across the fields near Sharpsburg. Thousands of eyes opened: blinking, uneasy. A million thoughts churned, enough to invisibly fill Antietam Valley. Two groggy armies were stirring, among them Georgian soldiers who had fought in the cornfield under Marcellus Douglass, members of the Irish Brigade, late of the Bloody Lane, and a regiment of Michiganders who had climbed that final hill. There were Louisiana Tigers, Pennsylvania Bucktails, Black Hats, and Red Caps. There were boys from Natchez and Pewaukee, Buffalo and Big Stone Gap, the 1st

Minnesota, 8th Florida, 58th Virginia, and 125th Pennsylvania. Everyone wondered whether the fighting would resume, and if so, when.

An alarming realization, evident in the harsh glare of the morning light, was how little the positions of the two armies had changed. This, despite a full day of ferocious battle. Of course, Burnside's men had fought to the far side of a bridge and then held their ground. Elsewhere on the field, it was often a matter of yards gained—or yards lost. Many soldiers were dismayed to find themselves in almost exactly the same spot they had occupied twenty-four hours earlier.

Yet the cost had been dear, as the roll calls revealed. For the 15th Massachusetts, a regiment that had marched into the West Woods 606-men strong, only to be savaged—surrounded by Rebels, fired on by confused Federals—just 174 were able to answer this morning's call. D. H. Hill, the mathematician turned general, rode down his line, addressing the "faithful few." As the morning drew on, many more men would come back. But it wasn't as if these returnees exactly swelled their units' combat readiness. Many were simply seeking familiarity. A soldier whose leg had been shot off hobbled to rejoin his regiment, using a pair of muskets as crutches. Some soldiers dragged themselves, teeth gritted, hands clutching earth. For these unfortunates, every priority had reshuffled. They drew on the last of their strength for a single focused goal: to die among friendly faces.

The odd musket shot rang out. Occasionally, a cannon shell traveled overhead. But it was as if the sounds of such weaponry had somehow transformed, taking on a languid almost inconsequential quality. Pay no mind. These were mere squeaks against the previous day's thunder. Besides, fresh noises now filled the air.

There was the scrape, scrape, scraping as shovels made contact with the strata of limestone that ran just beneath the Maryland soil. The day could only be expected to grow warmer. Already burial details were busy digging shallow graves for the dead.

Another sound was water call. Ordinarily, there was something festive about this bugle signal, calling cavalrymen, cannoneers, and anyone else tending a horse or mule to lead their animal to the nearest body of water for a drink. Here, water could be found in tantalizing abundance: Antietam Creek wended through the battlefield and nearby, for the truly thirsty beast, ran the Potomac. But on this day, countless animals lay upon the ground wounded, suffering. They recognized the water call. Many of them strained, but could not rise to their feet.

Fifty-five miles to the southeast, Lincoln set out once more on his familiar morning commute. After departing from the Soldiers' Home, with its ever-expanding graveyard for Union war dead, right on the grounds, he rode along Seventh Street Turnpike past the makeshift hospitals overflowing with wounded soldiers. Then a jog on Rhode Island Avenue before entering Iowa Circle, where Camp Barker came into view. "I used to see Mr. Lincoln almost every day," Anna Harrison, a fugitive slave who lived there would recall.

Maybe she saw the president this very day. Lincoln picked up Vermont Avenue, and continued toward his destination.

Outwardly, his commute was unremarkable: same half-hour travel time, same cavalry detail, same balmy September weather. Inwardly, it must have felt different for him today. According to McClellan's dispatch, the Union army had entered on the previous day into the most awful battle of the war, perhaps all of human history. This begged for further detail: Was it still in progress? Who was winning? Did Washington face imminent danger? But the general thrived on informational stinginess.

As if this wasn't enough, another matter also likely weighed heavy on the president's mind. It was *Thursday*. And it was on a Thursday, you may recall, that Willie had died.

That February evening, the president had slipped into the room in which Willie lay and lifted the cover from the boy's face for a look. Right then, it had hit Lincoln full, like nothing he could have imagined, a sorrow so consuming that it seemed to rattle his tall frame. He slumped into a chair, covered his own face with his hands.

For weeks afterward, Lincoln had marked Thursdays by shutting himself off in his bedroom, refusing to see anyone; had demanded these few hours at least to grieve, alone. With time, the sheer scorch of emotion quieted some for him—never really for his wife. But the pain remained. As he told an acquaintance, "ever since my little boy died, I find myself talking with him every day." Willie was really gone, yet he would never leave.

The White House, source of scant comfort for the president, must have seemed particularly unwelcoming on Thursdays. While Lincoln always chose to weave around the subject, Mary was more explicit, hinting that this shambling mansion was not without blame for the tragedy they had suffered. Their happy Springfield home lacked indoor plumbing. Not so the White House, fitted with pipes that drew water from the nearby Potomac. It was a questionable source, especially in wartime with thousands of soldiers now camped along the river's banks—and all that entailed. Microbiology was still a mystery at this time, but people certainly appreciated the healthful benefits of cleanliness. On more than one occasion, Mary had complained about the foul odor. Yet whenever Willie and Tad emerged parched from an hour's strenuous play, White House staffers fetched them cups filled with water, water piped in from the river.

Then again, there were so many possible culprits. There was the past winter's dreadful weather, and the wind-whipped pony ride the boys had taken on the White House grounds. There was the hubris of throwing a formal ball when Willie lay upstairs in his sickbed. Mary would never forgive herself. She barred the Marine Band from ever again playing its jaunty tunes at the White House. Even McClellan was a suspect. At the height of the "Onward to

Richmond" clamor, when Lincoln wondered if the army would ever pursue the enemy, the general had taken to his bed, apparently suffering from typhoid fever (an illness caused by dirty food or water, also potentially spread person to person). The president had paid McClellan a visit, bringing along Tad and Willie who always thrilled at the chance to meet military officers. The sorrow and blame were hard to sort into tidy little stacks; they just kept spilling into one another.

Now as Lincoln entered the White House, he must have been terribly uneasy. No one seemed to have much information about the battle in Western Maryland. It upped the president's distress, a feeling shared by others in Washington. "Our anxiety is intense," noted Navy Secretary Gideon Welles in a September 18 diary entry, adding that McClellan's communication style deserved part of the blame: "His dispatches are seldom full, clear, or satisfactory. 'Behaved splendidly,' 'performed handsomely,' but wherein or what was accomplished is never told."

Worry registered keenly, too, across an ocean, in a whole other country. It was as if sentiment could arc through the empty air like a cannon ball. Despite having no knowledge of the battle near Sharpsburg (news took roughly two weeks to travel to Britain), mere hours earlier Lord Russell had written a letter to Prime Minister Palmerston that contained the following: "the time is come for offering mediation to the United States Government, with a view to the recognition of the independence of the Confederates.... in case of failure, we ought ourselves to recognise the Southern States as an independent State."

Meanwhile, back on the battlefield, McClellan waited. Following a fitful night, racked by self-doubt, during which he entertained then abandoned the idea of resuming the battle at first light, he had instructed his generals to simply hold their ground. They were to refrain from initiating hostilities without further orders.

McClellan felt certain that there was no way to renew the fight until reinforcements arrived. Just as Lee had anxiously awaited A. P. Hill, McClellan had his own potential saviors in Darius Couch and Andrew Humphreys, a pair of Union generals who had promised to march all night bringing fresh troops. By sometime in the morning, those 12,000 soldiers were on the field, although they were exhausted from their rapid march. To this number add the 20,000 men who hadn't fired a shot the previous day, along with soldiers who had seen only light action, and McClellan could maybe cobble together 50,000 fighters (though he wouldn't have had the benefit of a precise tally). Nevertheless, many of these men were battle-weary, anxiety-ridden from horrors witnessed the previous day, or belonged to shattered commands.

Thus, McClellan waited. As he would later write in his official report, "the national cause could afford no risks of defeat."

One also detects something else at work in this hesitancy, something deeply poignant. Although McClellan had thousands of troops that could be thrown into a fresh fight, untold thousands had been killed, maimed, taken prisoner, or had simply vanished from the field. These were his men, the proud soldiers of the Army of the Potomac, a force that he'd molded and trained. On this morn, the commander who had once professed to being pained by every single death or injury among his men confronted a blood-bath. It left him so shaken that he became physically ill, suffering an intense bout of neuralgia.

Lee was also content to wait. He probably had half as many fight-ready soldiers as the Federals, though he also wouldn't have had a precise tally. What was clear was that his Army of North-ern Virginia had been similarly devastated. A delay suited him, as it provided a chance to begin conveying the wounded in ambu-lance wagons across the Potomac to safety. If at some point during the day the Union reopened the fight, well, he was prepared to simply react. Where McClellan saw only risk in battle, Lee saw opportunity.

The minutes grew to hours, and still no movement. Wild rumors began to circulate among the men. The Confederates had won a decisive victory. Tommy Meagher of the Irish Brigade had been killed. No, he had merely fallen from his horse, drunk, and it was the Union that had won. Lee and Longstreet were wounded. Correction, here was the latest skinny: Longstreet was dead; Stonewall Jackson had been taken prisoner along with 40,000 Rebs (more than fought in the battle, but no matter).

The soldiers began to grow restless. They took to exploring, at least within the confines of their immediate surroundings. Those on burial detail, or charged with carrying wounded comrades to field hospitals, were able to range further. What they saw was astonishing, a swath of heretofore peaceful countryside in ruins. Farmhouses were riddled with shell, barns turned to embers, crops trampled. One Union soldier was disturbed to see stacks of wheat, knocked over and scattered across a considerable area—such mindless waste. Wagons were upended, caissons blown to tarnation. The ground was littered with broken muskets, spent paper cartridges, and fragments of shell, blankets, haversacks, playing cards, and scraps of clothing. Elms and hickories were shot through with bullets, as if they were a menace that need be stopped in their tracks. And the bodies: everywhere and in every aspect, lying "thick as grasshoppers," as one soldier put it. Some were in orderly rows mirroring the battle lines from which they'd dropped. Others were wildly contorted, frozen in life's final excruciating moment.

Weirdly posed corpses drew special notice. Plenty were to be found. There was a dead Rebel whose musket barrel had filled with blood. The Federals who discovered him speculated that he'd been shot through the heart while in the act of loading, and his lifeblood had poured down the barrel. Near the Dunker Church, a Union soldier lay on his back dead, a pocket Bible splayed open across his chest. On the flyleaf was an inscription: "We hope and pray that you may be permitted by a kind Providence, after the war is over to return."

Counting became a kind of gruesome sport. A Confederate remained frozen in his last moment, shot in the act of climbing over a fence. Twenty-eight bullets were counted in his backside. Someone tallied 358 bodies lying in the Bloody Lane. Then the counter could count no more.

To be alive was lucky this day. Father Corby, chaplain of the Irish Brigade, held mass in a makeshift hut. All over the field, soldiers took the opportunity to write letters to loved ones. "I have lived through my first battle, and I am well," began George Fenno, private, 107th New York. "It gives me intensest pain to tell you of the death of my dear brother, your devoted husband Andrew," wrote a Texan in Hood's division.

McClellan wrote Nelly, providing assurance that her father and others on his staff were unharmed so far. Anxiety and lack of sleep had worn him down, he confided. But he reported that he had comported himself admirably: "Those in whose judgment I rely tell me that I fought the battle splendidly and that it was a masterpiece of art."

Even as he wrote this line, McClellan must have recognized it as hyperbole. Then again, it was meant for an audience of one, his wife, upon whom fell the thankless duty of tending his ego.

Presently, the first detailed battle account (remarkably accurate, too) arrived over the wires in Washington, sending the War Department's telegraph into urgent, clattering motion. The dispatch was not courtesy of McClellan, but came instead from George Smalley, the *Tribune* reporter. The telegraph office didn't even bother waiting for Lincoln's next visit. The dispatch was rushed to the White House, where it was devoured by the president.

How Smalley's dispatch ended up in Washington is a tale unto itself. Following the previous day's fighting, recall, he had set out for Frederick, site of the nearest available telegraph. By

3:00 A.M., when he finally reached his destination, the telegraph office was closed. So, Smalley lay down in the vestibule and tried to sleep. Upon arriving at work, the telegraph operator had found a reporter waiting. Smalley then fed his tale of the "greatest fight since Waterloo," directly to the operator.

Off it went, but, as was often the case with telegrams, the message didn't travel nonstop. After first being routed to Baltimore, it was supposed to be relayed on to New York. Turns out, the Baltimore operator was quite aware of the suspense gripping official Washington. He took it upon himself to reroute the message to the War Department. So it was that Lincoln got this privileged first peek at an item meant for a New York City paper.

Remember, too: Smalley had raced to Frederick in an effort to scoop the competition with news of the *first* day of a big battle. Like everyone else, he had fully expected the action to resume on September 18. Nevertheless, by fanning out across the field, the journalist and his team had done an admirable job of learning about everything that had transpired *so far*. Smalley sensed that the Union had gained slight advantage, particularly by crossing the Antietam via the Rohrbach Bridge. Thus, his conclusion: "If not wholly a victory tonight, I believe it is the prelude to a victory tomorrow."

It provided a first hint of how matters might turn out. At last, the president had some useful intelligence on the big battle in Maryland, and apparently the Union's prospects looked bright. Lincoln must have been greatly relieved. The War Department was good enough to relay Smalley's dispatch on to the *Tribune*. He would supplement this item, crafting a lengthy feature story from the team's pooled notes, though it wouldn't run until Saturday, three days after the battle. This account, in turn, would be picked up by papers in cities all over the Union. Smalley's dispatch would become a classic of war reportage, setting a standard that would hold for years to come.

By afternoon, it became clear that there wasn't going to be a fight this day. Both sides felt increasing urgency to retrieve wounded comrades before they succumbed to their injuries.

A rescue team from the 8th Connecticut sneaked up the same hillside that they'd boldly assailed the day before. They encountered one of their own, lying stiff, his teeth firmly fastened on an ear of corn from which he'd tried to extract some moisture to quench his raging thirst. For him, it was too late. But they found another comrade, wounded but still living, a mere boy, shot through the thigh and woozy from loss of blood. When they handed him a cup of water, he seized it and drank eagerly. Soon the young soldier began to revive, though he appeared to believe he was back home in Connecticut. "And from a *teacup* too," he said dreamily, as if sipping from fine china rather than regulation tin.

In some places, only a couple hundred yards separated the lines. Rescuers grew emboldened, traveling into this no-man's-land, and often getting shot at for their trouble. There were many instances in which soldiers risked their lives to aid the enemy's wounded.

Near the Bloody Lane, a Confederate officer lay crying out in agony. Colonel Edward Cross of the 5th New Hampshire dispatched a stretcher team to bear him to a field hospital. When Rebels spotted the white canvas stretcher, they mistook it for a flag of truce. Perhaps this was simply wishful thinking on their part, but their wish was ardently shared by the Federals. Soon the two sides had negotiated an informal ceasefire on this portion of the field.

Such truces broke out all along the lines. They were casually negotiated, taking the form: *You can cross our lines to retrieve your wounded, if we can cross yours.* But these little islands of grace were fragile, and prone to misunderstanding. Truce after truce collapsed, usually when a confused soldier fired upon rescuers. Thursday brought its share of fresh injuries and deaths, many involving men shot when truces broke down.

The afternoon dragged on. A light rain began to fall.

Back at the White House, Lincoln passed an uneventful day. He signed a couple of official letters. Maybe he paid a visit or three to the War Department cipher room hoping for a battle update, though none was forthcoming. Perhaps, too, he found time to talk with William Slade, one of his favorite staffers, and someone with whom the president had developed a special bond.

Slade—an African American man with olive skin, brown hair, and a little goatee—worked at the White House as an usher, a job that featured many and sundry duties. Slade purchased food for the kitchen staff to prepare, oversaw the maids, and made sure footmen were in the proper positions at state events.

On nights when Lincoln slept at the White House, Slade also acted as his valet, laying out his clothes, helping him with his toilet and grooming. Lincoln was in the habit of writing his thoughts on scraps of paper, then leaving them scattered about his quarters. (Sometimes they even wound up inside his stovepipe hat.) Slade dutifully gathered up these scraps and saved them for the president.

Lincoln valued Slade's discretion, often calling on him to deliver confidential messages. Over time, the role of trusted employee grew into a genuine friendship.

Lincoln and Slade were close in age, fifty-three and forty-seven, respectively. Both men had warm, expansive conversational styles and shared a similar sense of humor. The president appreciated Slade's ready collection of jokes, said to be able to "make a horse laugh." So, Slade gained yet another duty, this one in a rather more unofficial capacity: sometimes he kept Lincoln company when the president suffered from insomnia.

Slade lived at 464 Massachusetts Avenue NW, a five-minute walk from the White House. He had three young children: Andrew, Jessie, and Katherine, nicknamed "Nibbie." Willie's death followed by Mary's banishment of the Taft boys left Tad deeply lonesome. He grew increasingly disruptive, pestering the staff, bursting in on cabinet meetings. Fortunately, Slade's home became a haven for Tad, offering three young playmates.

Along with his key role at the White House, Slade enjoyed great prominence in the District's African American community. As an elder at the Fifteenth Street Presbyterian Church, he was a vital member of one of the most prominent houses of worship for blacks in Washington. He was also involved with the Columbian Harmony Society, dedicated to helping members of his race to obtain burial plots. Founded in 1825, this was one of the oldest African American mutual aid societies in the District. As well, Slade served as president of the Social, Civil, and Statistical Association, another mutual aid society, this one dedicated to collecting information on issues such as finances and educational attainment among blacks. The group's aim was to use data to help gain full citizenship rights for African Americans.

Naturally, Lincoln viewed Slade as a valuable source of information about the concerns of black people. When the two men talked, the subject often turned to slavery, and the thorny problem it posed. Slade, it appears, was also one of a handful of people in Washington aware of that handwritten document, tucked away in a White House desk, waiting.

At nightfall, Lee's army began to retreat. Long lines of soldiers and wagons wobbled over roads slick with mud, a consequence of the afternoon's rain. The air hung thick with fog. Torches marked Boteler's Ford, the crossing spot on the Potomac. The same Georgians who had opened the cornfield fight, rising up from a furrow to shower Duryee's men with lead, now closed the fight, guarding the ford. No doubt, they were shaken by the fate of their colonel, Marcellus Douglass, killed in the battle.

Peter Alexander, dean of Rebel war correspondents, witnessed this immense military maneuver. He wrote the following: "The trees and overhanging cliffs, and the majestic Blue Ridge loomed up in dim but enlarged and fantastic proportions, and made one feel as if he were in some strange and weird land of grotesque forms, visible only in the hours of dreams."

Lee oversaw the operation from the middle of the Potomac, astride Traveller. The horse stood knee-deep in the dark, roiling waters. The mood was funereal. On a bright morning, only two weeks earlier, the Confederates had entered the North by way of this same river, buoyed by the strains of "Maryland, My Maryland." The men retreated under cover of darkness and quietly, so quietly that a tale would grow up that the Southern soldiers had snuck away right under the nose of the sleeping enemy. Ridiculous: such stealth would have been impossible for an army as large as Lee's, especially with Federal pickets on watch. No, the Union army had had its fill of this fight, too, and was happy to see the Rebels go.

Last to cross was Maxcy Gregg and his South Carolinians, bane of those green New Englanders on that final hillside. At the midway point, Gregg's men encountered an ambulance wagon mired in the Potomac. The cowardly driver had simply unhitched the horses, abandoning a bevy of wounded and frightened soldiers. Twelve of the South Carolinians yoked themselves to the wagon and pulled it to the safety of the far shore.

"Thank god," Lee was heard to mutter as the last of his men crossed.

The feeling was mutual.

The next morning, McClellan crisscrossed the battlefield, assessing the situation. He traveled in an ambulance drawn by four gray horses. While Lee had entered Maryland in an ambulance, tending to an injured hand and wrist, the conclusion of the invasion found his rival confined to one instead, so emotionally shaken that he couldn't ride a horse. The Union commander was relieved to see that the Rebels had truly gone, though they had left behind their most critically wounded, along with thousands of unburied dead.

In the end, Lee had been the one to blink. The Confederate army had withdrawn from Northern territory and returned to Virginia. And though it was by the narrowest of margins—merely *a tactical draw*, some would argue—that river crossing spelled a victory for the Union. Somehow and most improbably, Little Mac had whipped Bobby Lee.

# CHAPTER 13

---

# SURGICAL PROCEDURES,
# LINCOLN'S PRESCRIPTION

*Back in Washington,* Lincoln waited in a state of unease. He must have felt as if he had been through a battle himself, suffering as he was from an array of maladies that all seemed to converge at once. His back ached; sharp pains coursed through his wrist, sprained during that recent fall from a horse; the corns on his feet were giving him great discomfort. To all of this, add the president's perennial duo, sleeplessness and anxiety—so much anxiety.

His most substantial piece of military intelligence had come from Smalley's dispatch, that partially written *New-York Tribune* article suggesting the Union stood poised for a great victory. Still, there was no reliable word on the battle's final result, least of all from McClellan. Lincoln had promised himself that if his general drove Lee from Maryland, he would use that occasion to issue an emancipation proclamation. But nothing was known with certainty. "We are still left entirely in the dark in regard to your own movements and those of the enemy," General-in-Chief Halleck telegraphed McClellan, "This should not be so."

Evenings at his Soldiers' Home cottage, the president tinkered with his proclamation. "From time to time I added or changed a line, touching it up here and there," he would recall.

He wrote notes to himself on little scraps of paper, as was his practice. He waited.

What Lincoln couldn't know is that Sharpsburg and the surrounding countryside had already gone through another transformation. No longer was this the site of an active battlefield. Seemingly in an instant the area had been consumed by a vast medical emergency, centered on the astonishing number of wounded soldiers the fighting had produced (more than 17,000—roughly 9,500 on the Union side and nearly 8,000 Confederates). At the same spots where men had rumbled in broad battle lines, muskets popping, cannons roaring, the action remained equally desperate, yet guided by wholly different considerations. So recently the goal had been to shoot men dead; now surgeons labored to save their lives.

Where McClellan and Lee were seasoned warriors, new skills were in demand. Throughout Western Maryland, from Sharpsburg to Frederick, from Keedysville to Boonsboro, and every spot in between, it seemed as if all the available structures—farmhouses, churches, shops, schools, sheds, even a bowling alley—had been converted into makeshift hospitals. A similarly impromptu Rebel medical complex sprang into existence across the Potomac in the safety of Virginia.

As befits such a shift, new leaders had come to the fore, most notably Jonathan Letterman, the medical director of the Army of the Potomac. Letterman selected the Pry house as his headquarters, the same ample farmstead where McClellan had tracked the battle. This was fitting, spoke to the shared sensibilities of the Union commander and his doctor in chief. For a general, McClellan had an unusual appreciation for medicine. Early in his career, while serving as a Crimean War observer, recall that he made a point of learning about the practices—and deficiencies—of European battlefield medicine. As a commander, he seemed so extraordinarily affected by injuries to his men. Such attitudes no doubt were shaped by his upbringing in a medically minded family, one where his own father had been among America's most distinguished surgeons. McClellan had handpicked Letterman as his medical director. And it was no accident that the general selected a graduate of Jefferson Medical College, the Philadelphia school founded by the elder McClellan.

Letterman—a gaunt, blunt-spoken man—proved an inspired choice. At thirty-seven years old, he was an army veteran who had been stationed all over the land: Florida, Minnesota, California, Fort Leavenworth in what was then Kansas Territory, and Fort Defiance in New Mexico Territory. Now that he was in charge, he brimmed with fresh ideas. During the days prior to the battle, while the armies shifted into position, Letterman had cased the surrounding countryside, identifying structures that could serve as hospitals, figuring out routes to reach them once the fighting began. Letterman deserves credit for refining the three-tiered battlefield evacuation system—dressing station to field hospital to general hospital—still in use in current times.

Another Letterman innovation was a dedicated military ambulance corps. During previous battles, transporting the wounded often fell to regimental musicians and civilian teamsters-for-hire. Predictably, buglers and cowherds were woefully unqualified to provide medical care. Under battle duress, they frequently drank the medicinal spirits—or simply bolted. The consequences could be disastrous. After Shiloh, thousands of wounded remained on the field, untended, in agony, while peach blossoms fluttered down, blanketing their war-torn bodies. After Bull Run, some injured soldiers lay where they had fallen for days. The lucky ones were able rise and make the twenty-five-mile walk back to Washington, dehydration and malnourishment compounding their injuries.

Letterman recognized this as unacceptable. Like McClellan, he was skilled at training men, and doing so quickly. Only recently, on August 2, the medical director had received authorization for his ambulance corps reorganization. During the intervening six weeks, he had worked tirelessly, designating soldiers in each regiment for ambulance duty, and providing them with at least a modicum of medical training. He also requisitioned a new type of ambulance, known as a Rosecrans wagon (named after one of its designers, General William Rosecrans).

The Rosecrans wagon represented a substantial upgrade. Before, a common style of Union ambulance had been a two-wheeled cart, akin to a wheelbarrow. While such compact carts had the advantage of battlefield mobility, riding in one could be agonizing, as they rattled over uneven ground, jarring the wounded, aggravating their injuries. "Gutbusters" the men called them, and begging to be removed was simply good sense. Better to lie on the ground and take one's chances than suffer such an excruciating hospital ride.

By contrast, the Rosecrans was, as billed, a wagon, not a wheelbarrow, designed to carry ten wounded soldiers. It featured cushioned benches and a canvas cover to protect the men from inclement weather. Most significantly, the Rosecrans wagon boasted a set of elliptical springs, providing rudimentary shock absorption.

Letterman had two hundred Rosecrans wagons on hand. Within forty-eight hours, every injured soldier had been evacuated from the field. The Rebels had left roughly 2,000 wounded behind in Maryland, and these men were picked up, too, and treated alongside the Federals. "Humanity teaches us that a wounded and prostrate foe is not then our enemy," Letterman once wrote.

How quickly soldiers received treatment depended on the seriousness of their injuries. Here, too, Letterman was a pioneer, helping to clarify triage, such a simple but essential concept. He demanded that his surgeons prioritize. A soldier who was slipping fast might be rushed onto an operating table—often nothing more than a door that had been removed and laid atop two barrels—while the less urgent cases waited, men lying on straw, lying on the ground, taking up every available inch in the barn or other makeshift hospital structure before spilling out into the open air. Soldiers with serious head or torso injuries stood no chance and could expect to be denied care. Given scarce time and resources, such cold calculus was necessary to save lives.

Western Maryland would be Letterman's laboratory, the place where he was finally able to put into practice ideas that had been churning in his mind for years. In the future, he would come to be known as the "father of battlefield medicine."

Meanwhile, Rebel relief efforts were concentrated in Shepherdstown, the first stop for Lee's army after crossing into Virginia via Boteler's Ford. The scenic little burg—situated atop the steep bluffs that lined the western side of the Potomac—was overwhelmed by an influx of injured, swelling its population to several times the usual 1,200. Not only were shops and churches called into service as hospitals, but so too were uncongenial spots, such as a dilapidated old factory that had been boarded up for years. Town resident Harry Snyder would recall, "After every available space indoors had been occupied, wounded and weary men stretched themselves upon the porches and in the yards, while many more lay along the streets in vacant places."

For most wounded Confederates, treatment was straightforward—amputation. Then again, same went for the Union soldiers across the Potomac. During the Civil War, amputations accounted for three out of four battlefield operations. This was Hobbesian medicine: brutish and quick.

But the instruments of war circa 1862—minie balls and chunks of shrapnel—were coarse, perhaps demanding a like medical response. Consider, for example, the ubiquitous .58-caliber minie ball, a projectile that measured half an inch in diameter. This hunk of soft lead traveled through the air slowly (compared to a modern bullet), and rather than piercing a body on impact, it flattened out and distorted, creating gruesome, gaping wounds. "The minnie ball striking a bone does not permit much debate about amputation," noted Theodore Dimon, a surgeon with the 2nd Maryland.

An experienced surgeon could perform the procedure in about ten minutes. Anesthesia was almost always used, notwithstanding the bite-the-bullet myth. To put a soldier under, surgeons had the choice of two common agents, each with its own set of benefits and downsides. Ether was highly effective, but also extremely flammable. When used during nighttime operations, there was an ever-present risk that burning candles or lanterns could trigger an explosion. Chloroform was the noncombustible choice, but getting the dose right was trickier, carrying the risk that a patient would go under and stay there.

Survival rates varied by type of amputation. With a finger amputation, the chance of living was 97 percent; for a portion of arm removed below the elbow, 86 percent; but one's odds dropped to 67 percent for a leg removed below the knee, and just 17 percent for a full-leg amputation at the hip joint.

Even after a successful operation, grave danger lurked. The role that microbes play in disease wasn't yet understood. As a consequence, surgeons often didn't bother to clean bonesaws, sponges, and other implements, introducing such dread afflictions as tetanus, erysipelas, pyemia, and hospital gangrene. Crowded conditions in the makeshift hospitals also contributed to the spread of disease. During the Civil War, diseases such as dysentery accounted for two thirds of all soldier deaths, proving far more perilous than muskets and cannons.

Physical ailments weren't the only danger, either. Many soldiers suffered from nightmares, heart palpitations, despondency, and crying jags. Some of them, it was noted, were easily startled by loud noises. Doctors of the era had a name for this bewildering collection of symptoms: "nostalgia." In the aftermath of a terrible battle, went the reasoning, certain men develop pathologically strong cases of homesickness. The diagnosis probably had a grain of accuracy. But it's likely that many of these soldiers were actually in the initial throes of what would later become known as shell shock, and today, as post-traumatic stress disorder. For some, the condition would linger on for years.

The hospitals hummed, both sides of the Potomac, tending to men broken in body, stricken in mind.

Such a big, vicious battle—the occasion for so much rivalry and rage—does not slip easily into quietude. It's like a spent bonfire, still marked by a bed of glowing embers. After Lee moved his troops across the Potomac, he left behind a detail to guard Boteler's Ford. Ostensibly, these men were there to ensure that the Federals didn't pursue his army into Virginia. But they were also a menace, positioned directly across the river. McClellan, practiced cogitator that he was, set to wondering whether Lee, though driven from Maryland, might not yet return. Yes, Bobby Lee had been whipped, but would he be content to stay that way?

The Confederate rearguard was under the command of artillery chief William Pendleton, one of the weaker links in Lee's hierarchy. A reputation for handwringing and gross ineptitude had earned him the nickname, "Old Mother Pendleton." Nevertheless, he arranged the forty-four pieces in the Rebel reserve brilliantly, selecting the choicest spots on the high Potomac bluffs, creating a formidable defense the equal of those Georgia boys at the Rohrbach Bridge. At his disposal, too, were roughly 600 soldiers, the ragged remnants of two depleted brigades. Some of these men no longer even had a musket, not that it mattered. Pendleton, whose expertise was artillery, had scant experience commanding infantrymen. From the Union side of the river, officers employed field glasses to track Pendleton's activities. In response, they arranged their own men and guns.

On the morning of September 19, ember fanned into flame. Missiles shrieked back and forth across the Potomac, as an artillery battle got under way. Cannons boomed then answered themselves in echo, their low, guttural reports bouncing off the steep bluffs. The din was terrifying, awesome, encompassing.

Perhaps the noise also served to mask some of the Rebel deficiencies. While Pendleton achieved an inspired artillery placement, he was saddled with an irregular collection of guns that included some short-range howitzers and about a dozen 6-pounders, a thoroughly outmoded weapon. Furthermore, he was low on ammo and fuses. By contrast, the Union side had positioned suitably long-range cannons and more of them, too (roughly seventy).

By dusk, the Federals had sized up Pendleton's force, and decided to press their advantage. A couple of regiments splashed into the Potomac, and began crossing at Boteler's Ford.

Pendleton ordered his men to drag the cannons to safety. But the operation was hampered by the fading light. It was difficult to account for his guns, difficult to account for his men—hard, really, to make much sense of anything. Soon enough, the enemy came charging over Virginia soil, its rifles aflash in the gloaming.

Old Mother Pendleton panicked. He set out across the countryside in search of Lee. Roughly three hours passed, it was just after midnight, before the artillery chief managed to locate the Rebel commander, asleep in the open air, beneath an apple tree. Pendleton awakened him with the chilling news that the entire Confederate reserve artillery had been captured.

"All?" asked a bleary Lee.

"Yes, General, I fear all," replied Pendleton.

Men who served with Lee saw him under pressure many times, noted the remarkable composure he brought even to the most precarious situation. This would be remembered as one of the few instances when the general was visibly shaken. It was the middle of the night. His army was spread out across the Virginia countryside. It was dangerously depleted from recent fighting. Not until 6:30 A.M. would a viable plan take shape.

As it turned out, A. P. Hill and his men were camped closest to Boteler's Ford. Thus, the role of saving the day fell yet again to

Hill, McClellan's old rival, who just three days earlier had marched his troops seventeen miles from Harpers Ferry, arriving in time to slam into the Union flank.

However, here's what none of the Confederate brass realized: after briefly trading fire with Pendleton's men, the Union forces—facing nightfall and uncertainty—had returned to Maryland without capturing a single cannon.

Come dawn on September 20, however, the Federals were poised to try again. Fresh troops—including regiments from Maine, Michigan, and Pennsylvania—had massed along the banks on the Union side of the Potomac. Nearly half this 1,700-man force was furnished by the 118th Pennsylvania, a green outfit that had only been in existence for three weeks. They were known as the "Corn Exchange Regiment" in honor of the Philadelphia-based agricultural futures market that had promised bonuses to each enlistee. They also had zero combat experience, having waited in reserve on September 17.

Yet again, Federal soldiers forded the Potomac. The men managed to capture three cannons, and repossessed another, as in: they seized a gun that had originally belonged to the Union, but had fallen into Rebel hands at Bull Run. (Back and forth went cannons, as if in a game of tug-of-war.)

On came A. P. Hill. A general cry of alarm went up among the Yanks. Men began to stream back across the Potomac. Still, the Corn Exchange Regiment held its ground. To onlookers, this seemed foolhardy. A courier arrived with an urgent message for Colonel Charles Prevost, exhorting him to lead his men to safety. Upon reading it, however, the colonel seemed to take issue with some fine point of military protocol. "I do not receive orders in that way," he announced haughtily.

Closer drew Hill's men. The Pennsylvania boys opened fire. It was then, to their great horror, that they discovered that many of their Enfields were defective. In some rifles, the little nipple on which a percussion cap is placed had simply broken off, making it impossible to ignite the powder in a cartridge. Others featured dud mainsprings, meaning the hammers couldn't strike hard enough to explode the percussion cap—with the same disastrous result. In the confusion, some of the rookies believed they were squeezing off repeated shots, when they were merely stuffing their barrels with unspent powder and multiple minie balls.

With Hill's men hot upon them, the 118th began to flee at last. But they were in an unfortunate position, backed up to the edge of a bluff. Men poured into a steep ravine, offering the only possible pathway down. Soon this route grew so choked with retreating soldiers that the best hope of escape lay in slipping over the lip of the bluff, then climbing down its sheer 60-foot face. Many Pennsylvanian boys lost their footing, plummeting to their death on the rocky riverbank below.

The Battle of Boteler's Ford resulted in seventy-three Union fatalities, all but ten coming from the luckless Corn Exchange Regiment. Confederate fatalities numbered thirty-six. It also sent a wave of fresh wounded (163 Yankee, 267 Rebel) pouring into those makeshift hospitals, both sides of the Potomac. With this final flare-up, the Maryland Campaign was at an end. For now, the two armies were done fighting, and they settled into camp life.

Lincoln had been wise to wait. Until the battle at Boteler's Ford, turns out, Lee really had been planning to reinvade Maryland. He was busily scheming another incursion into the Confederacy's *northern frontier* (his trademark-bold way of thinking about Union territory). Being a gifted strategist, the Confederate commander had no intention of returning to Sharpsburg, either. That would squander the element of surprise. Instead, he had been contemplating a Potomac crossing at Williamsport, Maryland, about ten miles upriver. Then came the late-night scare involving the artillery reserve, coupled with the last-gasp battle at Boteler's Ford, and he'd been forced to reevaluate the condition of his army. Lee concluded his men were simply too tired, hungry, ragged, and ill-shod to mount another attack. "I am, therefore, led to pause," he wrote to Jeff Davis.

By waiting, Lincoln also derived the additional benefit of letting newspaper accounts of the battle on September 17 accumulate. At this point, a critical mass existed, sufficient to convince the president that the Union had achieved an authentic victory.

Among the press, a consensus was even emerging on what to call the battle. At first, this had been an open question. In a diary entry, one Union soldier referred to the Battle of Meyer's Spring, inspired it seems by a modest aquatic feature that must have loomed large as he fought. The soldier was true to trend, at least, in suggesting a waterway, the standard Federal formula for battle names. Of course, a different one would receive the honor: Antietam Creek. In the South, the battle would come to be known as Sharpsburg, based on a nomenclatural tradition that looked to nearby towns or landmarks. Bull Run/Manassas; Wilson's Creek/ Oak Hills: in a civil war one can't expect the two sides to agree.

By whatever name, the Union had achieved victory and Lincoln stood ready to issue his proclamation.

Over time, however, he had become convinced of the wisdom of releasing it first in preparatory form, containing a threat about what would happen if the terms weren't met. Simply handing down an edict left no room for negotiation with the Confederacy. The president selected January 1, 1863, as the deadline. In those Southern states (or even discrete regions within those states) that remained in rebellion on that date, the US government would declare the slaves free. Setting a deadline, one hundred days hence, would provide the additional advantage of giving Northerners— many of them leery about tying the war to slavery—a chance to grow more comfortable with the idea.

In this trial version, Lincoln planned to dangle the possibility of gradual compensated emancipation. Although the border states had roundly rejected the president's overtures on this issue, it still made sense to offer the Confederate states "pecuniary aid" in exchange for freeing their slaves. The Union and Confederacy were already at war, so what was there to lose? Against a looming deadline, negotiations might be spurred between the two sides. If even one state—Georgia, say, or Alabama—accepted the offer and withdrew from the rebellion, the Confederacy would be that much the weaker. The president also intended a mention of voluntary colonization, hinting that the US government would continue to explore ways to prevail on free blacks to resettle in more welcoming countries. Lincoln was offering carrots, brandishing a stick.

But oh what leaden language! One of the most striking features of the document the president was preparing was its talc-dry legalese. This from a man capable of such soaring grandeur, able to summon "better angels" and sound "mystic chords of memory." Instead, he opted to use "thereof" six times, "hereby" thrice, as well as an "aforesaid," "thenceforward," and a "promulgated." For Lincoln, there was a time to appeal to hearts, and a time to convince minds. Now, the president was in full pragmatist mode. Karl Marx would compare Lincoln's historic document to "the trite summonses that one lawyer sends to an opposing lawyer."

Over the weekend of September 20 and 21, Lincoln tinkered, refining this opening legal salvo aimed at the Rebel states. He readied what would come to be known as the "preliminary emancipation proclamation."

Meanwhile, the massive medical emergency grew increasingly intense. As news accounts came pouring in, families North and South grew sick with worry. What information could be gleaned was often maddeningly incomplete.

The rosters of wounded that appeared in papers often featured first initials paired with last names. Consider, for example, one for the 11th Connecticut that appeared in the *Hartford Daily Courant*, and included the following: "T. Warner, Co. G, in jaw." Was it possible—pray let it be so—that more than one "T. Warner" served in the company? And what exactly did "in jaw" mean, anyhow? From afar, based on a two- or three-word description, it could be difficult to gauge the seriousness of an injury or even the identity of the victim.

Then, in the next instant, came the chilling realization: newspaper accounts tended to be several days old, so perhaps the soldier in question had already succumbed to his wounds.

Papers also made their share of errors. This was understandable, given the huge number of soldiers (more than 100,000) present at Antietam. A soldier's name and regiment might be correct, yet the roll of wounded may have assigned him the wrong rank.

Families clung to these variances. An incorrect detail, no matter how small, raised hopes that this might simply be a case of mistaken identity. It was known to happen. A family in Fond du Lac received news of the death of their loved one, Lieutenant Colonel E. S. Bragg of the 6th Wisconsin. That turned out to be wrong. Colonel Bragg had survived; Captain E. A. Brown had died. He left behind a wife and three children.

Families flooded into the region, where they fell into neat divisions, as if the battle were a bride, and the Potomac, a church aisle during her wedding. Those representing the Union wounded remained on the Maryland side, making the rounds of the hospitals surrounding Sharpsburg. Those looking for injured Rebels went to Shepherdstown, or other nearby Virginia communities where hospitals had been set up, such as Staunton.

A German-speaking mother arrived in Maryland, seeking her son, Charles Metzger, 4th New York. The sprawling collection of hospital tents and sheds proved totally overwhelming. With each one she visited, her spirits sank, as she learned that her son was not among those being treated. In the town of Frederick, she sat down on some steps and started to cry. A passerby, feeling her grief, offered to help out. During the next two hours, together they visited twenty hospitals in Frederick. No luck. But at the twenty-first, she scanned down a list and there it was: "Metzger Charles 4th New York." She rushed into the hospital, crying "mein sohn, mein sohn!"

John Gordon's wife had a very different reaction when she finally located him in a hospital. She stifled a blood-curdling scream. His face was grotesquely swollen, his body riddled with puncture wounds. As a member of the 6th Alabama, Colonel Gordon had fought in the Bloody Lane, where he claimed to have been shot five separate times. Mrs. Gordon parked herself by his bedside, insisted on helping with his care. The doctors instructed her to paint iodine three or four times a day onto a nasty wound on his left shoulder. "She obeyed the doctors, by painting it, I think, three or four hundred times a day," he would recall.

Silas Stowe made the long journey from Grafton, Massachusetts, to a hospital on the Hoffman farm, near Sharpsburg. Brother Jonathan of the 15th Massachusetts had been wounded in the leg during the West Woods action.

When Silas arrived, Jonathan greeted him with an agonized "Oh my god."

Jonathan had endured the amputation of his leg, followed by dizziness, chills, and diarrhea. The stump, to his surprise and dismay, gave him unremitting pain. Because he couldn't find a position where it didn't ache and throb, he couldn't even sleep. Now tetanus had set in.

He begged Silas to help cool his fever. Silas did what he could. Only six hours after his brother arrived at the hospital, Jonathan passed away. "Use more water—use it freely—ice water," were the young soldier's last recorded words.

On Monday, September 22, 1862, Lincoln settled into work at the White House. For the past few days, the president had been under the care of Dr. Issachar Zacharie, who had helped soothe his aching back, treated the corns on his feet.

Lincoln called a meeting of his war cabinet, signaling its importance by sending a messenger to make the rounds of the various departments. By noon, every member was present at the White House.

The president began the meeting in a curious way. He read aloud from a book by Artemus Ward, a humorist he enjoyed, selecting a short piece called "High-Handed Outrage at Utica." The cabinet members sat there stone-faced, puzzled. Lincoln kept on reading, punctuating parts he found especially funny with loud guffaws. "Gentlemen, why don't you laugh?" he asked at last. "With the fearful strain that is upon me night and day, if I did not laugh I should die, and you need this medicine as much as I do."

Presently, he set down the book. Lincoln's tall, black stovepipe hat sat nearby on his desk. According to Secretary of War Stanton's account of the meeting, the president reached into the hat and pulled out a document. Once again, he began to read out loud to his cabinet, the first airing of his preliminary Emancipation Proclamation.

Within hours, the full text had been released via telegraph, jangling through the wires and out across the land. The reaction, instantaneous and mixed, broke down very much along partisan lines. Conservative papers, such as the *Journal of Commerce*, condemned Lincoln's decision, while liberal-leaning papers, such as Horace Greeley's *New-York Tribune*, were laudatory. On the floor of Congress, Democrats expressed loud vocal outrage, while Republicans spoke in stentorian tones about justice and human dignity.

McClellan was incensed. Remember, only months earlier, he'd slipped Lincoln an impudent private communiqué, demanding that the president refrain from bringing the slavery issue into the war. Now, Lincoln had gone and done exactly that. In a letter to Nelly, the general faulted the "Presdt's late Proclamation" for making it "almost impossible for me to retain my commission & self respect at the same time. I cannot make up my mind to fight for such an accursed doctrine as that of a servile insurrection—it is too infamous."

For the benefit of his men, however, McClellan found it wise to take a more measured public stance. Sure, plenty of soldiers in the Army of the Potomac shared his disdain for Lincoln, but many also supported the president. That had to be taken into account. So, the Union commander opted to circulate a printed copy of the proclamation among his troops, now camped in the fields surrounding Sharpsburg. To Lincoln's words, McClellan tacked on a kind of appendix that he drafted himself. It included the line "The remedy for political error if any are committed is to be found only in the action of the people at the polls."

The polls: McClellan had just hinted at his fondest wish. In the upcoming midterms, he hoped the Republicans would be voted out of Congress, stymieing Lincoln and his foolhardy ideas about emancipation. Then, the general could continue to serve with self-respect.

The preliminary proclamation did pay one immediate dividend. Great Britain and France, a pair of countries that had been one Union battle loss away from meddling on behalf of the Confederacy, would pull away from their interventionist stance. Both countries had abolished slavery in their colonies. Now that the North was explicitly spelling out its war aims, aiding a Southern bid for independence became untenable. The window had pretty much closed on the Confederacy's efforts to gain diplomatic recognition. Throughout Europe, in fact, Lincoln's message registered with great clarity. "Everyone can understand the significance of a war where emancipation is written on one banner and slavery on the other," reported James Pike, the US minister to the Netherlands.

Most of all, Lincoln's message registered with black people. North and South, free and slave, they greeted the preliminary proclamation with wonderment, tempered in no small measure with skepticism. Had the president of the United States really just promised to free the slaves? Even on sunbaked cotton plantations in the most remote reaches of Dixie, there was a surprising level of awareness, as the news spread word of mouth, slave to slave.

Blacks everywhere pinned their hopes on January 1, 1863. But they also worried that Lincoln would go back on his word.

William Slade had a unique stake in the outcome as an African American, a White House employee, and a friend of Lincoln's. He'd gathered up those scraps of paper, the raw ingredients of the proclamation. He'd read them carefully, discussed slavery with the president. According to family lore, by the time Lincoln issued the document, Slade was familiar with every last word.

# CHAPTER 14

## The Dead of Antietam

*The space was well defined,* a ten- by four-inch rectangle. It was also uniformly white, looked almost like a porcelain tile. To the touch, however, it would have been moist and tacky.

Draw close . . . closer . . . absurdly so. This milk-white surface was composed of a million million atoms, every one akin to a tiny planet. Each individual atom, in turn, was shrouded by a constellation of electrons, like storm clouds gathered above the earth.

Light played across the porcelain-hued glaze. At whatever spots it struck, the electrons became agitated. The more intense the light, the greater the agitation. Around those million million tiny planets, the storm clouds swirled with increasing ferocity.

Of course, the people of this era knew nothing of atoms. Yet unknown forces affected their lives just the same. That these were undetectable didn't make them any less real. They existed as surely as the electric pulses that traveled over telegraph wires, bringing news of events in faraway places. They were as real as the stealthy microbes that killed Willie Lincoln.

A liquid washed across that ten-by-four surface. It spread like a puddle. Witness the miniature magic: when the liquid came in contact with the spots where the electrons had been agitated, specks of silver started to form. This was genuine silver, like one would find in an heirloom spoon. More silver appeared, organizing according to its own immutable rules. It clumped where the electrons were most agitated, but remained less concentrated elsewhere. The surface was transforming, porcelain giving way to tones of silver, finely calibrated, light in some places, dark in others.

An image started to emerge. Look closely. A dead Rebel lay on his back, one knee raised stiffly. It was as though he was trying to walk straight up out of this carnage, and into the sky.

Alexander Gardner had arrived. With his wooden box camera, he was busy documenting Antietam's ghastly aftermath.

The battlefield was strewn with bodies. Soldiers lay just where they had fallen. Even as a medical emergency gripped the region, designed to save the wounded, another fervent endeavor was in progress, this one for the benefit of the dead. A massive burial effort was under way.

The toll was unfathomable: 3,650 soldiers had been killed at Antietam (2,100 Union and 1,550 Confederates, according to best estimates). It marked September 17, 1862, as the deadliest day of the Civil War so far, a distinction that would hold to the conflict's end. In fact, the battle's twelve hours of mayhem resulted in a fatality count that still remains the highest for any day in American history.

Because the Union held the field, the work of burying the dead, both sides, fell to Federal troops. Sometimes it was a punishment, meted out to an unruly regiment, but more often a duty, assigned out of simple necessity. The weather remained unseasonably warm; this need be done quickly.

The men tied kerchiefs around their faces in an effort to ward off the unholy stench. Often, soldiers would roll a corpse onto a blanket. Then they'd take up a corner and pull the blanket-with-body over the ground like a sleigh. Another technique was to heat up a discarded bayonet, bend it into hook, and drag the deceased—anything to avoid physical contact. Lieutenant Origen

Bingham, 137th Pennsylvania, called it the "most disagreeable duty that could have been assigned to us," adding: "I would not describe to you the appearance of the dead even if I could, it is too revolting. You can imagine the conditions of the bodies when I tell you that they were slain on Wednesday and it is now Sunday."

The Federal fallen were buried first. It was grueling work, given that the fabled Maryland soil was shallow, a boon for crops, but not so good for planting bodies. Typically, the gravesite of a Union soldier was marked with a rough headboard, fashioned from a piece of scrap wood or the side of a hardtack box. On this, the deceased's name, rank, and regiment would be scrawled in pencil.

The body of Captain Werner von Bachelle, 6th Wisconsin, was recovered near the Hagerstown Turnpike, where he'd fallen during the cornfield fighting. His cap had slipped forward covering his eyes, his field glasses were shattered by bullets, and the captain's trusty Newfoundland lay across his chest, dead. The two were buried together on Miller's farm.

Less consideration was extended to the Rebels. Long, shallow trenches were dug and their bodies, tumbled in. A trench could contain upward of one hundred Confederates, laid out in long rows, sometimes stacked two bodies deep. As a courtesy, their undertakers might include a sign. "80 Rebels are buried in this hole," read one.

Gardner—a burly, hirsute Scotsman, aged forty-one—was present to document it all. Between September 19 and 22, he made his orderly way over the battlefield, traveling north to south, capturing the desolation that Antietam had wrought.

Gardner was something of a polymath. During his early life in Glasgow, he'd been a jeweler's apprentice, newspaper editor, amateur botany enthusiast, as well as a dabbler in "sun pictures," a term from the infancy of photography. After immigrating to America, he took a job in 1858 with Mathew Brady, one of the form's pioneers. Brady prided himself on shooting pictures of every president from John Quincy Adams onward, save for one (William Henry Harrison had died a month into his term).

Gardner would become manager of Brady's studio in Washington, DC. He did a bustling portraiture business among capital luminaries that included politicians, generals, merchants, and society wives. He also achieved a coup, as the first to photograph newly elected president Lincoln upon his arrival in Washington from Springfield.

By this time, a new photographic process was becoming popular. In decline was the daguerreotype, which captured a positive image on a silver-coated sheet of copper (*positive* denoting a one-off that could not be reproduced). The new standard, known as wet-plate collodion, required less expensive materials and generated a negative. A sitter could print multiple copies of a photograph to give to family members, or even a set of cartes de visite for handing out to business associates or sundry admirers. The process proved versatile, too, even making it possible to shoot three-dimensional images and then mass-produce them. A national fad was born, as photo aficionados began purchasing home stereoscopes, collecting 3-D prints, and treating their guests to glimpses of such wonders as Niagara Falls and the Great Pyramid.

With the opening shots at Sumter, the ever-enterprising Brady smelled opportunity. Warfare hadn't yet been adequately photographed, rich subject matter though it was. The Mexican War, fought during the very dawn of the medium, had produced some long-lost portraits of officers, ho-hum. More recently, Roger Fenton, an English photographer, had created a series of more than 350 images during the Crimean War. As a show of respect for the British military, however, the royal family had demanded that Fenton confine his work to undistressing fare—camp scenes and the like. The result was pretty tame, with one notable exception, the most famous photograph in the series, entitled "Valley of the Shadow of Death." It featured an array of spent cannonballs; no soldiers were even pictured. By merely offering this hint at the reality of warfare, Fenton managed to stir controversy, garnered international celebrity.

It got Brady's entrepreneurial wheels turning. No doubt, Fenton's work helped inspire his own ill-fated junket to Bull Run. But Brady's eyesight was growing increasingly poor, and capturing war images was a huge undertaking besides. So, he enlisted a team of photographers to travel with assorted sections of the Union army, engaged in various theaters.

For the past ten months, Gardner had accompanied McClellan and his men. He had even been designated official photographer of the Army of the Potomac, with the honorary rank of captain. Allan Pinkerton, the spy chief and fellow Scotsman, enlisted Gardner to take random pictures of Union campsites. By scrutinizing those images, it might be possible to pick out any Rebel agents who had infiltrated the Yankee ranks. Otherwise, Gardner's wartime output had not been exactly revelatory.

Then again, taking a photograph during a battle was impossible during this era. The equipment was unwieldy, the exposure time too long. Such limitations were precisely what had made special artists like Alfred Waud essential, as the only ones capable of capturing live action. Taking pictures after battles had also proved problematic for Gardner, at least while the Union remained mired in a losing streak. After all, one couldn't very well lug a camera onto a field held by an enemy.

With Antietam, all that changed. Gardner roamed the battlefield freely, parking his mobile darkroom (the What's-it Wagon) near the most compelling scenes. While he set up the camera on a tripod and focused the lens, James Gibson, acting as assistant, readied the glass plates that would become the negatives.

First, Gibson would pour on the collodion, a highly flammable mixture that included cotton soaked in nitric acid, along with alcohol and sulfuric ether. In the tight confines of the wagon, it required practiced wrist movements to spread it evenly over a glass plate. A speck of dirt or a wayward gnat could contaminate the collodion. The confines were dim-lit, too; speculation is that

Gardner fitted the wagon with little orange or red windows, creating an atmosphere similar to a modern darkroom.

As the ether and alcohol wicked off, the collodion began to grow tacky. At this point, Gibson would plunge the plate into a silver nitrate bath, rendering it light sensitive. The substance also turned his hands black. He would slide the plate into a light-tight case that looked kind of like a book.

Then he would run the case over to Gardner, who would slip it into his waiting camera. Removing the brass lens cap exposed the sensitized glass plate—typically for around ten seconds. Any movement at all and the image blurred; the exposure time was well suited to the dead. Then, back to the What's-it Wagon, where a developing agent was poured over the plate, drawing out those specks of silver, revealing the latent image. That was followed by water, lots of water (to arrest the process), a fixer (to freeze the image), then varnish (to protect it).

Gardner moved all over the field. He visited the battle's most notable sites, such as the Dunker Church, Bloody Lane, and Burnside Bridge. Along the way, he took a series of photographs, many of them stereographic, most of them featuring dead soldiers. Inside the What's-it Wagon, glass plates accumulated, a fragile record of warfare.

McClellan and Lee were separated by a river now, no mere creek. Days ticked by and the two generals didn't budge. Their armies were like a pair of heavyweight boxers who, following a bruising bout, retreat to their respective corners, dazed and broken. The Army of the Potomac, the Army of Northern Virginia: such proud fighting forces were now stilled. Both had been roughly handled, cruelly reduced.

The Union troops settled into camp in the hinterlands of Sharpsburg. Tents went up everywhere: crowded onto farm plots, gathered beneath apple trees, trailing up the hillsides, by churches, near the iron works, lining country lanes. The soldiers did their best to fall into a routine of roll call, drills, and guard duty. In off-hours, there were the usual diversions: chuck-a-luck and chess, jokes and stories. At least building a campfire was allowed once again. No enemy was present to notice or care.

The 51st Pennsylvania got their whiskey, along with a new stand of colors hand delivered by a citizens committee from Nor-ristown, Pennsylvania. The 35th Massachusetts was declared the filthiest regiment in its brigade, a distinction that seemed to fill its men with perverse pride.

For the first time since the battle, mail began to arrive. It brought welcome word from home. But there were many letters addressed to deceased comrades. Newspapers began to pour in, too, providing many soldiers with their first reliable accounts of Antietam. It was through news stories that battle mysteries were solved, rumors put to rest: *Yes, General Hooker had been carried from the field, but he wasn't dead. He'd merely been shot in the foot.* The Zouaves of the 9th New York were thrilled by an account of their heroics that appeared in a publication called *Wilkes' Spirit of the Times*. A tattered copy passed among the regiment as the men relived their glory.

The food was wretched. That was a given, but it also brought strange comfort. If anything smacked of normalcy, it was the vile rations. Some of the hardtack even came in boxes marked "York-town," a giveaway that the contents were left over from the Pen-insula Campaign. It inspired the men of the 16th Maine to make up a silly song to the tune of "The Battle Hymn of the Republic":
"Worms eat hearty in the commissary stores
While we go starving on."
But beneath the jokes, beneath it all, lay a great sorrow. A piece of common military wisdom holds that there's risk in keeping an army immobile for too long. The men are left with too much time to think, and it can wreak havoc on morale. This was not only a stationary army, but one that hadn't moved from the site of the last battle. The Federals held the field, leaving those fortunate enough

to still be alive surrounded by the dead. It served as a constant, painful reminder. In a diary entry, J. Franklin Dyer, a Union surgeon, lamented that "the atmosphere of the whole neighborhood is tainted."

The Rebels had the benefit, at least, of having vacated this mournful scene. A considerable portion of Lee's army set up camp on the outskirts of the town of Winchester, Virginia. Yet regret pursued these men even to their new quarters. They were the vanquished, after all. Since the beginning of August, they had been forever on the move, baked by the sun, pelted by rain, subsisting on green apples and the odd hunk of half-cooked dough, only to lose the big battle in Maryland. Where before they had been tattered but proud, they slipped into a state of decrepitude. The men developed an entire slang lexicon related to lice, calling them "tigers," "Zouaves," and "Confederates." To combat these vermin was known as "fighting under the black flag" or "flanking them out of position."

For the benefit of the good people of Winchester, some of Lee's men put on a parade. A "melancholy spectacle" is how resident Cornelia McDonald described the line of barefoot, haggard, hungry soldiers who shuffled past, adding: "I could not help thinking that in case of an onset by the Yankees, our defenders could be easily put to flight."

Winchester was only thirty miles from Sharpsburg. McClellan certainly commanded the larger, fresher army (all things being relative). Had he been less risk-averse, he might have hastened into Virginia in pursuit of the Rebels. Then again, the Union general believed he'd already achieved his mandate by chasing Lee from Northern territory. He'd even broken his telegraphic silence at last, crowing: "Our victory was complete. The enemy is driven back into Virginia. Maryland & Penna. are now safe."

Lincoln hadn't bothered to send a congratulatory telegram. In fact, he hadn't responded at all. "Not yet even have I a word from anyone in Washn about the battle of the Antietam," McClellan complained in a letter to Nelly.

It struck him as odd. Ordinarily, he found the president such an eager correspondent, asking questions, making demands, prying into military matters that were utterly beyond his grasp. What was with the sudden silence?

McClellan stewed.

Meanwhile, the death toll kept climbing. Along with the 3,650 soldiers killed on September 17, roughly 2,000 more would succumb to their wounds in the days, weeks, and months following the battle.

Charley King was just one among this frightful multitude. Early in the war, while still only a schoolboy, he had grown enthralled when the 49th Pennsylvania drilled near his home in the town of West Chester. He loved spending time among the soldiers. He begged his family to let him join up. A captain with the 49th suggested to his parents that enlisting as a drummer boy was a sensible option. Drummers are noncombatants, he assured them, and remain behind the lines, safe from harm. Although filled with worry, Mr. and Mrs. King allowed Charley to join the Union army.

At Antietam, amid the ceaseless barrage, one particular Rebel shell soared above the Union men, traveled well beyond the front lines, before raining shrapnel onto the 49th Pennsylvania. Several members of the regiment were hit, including drummer Charley, who was carried to the rear. Several days later, he died. Charley King was just thirteen, the youngest soldier killed in the Civil War.

George B. Anderson, the Confederate general struck in the ankle by a minie ball during the Bloody Lane fighting, set off on a medical circuit, Shepherdstown to Staunton, Virginia, to his home in Raleigh, North Carolina. There, the wound became infected, and a doctor amputated his foot. Anderson would die on October 17, one month after the battle. Union general Israel Richardson, also wounded at the Bloody Lane when a piece of shell lodged in his shoulder, would survive until November 3. With the deaths of Anderson and Richardson, the number of major generals killed by the battle rose to six, three from each side.

Just as family members traveled great distances to join injured soldiers in the hospitals, so too did they descend on the battlefield to recover the remains of dead loved ones. Often, they would arrive bearing letters instructing them on how to find the gravesite in question. Such letters might direct them to a section of the field where the soldier lay buried (near the Bloody Lane, say), or provide the name of a farm or landmark. Typically, the missives were written by comrades in the deceased soldier's regiment, perhaps hailing from the same hometown.

Henry Ainsworth and Roland Bowen were friends since childhood from the village of Millbury, Massachusetts. Both served together as privates with Company H of their state's 15th regiment. When Ainsworth was killed at Antietam, Bowen undertook the solemn duty of writing his friend's father about his son's burial location.

As it happened, the 15th Massachusetts had suffered so many losses in the West Woods massacre that individual burial proved difficult. Instead, many of the men were laid to rest in trenches, treatment usually reserved for the Rebels. "Mr. Ainsworth," wrote Private Bowen, "this is not the way we bury folks at home."

Bowen did his best to describe the location: "The trench in wich Henry is buried is situated near a log cabin just out side the garden fence. I believe its on the West side." There should be a board marked "15th Mass. buried here," he added helpfully.

The private also explained that there were forty soldiers crowded into the trench. "Henry is the 3rd corpes from the upper end on the top tier next to the woods," he wrote.

It appears that Bowen's instructions were sufficient and Mr. Ainsworth was able to bring Henry home for a proper burial in a Millbury cemetery. But this was not exactly a streamlined process.

Grief-racked relatives were frequently known to break down under the stress of attempting to find a deceased loved one, aided only by a confusing, albeit well-meaning, set of written directions.

This gave rise to a macabre business. For a fee, enterprising locals would conduct visiting relatives over the battlefield and help them locate gravesites. The body then had to be dug up. Before the soldier could be conveyed home, he had to be embalmed and placed in a coffin. Otherwise the railroads refused to provide transport.

Coffins cost around $5. Embalming was downright expensive, typically $25 for a private and $50 for an officer. It was a very new process, at least in its modern formulation (Egypt and other ancient cultures had long ago developed methods for preserving bodies). While Jonathan Letterman is father of battlefield medicine, Thomas Holmes is the father of embalming, thanks to work he did to advance the field during the 1850s. After Elmer Ellsworth was killed, Holmes embalmed the little colonel's body before that final train journey back to Mechanicville, New York.

Of course, Southerners generally didn't even have the option of claiming the bodies of their loved ones following Antietam. Not only were Rebels jumbled together in trenches, making identification near impossible, but the battlefield was enemy territory.

All this while, displaced residents were returning to Sharpsburg. The town was in shambles, as they were distressed to learn. Scarcely a house had escaped damage, pocked with bullet holes or slammed by shells, fallen bricks strewn all about. On entering their home on Main Street, the Smith family found two dead Rebels in the kitchen. One still clutched a handful of pilfered onions. Another resident discovered that a shell had exploded in front of his house, loosing a fragment that burrowed through several doors before entering his pantry. Awaiting him on a shelf sat a broken jar of honey and the offending hunk of iron. Aaron Fry found that a shell had traveled through one of his home's walls before entering a chest filled with bedding. Unfolding a sheet, he noted with bemusement that there was a neat hole in each individual square. The Lutheran Church (site of a Rebel wigwag station during the battle) was so badly damaged that it would soon have to be torn down.

The farmsteads in the surrounding countryside were devastated. Fences were toppled, crops trampled, sheds and other outbuildings knocked down, set afire, or riddled with shell. It would be years before the land returned to the kind of agricultural abundance that had existed before the battle.

Livestock had been slaughtered for food—or carelessly set free. Pantries had been stripped bare. "The only thing my wife and I had left was five hungry children," lamented Jacob Houser.

Sometimes the culprits were Rebels, but sometimes Yankees, depending on the location of the farm. This distinction mattered. When farmers began submitting claims to the US government, they were informed that only damages done by Federal troops would be covered. Anything caused by the Confederates—well, that had to be written off as a hazard of war. Farmer Otto submitted a claim for $2,350.60, and the Pry family assessed their property's damage at $2,459. It would require years to settle these claims, with both parties recovering only a fraction of the requested amount.

Adding to the insult, the farmers' fields had been turned into burial grounds. William Roulette counted seven hundred graves on his land, a number that left him fuming and mortified. Whereas many of the Union bodies on the farmsteads would be claimed, the Rebels remained. Eventually, those bodies would be dug up, too, and many would be reinterred at a Confederate cemetery established in Hagerstown, Maryland. Not one could be identified. Roughly 2,500 men who had died at Antietam and in the earlier battle at South Mountain were buried in a single mass grave.

Not long after the battle, a placard went up in Manhattan, 250 miles away. It appeared on a wall at 785 Broadway, just below East 10th Street. The placard was small, with dimensions that weren't much different from a photographic glass plate. Given the message, however, the sign needn't be large: "The Dead of Antietam."

It could whisper and still draw a crowd.

The Broadway amblers arrived in droves, climbing the stairway to Mathew Brady's second-floor gallery to view the exhibit. The atmosphere was electric. The visitors waited eagerly for their turn to lean over and peer into one of the stereoscopes. What greeted them was astonishing, like nothing they had ever seen on the pages of *Harper's*. Here were dead soldiers in full 3-D, rendered with stunning clarity.

There was something curiously casual about the scenes. A soldier's arm might be flopped across his chest, as if he were sleeping. Another might be lying on the ground with his trousers partially open. It seemed undignified, almost brazen. Homely little details abounded, seemed bent almost on hijacking the scenes: discarded shoes, cartridge boxes, the grass, its texture, and fencing, so much broken wooden fencing. Everything was suffused in a harsh noonday glare, short on shadow, making more fanciful interpretations futile.

These men were dead! Tearing one's eyes away proved impossible.

Reproductions of the stereographs featured in the sensational show soon went on sale. This spurred a brisk mail-order business among collectors across the Union states.

Oliver Wendell Holmes—physician, *Atlantic Monthly* columnist, eminent Bostonian—purchased a set. Not only was Holmes a photo enthusiast, but he had actually traveled to Sharpsburg, where he'd spent a panicked few days searching the hospitals for his son and namesake, shot through the neck in the West Woods. To his great relief, he managed to locate Captain O. W. Holmes Jr. of the 20th Massachusetts, found him alive and surprisingly well. (The bullet had missed his spine as well as critical blood vessels.) Upon receiving his order of stereographs, however, the emotions from that visit flooded back over the senior Holmes. The verisimilitude of the "terrible mementos" stunned him. "These wrecks of manhood thrown together in careless heaps or ranged in ghastly rows for burial were alive but yesterday," he marveled.

Wisely, Gardner took the step of copyrighting some of the most compelling images in his own name. He was quite aware of what he had captured. He knew its value. In fact, he would soon end his association with Brady and set out on his own as a photographer.

Then again, everyone appeared to recognize the importance of these images. By photographing the dead at Antietam, a cultural line had been crossed and there was no going back. The images were both sacred and profane. So, this is what war looks like. So, this then is what is happening on those faraway fields. And with that realization, came a question: If men are dying, shouldn't their sacrifice be in service of a worthy purpose, a truly glorious cause?

# CHAPTER 15

———

# BY PROCLAMATION

*On October 2,* Lincoln arrived at Antietam. The previous day, he had traveled by train from Washington, DC, to Harpers Ferry, now restored to Northern control. Never before had a US president visited a battlefield so soon after the fighting. First the unaccustomed silence between Lincoln and McClellan, and now—all of a sudden—the president had arrived in person. He wore a dark suit. Encircling his stovepipe hat was a strip of black crepe, an emblem of mourning for the son he'd lost this bitter year.

McClellan was eager to conduct Lincoln over the battleground, site of what the general had termed his "masterpiece of art." Naturally, he led the president to the Pry farmstead, the commanding spot from which he'd watched the action unfold. As always, McClellan had surrounded himself with numerous staff members. But Lincoln was accompanied by a retinue of his own, a traveling party of five, consisting of a Union general, munitions expert, railroad executive, and two old friends from Springfield.

The presence of this other general appears to have particularly unsettled McClellan. His name was John McClernand—a slurred version of McClellan, very nearly. Like McClellan, he was a Democrat and admirer of Stephen Douglas. Yet he'd seen action in the Union's Western Theater and hailed from Illinois, Lincoln's home state. What exactly did this mean?

Nevertheless, McClellan seized his moment. He narrated the battle action for the president, pointing out various landmarks in the distance, describing how events had unfolded. They must have made for an awkward pair: McClellan puffed up in his military finery, Lincoln towering over him. Gathered around the president and his commander were the respective entourages. One imagines the general launching into a carefully modulated soliloquy, designed to impress some key matters on Lincoln (the odds were prohibitive, the foe formidable, the victory decisive) while reflecting maximum glory back onto himself. Certainly McClellan would not have stinted on verbiage, spinning out the tale at his leisure, taking time to—

"—Let us go and see where Hooker went in," Lincoln interrupted.

McClellan was crestfallen. The president appeared fixated on still a different general, as if Hooker deserved the credit for the victory at Antietam.

The parties split up, planning to reconvene near Miller's farm. From there, they could retrace the Union's advance through the corn early on the morning of September 17. Because McClellan and his staff were on horseback, they set out across the fields and forded the Antietam. Lincoln was traveling in an ambulance wagon, so his party opted to take a different route. Apparently, he cut a somewhat comical figure, scrunched into the wagon bed, his knees nearly touching his chin as he bumped along the country lanes.

McClellan waited for Lincoln. But somehow the two parties became separated. Lincoln would end up touring Antietam without the general. As the president traveled over the battlefield, he passed a burial trench marked by a sign: "Here lies the bodies of sixty rebels. The wages of sin is death!" He also saw the charred remains of dead horses. There were so many dead horses: the sad fate of these heavy, bloated creatures was to be dragged by chains attached to living horses, arranged in piles, and set afire. This was a landscape bereft: all the more reason for the president to pay a visit (as some accounts hold that he did) to one of Antietam's most conspicuous survivors, the little Dunker Church, battered but standing.

Lincoln and McClellan were reunited the next day when they reviewed the troops together. Bands played, cannon boomed in salute, the men stood at rigid attention. Every effort was made to create a suitable military showing, yet there was no way to disguise the depleted ranks, tattered flags, and torn uniforms.

Lincoln brought a solemn dignity to the proceedings. This was duly noted by the soldiers, many of whom perceived a president afflicted by a heavy mood of his own. "Mr. Lincoln was manifestly touched at the worn appearance of our men, and he, himself, looked serious and careworn," Rufus Dawes of the 6th Wisconsin would write.

The soldiers of the 20th Maine combed their hair and brushed their uniforms. They polished their muskets with soapstone and emery paper. When their turn for review came, a thirty-four-year-old lieutenant colonel named Joshua Chamberlain was moved by how intensely Lincoln engaged with the men, yet wordlessly, relying on nothing more than his gaze. As Chamberlain would recall: "We could see the deep sadness in his face, and feel the burden on his heart . . ."

The 20th Maine had been held in reserve during the battle. But Chamberlain and his men would become hotly engaged during a future Northern incursion by Lee, and would emerge as great heroes. That, in turn, would result in another battlefield visit by the president, this one accompanied by a fabled address.

In the afternoon, Lincoln and McClellan visited Stephen Grove's farm on the outskirts of Sharpsburg. Although a resident of Union Maryland, Grove was also a slaveholder. Now that his farm had become a temporary hospital, fittingly, it tended to the wounded of both sides. Lincoln walked through the tent city that had sprung up on Grove's land. He wended his way among the straw pallets, shaking hands with the injured Union soldiers. But then the president announced that he would also be amenable to shaking the hands of wounded Confederates. He bore these men no ill will, he explained. Soon Rebels began to reach out and shyly grasped Lincoln's hand.

While riding in an ambulance wagon near the Grove farm, Lincoln requested that Ward Lamon, one of his traveling companions, sing him a song. Lamon, a one-time legal colleague of Lincoln's, now serving as the president's bodyguard, possessed an extensive repertoire, knew exactly what would suit the mood of his old friend. In a rich baritone, he broke into "Twenty Years Ago," a mournful ballad and Lincoln favorite:

> I visited the old churchyard,
> And took some flowers to strew
> Upon the graves of those we loved
> Some twenty years ago.

The ambulance wagon bumped along. Lincoln's knees drew up even nearer his chin. His face drooped with melancholy.

On October 4, the president boarded a special train at Frederick, Maryland, and returned to the capital.

Lincoln and McClellan emerged from the visit with very different notions about what had been accomplished. The president had now witnessed the army firsthand. The war-torn regiments that he'd reviewed left him heartsick. But he was also aware that McClellan had held many troops in reserve during the battle and that fresh Federal units were arriving in Western Maryland every day, replenishing the ranks. While encamped, a number of regiments that took a beating at Antietam had recovered sufficiently to be combat ready once again. Altogether, McClellan commanded a sizeable fighting force.

Lincoln wished his general to pursue Lee into Virginia at a time when the Rebels were camped nearby, yet in disarray, while the weather remained good, the roads passable. It was October. The time to move was now. An opportunity existed to score a decisive victory against a weakened Confederate army, perhaps even to win the war. Lincoln felt certain that he had communicated all of this to his general. "I went up to the field to try to get him to move, and came back thinking he would move at once," he would recall.

For his part, McClellan came away from the president's visit both shaken and cocksure—classic Little Mac. The presence of General McClernand had been disquieting. (McClellan referred to him as a "Western officer" in an anxious letter to Nelly.) The episode where Lincoln didn't show at the rendezvous point near Miller's farm was impossible to ignore.

Yet McClellan was pleased that he'd found other times during the visit to speak with the president one-on-one. He felt confident that he'd won Lincoln over to his point of view; namely, that the army required time to build strength, and that pursuing the Rebels into Virginia opened up new and needless risks. "I urged him to follow a conservative course," McClellan would recall, "and supposed from the tenor of his conversation that he would do so. He more than once assured me that he was fully satisfied with my whole course from the beginning; that the only fault he could possibly find was that I was perhaps too prone to be sure that everything was ready before acting, but that my actions were all right when I started."

So, it must have come as a surprise when on October 6 (just two days after the president's departure), the general received a telegram ordering him to cross the Potomac at once and give chase to the Rebels.

McClellan didn't move. He dragged and delayed per usual. Several days passed, and then came a debacle.

J. E. B. Stuart, Lee's cavalry commander, set out with a party of 1,800 horsemen and succeeded in riding completely around McClellan's supine army.

The maneuver was part reconnaissance mission, designed to get a read on the disposition of the Union forces in the aftermath of Antietam. Over three days, Stuart and his men made a 130-mile circuit, crossing the Potomac at a spot called McCoy's Ford, then riding through Western Maryland and north into Pennsylvania, along the way passing within a few miles of a sleepy little town called Gettysburg. Stuart's cavalry was the doughnut and McClellan's army, the hole in the middle.

The maneuver was also part raid. After all, Stuart was accompanied by 1,800 men—way more than the number required for mere reconnaissance—among them William Henry Fitzhugh Lee, known as "Rooney" Lee, a colonel with the 9th Virginia cavalry and second son of the Rebel commander. The men cut telegraph lines, destroyed railroad boxcars, and blew up an ammunition depot. They broke into warehouses and other storage facilities, making off with overcoats and underwear as well as five thousand muskets, pistols, and sabers. They stole 1,200 horses.

Perhaps most of all, Stuart's expedition was a kind of thumbed-nose insult. In Mercersburg, Pennsylvania, the men made a show of purchasing shoes and boots from local merchants, though with Confederate scrip. While in Chambersburg, Pennsylvania—a town they ransacked with special abandon—Stuart and his top lieutenants signed the register of the Franklin Hotel, even used their real names. The raiding party then rode back into Virginia via White's Ford, selecting a different Potomac crossing for the return journey, maintaining the element of surprise. McClellan's pursuit, such as it was, proved utterly ineffectual. Stuart didn't lose a single man.

Lincoln was furious. Whereas the president and his commander had lately fallen into a period of telegraphic silence, the wires now fairly vibrated as messages volleyed back and forth between Washington and Western Maryland. In the wake of the

J. E. B. Stuart humiliation, Lincoln demanded that McClellan mobilize at once. The general responded with a series of excuses and justifications: the army needed more soldiers, more supplies, more time. The fear that Braxton Bragg, commander of one of the Confederacy's western armies, might combine forces with Lee became a fixation for McClellan. Bragg was known to be about 400 miles away.

It seems that McClellan was prepared to settle his army into winter quarters and declare the '62 fighting season at an end. He relished the idea of planning his next move carefully and at leisure. In the spring, he envisioned a fresh attack on the Rebels, one as grand and daring as the Peninsula Campaign, but successful this time.

Lincoln would have none of it. On October 13, the president stayed up all night at the Soldiers' Home, discussing the McClellan problem with Vice President Hannibal Hamlin. That same day he had sent a long missive to his general. This was a letter, not a telegram; Lincoln had a lot to say, starting with an allusion to the pair's recent meeting at Antietam: "You remember my speaking to you of what I called your over-cautiousness? Are you not over-cautious when you assume that you can not do what the enemy is constantly doing? Should you not claim to be at least his equal in prowess, and act upon the claim?"

The president reminded McClellan that he was currently about as close to Richmond as Lee. Why not set off on a race toward the Confederate capital? If McClellan arrived first, it could spell ultimate victory. If Lee intercepted him, then that would become the occasion for a showdown against a weakened force. "[T]ry to beat him to Richmond on the inside track," Lincoln implored. "I say 'try'; if we never try, we shall never succeed."

By now, he knew his general well. He had poured on the vinegar, so he closed on a note of ego-soothing honey. "This letter is in no sense an order. Yours truly A. Lincoln."

McClellan got the message at last. On October 26, he mobilized his forces, although he did so armed with a fresh Pinkerton intelligence report indicating that his foe's strength had swelled to 130,000, drastically larger than its actual size. Crossing the Potomac took the men a full week, whereas Lee had done it in a single night. Once in Virginia, McClellan inched forward. "We moved with McClellan rapidity, slow but a little every day," Austin Stearns, a corporal with the 13th Massachusetts, wrote in his diary, adding: "at the rate we moved, the youngest amongst us would be grey before we could reach Richmond . . ."

October slid into November. The first snows were soon to fall upon McClellan and Lee's encampments, signaling the arrival of weather as unseasonable as on that warm day in September.

It was proving wise on Lincoln's part to have called for a hundred-day wait between the preliminary Emancipation Proclamation and the final decree. The glow of the recent victory at Antietam had little dimmed. Yet with the passage of time, resistance to the proclamation among certain Northerners was starting to soften. Of course, the South remained no closer to laying down arms and meeting the terms.

During the autumn of 1862, Lincoln had the opportunity to further refine his position. He decided he would unsweeten the deal, removing some of the incentives that had been offered in the initial version. Come the new year, he was determined to declare slaves in the states and regions still in rebellion instantly free— no gradual emancipation, no compensation. The South had had ample time to weigh the offer; now that dangled carrot was to be yanked away. Likewise, he opted to strike the reference to voluntary colonization, long a sore point for many African Americans.

At the same time, the president decided to include a critical new provision: black men would be invited to enlist in the army. It would serve as an acknowledgment of their abilities, and as a means of more closely connecting them to the Union cause. But make no mistake: this also represented a fattening of that stick

Lincoln intended to wield against the Confederacy. Offer slaves the opportunity to fight against their masters—indeed, to fight against the very institution of bondage—and they might be induced to flee northward to join the Federal forces. As he would later write: "The colored population is the great *available* and yet *unavailed* of, force for restoring the Union." (Roughly 180,000 African Americans would serve in the Union army during the Civil War, accounting for about 10 percent of its total strength.)

By the autumn of 1862, Lee had also made a fateful decision about emancipation, regarding his own slaves. He had concluded that he had no choice but to set them free. Despite the timing, this had absolutely nothing to do with Lincoln's pending proclamation. Instead, it stemmed from a court order related to the Arlington mansion, handed down earlier in the year. The order specified that regardless of the property's finances, Lee's slaves must be freed within the five-year timeframe specified in Custis's will. Lee would have been quite content to keep them in bondage indefinitely, but a Virginia state court ruled otherwise. (The decision was rendered by a Confederate judicial body rather than under authority of the Union, which occupied Arlington.)

Lee opted to hold onto his slaves until the turn of 1863 anyway, just beyond the five-year anniversary of Custis's death. Among those set free would be Perry Parks and Michael Meredith, the two slaves Lee appears to have brought with him to Antietam.

As for Arlington, it would soon become the site of a freedman's village. Within Washington's city limits, the areas set aside for runaway slaves, including Camp Barker, were becoming increasingly crowded. Arlington offered open land where the freed blacks could earn their own incomes, growing wheat and potatoes. Some of Lee's former slaves would settle in the village.

The burial ground at the Soldiers' Home (the Union's first national cemetery) had become overcrowded, too. Thus, along with playing host to a lively village, Arlington would also soon become a final resting place for the dead. Lee's property was located conveniently close to the District and offered ample acreage as well as a pastoral setting. Such attributes made it ideal for a new national cemetery. The choice was also meant as a taunt, and a solemn reminder. If the Confederate commander ever returned to Arlington, no respite could be found; his own yard would be filled with the buried bodies of Union soldiers.

Lee was soon to suffer many losses, but this one would slow burn over the years. Never again would he live in his beloved home.

On November 7, the assistant adjutant general of the War Department set out on a special train from Washington. The man was on an errand as serious as his official-sounding name: Catharinus P. Buckingham. He carried two sealed envelopes, along with explicit instructions straight from President Lincoln. Buckingham traveled by rail to as close as he could get to the Union encampments in Virginia. Then he switched to a horse and rode through a blinding snowstorm until he found Ambrose Burnside.

Buckingham handed the first of the envelopes to the general. It contained a letter offering Burnside command of the Army of the Potomac. As a replacement for McClellan, Lincoln had considered McClernand, he'd considered Hooker (he'd thought about so many generals), but Burnside had emerged as his choice.

Burnside did not greet the news with pleasure. In fact, he was visibly shaken. As a modest man who had once been close friends with McClellan, he was put in a real bind by the offer. Buckingham had firm instructions to make sure Burnside accepted the post before proceeding to step two in his assignment. If Burnside said no, Buckingham was supposed to return to Washington at once. Apparently, Burnside raised a series of vehement objections, recounting what he saw as his own deficiencies in experience, leadership ability, and confidence. But Buckingham told him that if he didn't accept, the post would go to Hooker, one of the few men Burnside disliked. He agreed to take the job.

Together, Buckingham and Burnside went to McClellan's headquarters. It was 11:00 P.M. Upon entering McClellan's tent, they found the general occupied, writing a letter to Nelly. Buckingham handed him the second envelope. As McClellan read the contents, he showed no expression whatsoever. Upon finishing, he said little. He simply bid the two men a terse goodnight.

Then, McClellan completed the letter to his wife, filling her in on the "interruption" that had just occurred. He wrote: "Of course I was much surprised—but as I read the order in the presence of Genl Buckingham, I am sure that not a muscle quivered nor was the slightest expression of feeling visible on my face, which he watched closely."

McClellan continued for a couple more paragraphs, jotting down his real-time impressions of the just-completed events.

"They shall not have that triumph," he wrote, proud that he'd concealed his emotions, thereby denying his enemies something to savor.

"They have made a great mistake," he asserted, certain that vindication awaited him.

"Do not be at all worried—I am not," he assured Nelly.

He closed on a note of defiance, delivered in regal first-person plural no less: "Our consolation must be that we have tried to do what was right—if we have failed it was not our fault."

Sacking McClellan when he did was a canny move on the part of the president. Lincoln had waited until the midterm elections were over. Otherwise, a Republican firing such a high-profile Democrat might have had serious political repercussions.

As it was, the president's party still took a beating in the midterms. The Republicans lost twenty-two seats in the House of Representatives. They also lost the governorships in New York and New Jersey, and gave up their majorities in the state legislatures of Indiana, Illinois, and New Jersey. However, even after losing those twenty-two seats, the Republicans still retained control of the House. What's more, they gained five seats in the Senate.

In American politics, then as now, the out party tends to take control of Congress during midterms, serving as a check on the in party. That this didn't happen in 1862 owes in large part to the victory at Antietam.

Lincoln had relied on McClellan, a man who was laissez-faire on slavery, for a crucial Union battlefield win, prompting the issuance of the preliminary proclamation, followed by McClellan reverting to his usual hesitancy in pursuing the enemy, but the president had remained patient, first reaping the political benefits during the midterms before firing the general whose victory had started the whole sequence in the first place. The ironies nest inside ironies like Chinese boxes. But there's also a simpler way to look at the matter: Lincoln had played it perfectly.

———

To bid adieu to his men, McClellan composed a farewell bulletin that circulated among the soldiers in camp. "In parting from you," he mooned, "I cannot express the love and gratitude I bear for you."

Love, always love: even at this late date, an extraordinary bond existed between the commander and his army. He arranged one last review—suitably grand. Soldiers formed a line that stretched for three miles. Tears streamed down faces as McClellan rode past on Daniel Webster, his handsome bay horse. Some men dropped their muskets and followed after the general. The Irish Brigade's standard bearers threw down their emerald flags, hindering his progress. But McClellan was resolute. He halted his horse and patiently waited for the men to gather up the flags.

The scene was repeated when McClellan boarded the train that would convey him away. Some troops uncoupled his railcar.

Yet again, he waited—a model of steadfastness. At last, the car was reconnected, and off chugged the train with McClellan standing on the rear platform, calling out "Good bye, lads."

The general was bound for Trenton, New Jersey, where he'd been ordered to go and await further orders. Trenton hadn't been the site of significant military action since 1776.

The general would wait and wait. There would be one final episode—this one the biggest Chinese box that encloses all the others—when McClellan emerged from exile in 1864 to run against Lincoln as the Democratic Party's candidate for president of the United States—and lost.

And now, at last: New Year's Day. Enter 1863, full of promise and peril. It had the advantage at least of being a fresh start, chronologically; it had the advantage at least of not being 1862.

The waning days of the previous year had not been good. Burnside's debut as an army commander was a nightmare; his deepest fears about his own shortcomings were confirmed over four bleak days in mid-December when his men suffered a crushing defeat at the Battle of Fredericksburg. Some worried that a fresh Union loss had dampened Lincoln's willingness to proceed with his emancipation plans. Only the day before, on New Year's Eve, a group of abolitionists had visited the White House, where they attempted to draw out Lincoln and discover his intentions. But the president remained tight-lipped on the subject. He was inscrutable. "Will Uncle Abe Lincoln stand firm and issue his promised proclamation on the first of January, 1863," asked George Templeton Strong in his diary, adding: "Nobody knows . . ."

At the White House, the Lincolns were holding a New Year's Day levee, a tradition dating back to Washington's presidency. This was the first major public event the family had hosted since Willie's death. The previous night, Lincoln hadn't slept a wink; so much was on his mind. The floorboards creaked as the president paced: all through New Year's Eve, back and forth; back and forth, all through the dawning hours of 1863. It was a Thursday, too, assuring that a note of grief would creep into the festivities.

The levee was held in the Blue Room. Guests began to arrive at 11:00 A.M., starting with various government officials, such as congressmen, Supreme Court justices, and members of the diplomatic corps. A small group of War of 1812 veterans, ancient now, wearing cockades in their hats, were here as honorees. Present, too, were several members of the cabinet, including Navy Secretary Gideon Welles, who had accompanied Lincoln on that carriage ride the previous summer when the president first shared his ideas about freeing the slaves.

At noon, the levee was thrown open to the public. By this time, a huge crowd had gathered on the White House lawn. Now they came flooding through the doors. Preserving order fell to a small detachment of Pennsylvania soldiers. These men may have concluded that battle was less demanding than crowd-control detail—perhaps safer, too. "The press was tremendous," according to one account, "and the jam most excessive; all persons, high or low, civil, uncivil, otherwise, were obliged to fall into an immense line of surging, crowding sovereigns . . ."

Lincoln stood on one side of the Blue Room, greeting the menfolk. Across the room stood Mary, greeting the ladies. She wore black mourning attire complete with a veil, such a contrast to the white satin dress with a long train from the party back in February. The Marine Band, which had provided the musical entertainment that evening, was playing once again, its banishment lifted. The musicians were striking up jaunty tunes. Mary appeared distracted. At one point, she was heard to say: "how much we have passed through since last we stood here."

Mary simply found the event too painful. Midway through, she slipped off. Lincoln remained. Conspicuous, unmistakable, standing a head taller than most in the surging, jockeying crowd, the president greeted and joked and shook hands. And shook hands. And shook hands.

Meanwhile, across the land, people gathered to await news of the proclamation. African Americans were in especial suspense. The very date (January 1) contributed to the anxiety. Among the enslaved, you see, New Year's Day had come to be known as "Heartbreak Day." It was a day when masters, reckoning with their finances, tended to make consequential decisions, such as selling slaves to distant plantations and breaking up families in the process.

In Washington, DC, more than three hundred former slaves crowded into a little schoolhouse at the corner of Twelfth and Q Streets. In Brooklyn, an all-day vigil was in progress at the Bridge Street African Methodist Episcopal Church. Even in the South, many slaves awaited those grapevine dispatches, passed person to person. The sense of optimism was palpable, but so too the worry: *Please don't let this be just another day of disappointment, another Heartbreak Day.*

At the Tremont Temple in Boston, a special Thursday service was under way, attended by a large crowd, both black and white. A relay system had even been put in place, featuring a series of messengers positioned between the nearest telegraph office and the church. The moment news went out over the wires, the people gathered here could expect to receive word. While the crowd waited, various speakers took to the pulpit, among them such abolitionist lights as Frederick Douglass, William Wells Brown, Anna Dickinson, and William Nell, a journalist and Boston postal clerk distinguished as the first black person to be employed in the federal civil service. The hours ticked by. "Every moment of waiting chilled our hopes, and strengthened our fears," Douglass would recall.

On this New Year's Day, too, at Camp Saxton near Port Royal in the South Carolina low country, a regiment of black soldiers waited. *Black soldiers*: this was as extraordinary as it sounds. African American military units weren't even supposed to exist, right? Yet here one was, the result of a unique set of circumstances.

As it happened, Port Royal had been under Union control as a military district for more than a year. During that time, it had become the site of a kind of experiment, where freed blacks worked the same plantations where once they had been enslaved. The War Department had even granted secret permission for a military regiment to be raised, composed of former slaves. It was called the 1st South Carolina Volunteers (later the 33rd United States Colored Infantry). The regiment's leader was a white man, Colonel Thomas Wentworth Higginson, a Cambridge, Massachusetts clergyman, abolitionist, and literary mentor to Emily Dickinson.

The 1st South Carolina was throwing a levee of its own. At Camp Saxton, a platform had been set up in a grove of live oaks. Residents of the surrounding area, both black and white, drifted by throughout the morning, joining a group of dignitaries down from the North. The crowd feasted on barbecued ox meat. They toasted Lincoln's health with molasses-sweetened water.

From the platform, the preliminary Emancipation Proclamation was read aloud. A ceremony followed, in which the 1st South Carolina was presented with a pair of silk flags donated by some New York Samaritans. The flags were received by the unit's standard bearers, Sergeant Prince Rivers and Corporal Robert Sutton. One was a regimental flag and the other, adorned with stars and stripes.

It was at this point that an elderly black man spontaneously broke into song, his voice creaking and hesitant at first. Two women blended with him, and together their voices lifted above the crowd. Soon others joined in:

My country, 'tis of thee,
Sweet land of liberty,
Of thee I sing!

It was a stirring moment, but wistful. That this experiment would go forward was not yet assured.

The White House levee ended around 3:00 P.M. An exhausted
Lincoln repaired to his second-floor office, where a finalized version of the Emancipation Proclamation awaited him, five pages,
carefully rendered by an official government calligrapher. The
president was accompanied by Secretary of State Seward, Seward's
son, and two other witnesses.

On Lincoln's desk lay a steel-tipped pen. It had been promised to abolitionist senator Charles Sumner, as a memento of this
historic occasion. The pen was rather worse for wear. Its wooden
stem was covered with little pocks and indentations, the result of
being gnawed on by Lincoln, a nervous habit.

The president dipped the pen in an inkwell. He paused. During
the levee, he must have shaken a thousand hands. His arm felt
stiff and numb. If his signature was shaky, he worried, it might
appear that he had wavered, might seem as if he had "some compunctions." That's how he put it. This document would be closely
scrutinized—of that he was certain.

Lincoln—the instrument of providence—had no compunctions. He had made up his mind. He put pen to paper. He signed
his name to the proclamation, bold and true. Then he looked up at
those gathered around his desk, and smiled a weary smile.

"That will do," said Old Abe.

# Further Explorations

Antietam battlefield is a national park—and national treasure—so scrupulously maintained that certain spots feel unchanged from September 17, 1862. Other important sites related to the battle can be found throughout the surrounding region in towns, such as Sharpsburg and Shepherdstown, even nearby Washington, DC. What follows is a brief guide, suggesting places to visit, and, in some cases, accompanying texts to read, so as to get a rich Antietam experience.

## Antietam National Battlefield

At the visitor center, start out by viewing the paintings of James Hope. As a captain with the 2nd Vermont, Hope was present for the battle and his heroic-scale canvases are a great way to get into an epic frame of mind.

Consider getting a battlefield tour from one of the highly knowledgeable Antietam guides. (Book an experienced guide through the visitor center; don't take your chances with a freelancer.) A guide can cover the entire battle in two or three hours.

On the battlefield, it's easy to find spots where modernity simply melts away. While standing in the Bloody Lane, my guide upped the suspense by reading aloud from a vivid and immediate account of the action: *Reminiscences of the Civil War* by John

Gordon of the 6th Alabama. I half expected blue-coated Federals to come pouring over the ridge in front of me.

Reading from a contemporaneous account is a great way to bring the battle action to life. Fortunately, many of the old books that I used in my research can be obtained easily (and free) through various online archives. Because the battle unfolded in distinct stages (Cornfield, West Woods, Bloody Lane, Burnside Bridge), you'll want to consult accounts by soldiers who took part in a particular piece of the action. For the Cornfield, consider Rufus Dawes's fine *Service with the Sixth Wisconsin Volunteers*. For the West Woods, I highly recommend the stirring letters of Private Roland Bowen, 15th Massachusetts, who lost a friend from his hometown during the fighting. See *From Ball's Bluff to Gettysburg . . . and Beyond*.

At the southernmost reaches of the battlefield, you'll encounter the most dramatic terrain. This is the site where the Burnside Bridge (circa 1836 and still standing) crosses Antietam Creek. Check out the stately Burnside Sycamore tree, present at the battle as a young sapling. Here, on either side of the Antietam, there are paths that can give you a taste for the daunting task that faced each side: for Union troops, crossing a creek, and for Confederates, defending against that crossing.

If you're feeling ambitious—or want some vigorous cardio—walk the Final Attack Trail. While merely carrying a reporter's notebook, I found this plenty challenging, and can scarcely imagine climbing this steep, three-quarter-mile hillside in chafing brogans, weighted down by gear, bearing a musket, and under withering fire all the way. Once again, contemporary accounts can enliven the experience. *The Hawkins Zouaves (Ninth N. Y. V.): Their Battles and Marches* by J. H. E. Whitney, provides the gripping tale of the 9th New York's slog up this final hillside. To get the opposing perspective (what it was like to be a Rebel awaiting the oncoming Federals) look to *John Dooley, Confederate Soldier: His War Journal*.

During your battlefield visit, you'll see a number of farmhouses. Some are still worked today by modern-era farmers. However, Pry

House is open to the public and notable as the site of Union commander George McClellan's field headquarters. Only feet from the house, you can visit the exact spot where Little Mac watched the action unfold, and enjoy a panoramic view of the battlefield.

Meanwhile, Robert E. Lee spent much of the morning on a promontory just outside Sharpsburg. Today, it's the site of Antietam National Cemetery, ironically a burial spot exclusively for the battle's Union dead. Captain Werner von Bachelle of the 6th Wisconsin is buried here, presumably sharing a grave with the faithful dog that died at his side. There's also a monument dedicated to four unknown soldiers from the Irish Brigade who were reinterred here after their remains were discovered on the field— in 1988!

Antietam is like a vast, outdoor museum, spread out over roughly 3,200 acres. If you find yourself drawn deeper into the subject, the battlefield rewards repeat visits. You can delve into a seemingly endless array of topics, following in the footsteps of Lincoln during his visit there, say, or even tracing the movements of a single regiment over the course of that fateful day.

If you happen to be a photography buff, William Frassanito's *Antietam: The Photographic Legacy of America's Bloodiest Day* is invaluable. Frassanito carefully reconstructs Alexander Gardner's progress over the field, identifying the precise spots where he captured his landmark images.

If you can carry a tune, Ward Hill Lamon's *Recollections of Abraham Lincoln* is the book for you. While visiting the battlefield, Lincoln's old friend Lamon sang his favorite song, the mournful "Twenty Years Ago." The lyrics appear on page 237. You can also find modern recordings of the song online.

## SHARPSBURG, MARYLAND

Little Sharpsburg was overwhelmed by the arrival of roughly 100,000 Union and Confederate soldiers. Today, more than 150 houses, churches, and other structures from the time of the battle are still standing, many of them marked with iron "Antietam 1862" plaques. The impact on the town is still very much in evidence. Check out the cannonball hole in the wall of the house at 109 West Main Street, home of Augustin Biggs in 1862. The Reformed Church (117 West Main Street) features a stained-glass window that's a gift from veterans of the 16th Connecticut, a regiment whose wounded received care in the church when it served as a temporary hospital following the battle.

Also still standing is the Kretzer House (128 East Main Street), where a number of townspeople hid in the basement while the battle raged. As Theresa Kretzer would recall: "We didn't have any breakfast—you bet we didn't—and no dinner was got that day, or supper—no, indeed! We had to live on fear." Her vibrant account, offering the rare perspective of a civilian caught up in the fighting, appears in Clifton Johnson's *Battleground Adventures: The Stories of Dwellers on the Scenes of Conflict in Some of the Most Notable Battles of the Civil War* (pages 118–124).

## FREDERICK, MARYLAND

For anyone interested in the vast emergency that followed Antietam, a must-visit is the National Museum of Civil War Medicine in Frederick (roughly a half-hour drive from the battlefield). On permanent display is an impressive collection of period surgical implements including amputation knives, bone files, bullet extractors, and fleams (for bleeding patients). An exhibit devoted to Jonathan Letterman, the Union medical director, includes a desk that he may have used at Antietam. The Clara Barton exhibit features her trunk bed, a suitcase that opened into a cot—perfect for this no-nonsense medical pioneer.

The museum serves as a thoughtful, carefully curated reminder that Antietam didn't end with its last shots. The battle resulted in more than 17,000 wounded Union and Confederate soldiers. An especially affecting exhibit is devoted to stories of the care received by specific soldiers. For example, Patrick Doyle of the 69th New York was shot in the right arm at Antietam and underwent a series of operations, culminating in an amputation near his shoulder. He was fortunate enough to survive, although he remained in the hospital until December 9, 1864. The actual bones from Doyle's lost arm are on display, something I found unsettling, though it also brought home the reality of the battle and its human toll.

A five-minute walk from the museum (at the intersection of S. Market and W. All Saints streets) is the place where on October 4, 1862, Lincoln boarded a train to return to the capital after his visit to Antietam. The train station is long gone, but a placard marks the spot and includes a portion of the impromptu speech the president delivered to the gathered Frederick townsfolk: "May our children and children's children, for a thousand generations, continue to enjoy these benefits conferred upon us by a united country ..."

## SHEPHERDSTOWN, WEST VIRGINIA

Fortunately, you can follow in the footsteps of Lee's retreating army and cross the Potomac without so much as getting wet. Simply walk or drive across the James Rumsey Bridge. Keep in mind that Boteler's Ford, the precise spot where this massive maneuver took place, is about 100 yards to the south of the bridge.

Once across, you'll be in Shepherdstown, located in modern-day West Virginia though it was part of Virginia circa 1862. Like Sharpsburg, little Shepherdstown was besieged by the battle and its aftermath. For a superb recounting, see "A Woman's Recollections of Antietam," by town resident Mary Bedinger Mitchell in *Battles and Leaders of the Civil War, volume 2.*

Not to be missed is the Elmwood Cemetery, a Confederate counterpart to the Union burial ground at Antietam battlefield. It contains the graves of 114 Rebels killed in the battle, about half of whom have headstones that include a name and regiment (the other half are marked "unknown soldier"). To view these moss-covered old stones; to barely decipher inscriptions such as Private Richard Watters, Co. A, 8th Georgia or N. L. Farnham, Co. D, 5th Florida; to realize that this tiny band of soldiers represents some of the only Confederate dead from Antietam whose names are preserved for posterity on headstones—it's heartrending.

In contrast, the Washington Cemetery in Hagerstown, Maryland, contains a patch of open ground, bounded by two small markers that identify the final resting place for roughly 2,500 Confederates killed at South Mountain and Antietam. Such a massive yet anonymous burial plot is poignant in its own way.

## Washington, DC

As Antietam got underway, Lincoln was fifty-five miles away at the Soldiers' Home. The president's neo-Gothic cottage with gingerbread trim still stands and is open to the public for visits and tours. At the time of the battle, it served as the First Family's country retreat, a place to get away from the hectic White House and stifling capital heat. Here, the president padded about in slippers, lounged on the broad breezy veranda, and sought relief from a recent personal tragedy, the death of his eleven-year-old son, Willie.

The cottage is also where Lincoln did considerable work on the Emancipation Proclamation. Sometimes he would write his thoughts on scraps of paper that he'd carry with him to the White House. Contact with African Americans—as employees and sometimes as friends, both at his cottage retreat and the White House—played an essential role in the creation of the document that Lincoln would call "the central act of my administration." This subject is covered in *They Knew Lincoln*, by John E. Washington, an important but long out-of-print book reissued in 2018 by Oxford University Press.

# NOTES

## AUTHOR'S NOTE

xi   **a quarter of Gould's regiment:** *The Civil War Journals of John Mead Gould, 1861–1865*, ed. William B. Jordan Jr. (Baltimore: Butternut and Blue, 1997), 197n.

xi   **Gould helped him from the field:** John Mead Gould, *Joseph K. F. Mansfield, Brigadier General of the U.S. Army* (Portland, ME: Stephen Berry, Printer, 1895), 16.

xi   **"how *mighty* easy":** Gould to Ezra Carman, April 7, 1877, box 1, folder 5, Ezra A. Carman Papers, NYPL.

xi   **remain in the army:** *Civil War Journals of John Mead Gould*, ii.

xi   **worked as a bank teller:** "The Biography of John Mead Gould," at http://www.johnmeadgould.com/jmgould.html.

xii   **"Confederates are the better correspondents":** "Fighting Them Over," *National Tribune*, August 25, 1892.

xii   **company of graying former Rebels:** Gould, *Mansfield*, 13.

xii   **"snap a little kodak":** *National Tribune*, August 25, 1892.

xii   **identified the precise spot:** Gould, *Mansfield*, 20–21.

xii   **"Those things make me":** Gould to Carman, March 24, 1877, box 1, folder 5, Carman Papers, NYPL.

xii   **house on Pearl Street:** "The Biography of John Mead Gould."

xiii   **more than 3,500:** Antietam Battlefield Board.

xiii   **"Jeff Davis will proclaim":** Charles Loring Brace to Frederick Law Olmsted, September 12, 1862, printed in *The Papers of Frederick Law Olmsted: Defending the Union*, vol. 4, ed. Jane Turner Censer (Baltimore: Johns Hopkins University Press, 1986), 415.

xiv   **"last card":** Francis B. Carpenter, *Six Months at the White House: The Story of a Picture* (New York: Hurd and Houghton, 1867), 21.

xv   **"radical views":** George McClellan to Abraham Lincoln, July 7, 1862, printed in *The Civil War Papers of George B. McClellan*, ed. Stephen W. Sears (New York: Ticknor & Fields, 1989), 345.

## CHAPTER 1. HELL COMES TO SHARPSBURG

1   **lit at nightfall by Confederate soldiers:** Ezra A. Carman, *The Maryland Campaign of September 1862*, vol. 2, ed. Thomas G. Clemens (Eldorado Hills, CA: Savas Beatie, 2012), 40.

1   **"you could make a hole":** Milton Laird, 5th Pennsylvania, quoted in *To Antietam Creek: The Maryland Campaign of September 1862*, by D. Scott Hartwig (Baltimore: Johns Hopkins University Press, 2012), 646.

2   **meal of dry coffee grounds:** David L. Thompson, "With Burnside at Antietam," *Battles and Leaders of the Civil War*, vol. 2, ed. Robert Underwood Johnson and Clarence Clough Buel (New York: Century Co., 1887), 660.

2   **smell of clover trampled underfoot:** Miles Clayton Huyette, *The Maryland Campaign and the Battle of Antietam* (Buffalo, NY: self-published, 1915), 28.

2   **"When was the fight to begin?":** Thomas L. Livermore, *Days and Events, 1860–1866* (Boston: Houghton Mifflin Company, 1920), 129.

2   **soldier tripped over a pet dog:** Thompson, "With Burnside at Antietam," 660.

3   **arrived from god-knows-where:** See Carman, *Maryland Campaign*, vol. 2, 43, which mentions that Mansfield's XII Corps remained on the move at 2:30 A.M.

3   **Rebel horses grew spooked:** Gen. G. Moxley Sorrel, *Recollections of a Confederate Staff Officer* (New York: Neale Publishing Company, 1905), 110.

3   **roughly 5:45 A.M.:** Sunrise at Sharpsburg, Maryland, on September 17, 1862, was at 5:43 A.M. according to R. L. Duncombe, director, Nautical Almanac Office of the United States Naval Observatory in Washington, DC. See James V. Murfin, *The Gleam of Bayonets: The Battle of Antietam and Robert E. Lee's Maryland Campaign* (Baton Rouge: Louisiana State University Press, 1965), 418.

4   **about 65 degrees:** Ibid., 212.

4   **"swift flowing water":** Ted Alexander, *The Battle of Antietam: The Bloodiest Day* (Charleston, SC: History Press, 2011), 59.

4   **maple, sycamore, and witch hazel:** Interview JM with Joe Calzarette, Antietam natural resources manager, August 10, 2016.

4   **Great Wagon Road:** *The Stone Houses of Antietam Walking Tour* (Sharpsburg, MD: Sharpsburg Historical Society, 2010), 1.

5   **six good springs and twenty-one wells:** John W. Schildt, *Drums Along the Antietam* (Parsons, WV: McClain Printing Company, 1972), 37–38.

5   **consisting of eight streets:** *Antietam National Battlefield Historic Resource Study: Sharpsburg and the Battle of Antietam* (National Parks Service, 2008).

5   **masons, millers, potters:** 1860 Census, for professions.

5   **hailing from England, Scotland, France:** Kathleen A. Ernst, *Too Afraid to Cry: Maryland Civilians in the Antietam Campaign* (Mechanicsburg, PA: Stackpole Books, 1999), 3.

5   **Irish workers had built a stretch:** Interview JM with Vernell Doyle, Sharpsburg Historical Society, April 27, 2016.

6   **Samuel Poffenberger:** Ernst, *Too Afraid to Cry*, 116.

6   **The Mumma family:** Keven M. Walker, *Antietam Farmsteads: A Guide to the Battlefield Landscape* (Sharpsburg, MD: Western Maryland Interpretive Association, 2010), 54, 58.

6   **An old couple:** Ernst, *Too Afraid to Cry*, 139.

6   **the Kretzer family:** Ibid., 136.

6    **about 55,000 men:** Troop numbers are notoriously hard to pin down. This snapshot of Federal soldiers on the field when the battle began based on the most authoritative source: Daniel J. Vermilya, *"Perceptions, not Realities . . .": The Army of the Potomac in the Maryland Campaign* (Sharpsburg, MD: Save Historic Antietam Foundation, 2012), 22. Note that JM rounded up from 54,000 (Vermilya's number) to "about 55,000," in consultation with Vermilya, March 4, 2018.

6    **additional 16,000 Federals:** Ibid.

6    **roughly 35,000:** This number is drawn from the most authoritative source on Confederate troop strength: Carman, *Maryland Campaign*, vol. 2, 598–599. Note that JM arrived at "roughly 35,000" by subtracting A. P. Hill's 2,568 men (still at Harpers Ferry when the battle began) from Carman's total of 37,351. Also note: At 5:45 A.M., Lafayette McLaws's division of roughly 3,000 men and Richard H. Anderson's 3,400 were crossing the Potomac at Boteler's Ford and hadn't yet arrived at the battlefield proper. See Ezra A. Carman and E. B. Cope, Antietam battlefield, day break map, *Atlas of the Battlefield of Antietam* (Washington, DC: Secretary of War, 1908), 1.

7    **just started using his middle initial:** Elizabeth Brown Pryor, *Reading the Man: A Portrait of Robert E. Lee Through His Letters* (New York: Viking, 2007), 300.

7    **at least three major battles:** Vermilya, *Perceptions, not Realities*, 9.

7    **The Confederate support apparatus:** Dr. Jay Luvaas and Col. Harold W. Nelson, eds., *The U.S. Army War College Guide to the Battle of Antietam* (New York: Harper & Row, 1988), 279.

7    **better-provisioned Federal army:** Ibid., 281.

8    **the Bucktails:** "'The Bucktails' Historical Marker," ExplorePAHistory.com, http://explorepahistory.com/hmarker.php?markerId=1-A-1EA.

9    **right eye of a Jeff Davis:** Robert V. Bruce, *Lincoln and the Tools of War* (Indianapolis: Bobbs-Merrill Company, 1956), 110.

9    **"My costume consisted":** Alexander Hunter, "Battle of Antietam," *Southern Historical Society Papers*, vol. 31 (Richmond: Southern Historical Society, 1903), 40.

9    **"We are a dirty, ragged set":** Private Theodore Fogel, 2nd Georgia, to mother and father, October 13, 1862, box 1, folder 11, Stuart A. Rose Manuscript, Archives & Rare Book Library, Emory University.

10   **flying a white silk flag:** Lieutenant-Colonel Benjamin F. Cook, *History of the Twelfth Massachusetts Volunteers* (Boston: Franklin Press, 1882), 21.

10   **"The post of danger":** James M. McPherson, *For Cause and Comrades: Why Men Fought in the Civil War* (New York: Oxford University Press, 1997), 84.

11   **Joseph Pierce:** "Joseph Pierce," Antietam on the Web, http://antietam.aotw.org /officers.php?officer_id=8900&from=results.

11   **three light-skinned African Americans:** Alexander, *Battle of Antietam*, 26.

11   **"free able-bodied white male":** "Laws of the United States, Published by Authority, Second Congress of the United States," *Columbian Centinel* (Boston), June 2, 1792.

11   **"found competent":** "The Militia Act of 1862," the Freedmen & Southern Society Project, http://www.freedmen.umd.edu/milact.htm.

11   **As many as eight women:** Maggie MacLean, "Women of Antietam," *Civil War Women*, posted October 29, 2014, https://www.civilwarwomenblog.com/women -of-antietam/.

12 **Muskets predominated:** Details about muskets drawn from multiple sources, including William Sagle, Antietam guide, tour with JM, April 27, 2016. Of course, there's no substitute for watching a musket being loaded and fired. Fortunately, there are many excellent videos available online featuring demonstrations using replicas of Civil War–era muskets and ammunition. See, for example: "Musket Drill and Cannon Firing" from the Gettysburg National Military Park Visitor Center available on YouTube.

13 **And then, there were the cannons:** Details about cannons drawn from multiple sources, including Curt Johnson and Richard C. Anderson Jr., *Artillery Hell: The Employment of Artillery at Antietam* (College Station, TX: Texas A&M University Press, 1995). For further information about Civil War cannon, watching a video online is worthwhile. "Civil War in Four Minutes: Artillery," produced by the Civil War Trust and featuring historian Gary Edelman is highly recommended.

13 **forty-five 6-pound cannons:** *Artillery at Antietam* booklet (Sharpsburg, MD: Western Maryland Interpretive Association, 2012).

14 **types of cannon shot:** Ibid.

14 **throats of side-by-side horses:** Alexander, *Battle of Antietam*, 59.

15 **piece of a soldier's skull:** Ibid.

15 **McClellan intended to use his army:** Drawn from multiple sources, including George McClellan, "Second Preliminary Report," October 15, 1862, Antietam on the Web, http://antietam.aotw.org/exhibit.php?exhibit_id=19.

15 **"ball had opened":** E. E. Stickley, "Wounded at Sharpsburg," *Confederate Veteran*, September 1917.

## Chapter 2. Stakes

16 **a dedicated early riser:** William H. Herndon and Jesse W. Weik, *Abraham Lincoln: The True Story of a Great Life*, vol. 2 (New York: D. Appleton and Company, 1909), 225.

16 **long-suffering insomniac:** drawn from multiple sources, including John E. Washington, *They Knew Lincoln* (New York: E.P. Dutton & Co., 1942), 110.

16 **nearly twenty-four hours earlier:** The most recent telegram that Lincoln would have received from General McClellan in the field was addressed to Henry Halleck, dateline Sharpsburg, 7:00 A.M., September 16. The telegram indicated uncertainty about when or whether a battle would take place. This telegram is printed in *The Civil War Papers of George B. McClellan: Selected Correspondence, 1860–65*, ed. Stephen W. Sears (New York: Ticknor & Fields, 1989), 465.

16 **at the Soldiers' Home:** Earl Schenck Miers, ed., *Lincoln Day by Day: A Chronology, 1809–1865*, vol. 3 (Washington, DC: Lincoln Sesquicentennial Commission, 1960), 140.

16 **an entire community:** Description of Soldiers' Home drawn from multiple sources, including Matthew Pinsker, *Lincoln's Sanctuary: Abraham Lincoln and the Soldiers' Home* (New York: Oxford University Press, 2003), and JM tour on December 2, 2016.

17 **"grievously altered":** Michael Burlingame, ed., *Lincoln Observed: Civil War Dispatches of Noah Brooks* (Baltimore: Johns Hopkins University Press, 1998), 13.

17 **"His hair is grizzled":** Ibid.

19 **"Bombardment of Fort Sumter!":** *Charleston Mercury*, April 13, 1861, http://teachingushistory.org/lessons/Bombardmentofsumter.htm.

19 **In St. Augustine:** Marcia Lane, "Oldest City Goes to War," *St. Augustine Record*, April 10, 2011.

19 **In Goldsboro, North Carolina:** James M. McPherson, *For Cause and Comrades: Why Men Fought in the Civil War* (New York: Oxford University Press, 1997), 17.

19 **in Richmond:** David Detzer, *Dissonance: The Turbulent Days Between Fort Sumter and Bull Run* (New York: Harcourt, 2002), 42.

19 **Blue Union neckties:** Ernest A. McKay, *The Civil War and New York City* (Syracuse, NY: Syracuse University Press, 1990), 58.

19 **Currier & Ives:** "The Civil War in Art," Art Institute of Chicago, http://www.civilwarinart.org/items/show/63.

19 **Trinity Church's spire:** George Templeton Strong, *Diary of the Civil War, 1860–1865* (New York: Macmillan, 1962), 124.

20 **"jubilant as if they":** Louise Wigfall Wright, "Memories of the Beginning and End of the Southern Confederacy," *McClure's Magazine*, September 1904.

20 **"a lady's thimble":** James A. McPherson, *Battle Cry of Freedom* (New York: Oxford University Press, 1988), 238.

20 **"so much bliss":** Mary Lincoln to Hannah Shearer, November 20, 1864, printed in *Mary Todd Lincoln: Her Life and Letters*, ed. Justin G. Turner and Linda Levitt Turner (New York: Knopf, 1972), 189.

21 **two young boys:** Biographical details about Willie and Tad Lincoln drawn from multiple sources, including Ruth Painter Randall, *Lincoln's Sons* (Boston: Little, Brown and Company, 1955).

21 **cleft lip and palate:** John M. Hutchinson, "What Was Tad Lincoln's Speech Problem?" *Journal of the Abraham Lincoln Association* (Winter 2009).

22 **"blinded to his children's faults":** William Herndon to Jesse W. Weik, February 18, 1887, printed in *Herndon on Lincoln: Letters, William H. Herndon*, ed. Douglas L. Wilson and Rodney O. Davis (Galesburg, IL: Knox College Lincoln Studies Center, 2016), 237.

22 **"raising a battalion":** Willie Lincoln to Henry Remann, September 30, 1861, quoted in Randall, *Lincoln's Sons*, 110.

23 **Elmer Ephraim Ellsworth:** Biographical details about Ellsworth drawn from multiple sources, including Ruth Painter Randall, *Colonel Elmer Ellsworth* (Boston: Little, Brown & Company, 1960).

25 **"long after the rebellion":** *New York Times*, May 25, 1861.

26 **Shiloh was such a battle:** Description of Shiloh drawn from multiple sources, including Winston Groom, "Why Shiloh Matters," *New York Times*, April 6, 2012.

28 **Son Willie caught a cold:** Description of Willie Lincoln's illness drawn from multiple sources, including Randall, *Lincoln's Sons*.

28 **efficacious remedies available:** Jean H. Baker, *Mary Todd Lincoln: A Biography* (New York: W. W. Norton & Co, 2008), 209.

28 **more than five hundred guests:** Description of the February 5, 1862, White House gala drawn from multiple sources, including Benjamin Perley Poore, *Perley's Reminiscences of Sixty Years in the National Metropolis*, vol. 1 (Philadelphia: Hubbard Brothers, Publishers, 1886).

28  **white satin dressed trimmed with black lace:** Elizabeth Keckley, *Behind the Scenes, or, Thirty Years a Slave, and Four Years in the White House* (New York: G. W. Carleton & Co., 1868), chap. 6.

29  **The Lincolns kept breaking away:** Poore, *Reminiscences*, 121.

29  **"I am in favor":** Ibid., 120.

29  **official business of the presidency:** Miers, *Lincoln Day by Day*, vol. 3, 94.

29  **Valentine's Day:** *Washington Star*, February 14, 1862.

29  **In a cavernous, formal bedchamber:** Description of the furnishings of Willie's room drawn from Daniel Mark Epstein, *The Lincolns: Portrait of a Marriage* (New York: Ballantine Books), 358.

30  **"my boy is gone":** Harold Holzer, *Father Abraham: Lincoln and His Sons* (Honesdale, PA: Calkins Creek, 2011), 128.

32  **"The present seems to be":** Robert E. Lee to Jefferson Davis, September 3, 1862, printed in *The Papers of Jefferson Davis*, vol. 8, ed. Lynda Lasswell Crist (Baton Rouge: Louisiana State University Press, 1995), 373.

32  **"coming elections":** Lee to Davis, September 8, 1862, printed in *The Wartime Papers of R. E. Lee*, ed. Clifford Dowdey and Louis H. Manarin (Boston: Da Capo Press, 1987), 301.

32  **so-called Copperheads:** Discussion of Copperheads drawn from multiple sources, including Jennifer Weber, *Copperheads: The Rise and Fall of Lincoln's Opponents in the North* (New York: Oxford University Press, 2006).

33  **included 150 enslaved blacks:** Kathleen A. Ernst, *Too Afraid to Cry: Maryland Civilians in the Antietam Campaign* (Mechanicsburg, PA: Stackpole Books, 1999), 12.

34  **Rebel flags might go up and stay up:** Although Lee's army received an unexpectedly cool reception en route to Sharpsburg, there was still plenty of pent-up sympathy for the Confederacy in Maryland, a deeply divided border state. A Rebel victory at Antietam might well have sparked an upsurge in such sentiment. In fact, three weeks after the battle, a pro-Confederate crowd in Emmitsburg, Maryland, welcomed J. E. B. Stuart and his cavalry raiders; see Emory M. Thomas, *Bold Dragoon: The Life of J. E. B. Stuart* (New York: Vintage Books, 1988), 176.

35  **"Demandez au government anglais":** James M. McPherson, *Crossroads of Freedom: Antietam* (New York: Oxford University Press, 2002), 58.

35  **"If this should happen":** Lord Palmerston to Lord Russell, September 14, 1862, printed in *The Life of Lord John Russell*, vol. 2, by Spencer Walpole (London: Longmans, Green, and Co., 1889), 349.

36  **Lee had his eye set on Harrisburg:** John G. Walker, "Harpers Ferry and Sharpsburg," *Century Illustrated Monthly* magazine, June 1886.

36  **"I believe it possible":** Louis M. Starr, *Bohemian Brigade: Civil War Newsmen in Action* (Madison: University of Wisconsin Press, 1987), 132.

## CHAPTER 3. THE CORNFIELD

39  **a little white schoolhouse:** Alpheus Williams to "My Dear Daughters," September 22, 1862, printed in *From the Cannon's Mouth: The Civil War Letters of General Alpheus S. Williams*, ed. Milo M. Quaife (Detroit: Wayne State University Press, 1959), 129.

39 **The stalks stood taller than a man:** Rufus Dawes to Ezra Carman, July 7, 1896, Ezra A. Carman Papers, National Archives.

39 **covering 30 acres and owned by David Miller:** Miles Clayton Huyette, *The Maryland Campaign and the Battle of Antietam* (Buffalo, NY: self-published, 1915), 34.

40 **1,100 strong:** Ezra A. Carman, *The Maryland Campaign of September 1862*, vol. 2, ed. Thomas G. Clemens (Eldorado Hills, CA: Savas Beatie, 2012), 58.

40 **"trembling fingers":** Alan D. Gaff and Maureen Gaff, "The Dread Reality of War," essay published in *Giants in Their Tall Black Hats: Essays on the Iron Brigade*, ed. Alan T. Nolan and Sharon Eggleston Vipond (Bloomington: Indiana University Press, 1998), 70.

40 **"quaked so they would scarcely":** Ibid.

40 **"queer choking sensation":** *An Irishman in the Iron Brigade: The Civil War Memoirs of James P. Sullivan, Sergt., Company K, 6th Wisconsin Volunteers*, ed. William J. K. Beaudot and Lance J. Herdegen (New York: Fordham University Press, 1993), 45.

40 **"it is terrible to march":** John Mead Gould, *History of the First-Tenth-Twenty-Ninth Maine Regiment* (Portland, ME: Stephen Berry, 1871), 236.

41 **file closers:** Details about file closers drawn largely from William Sagle, Antietam guide, "Cornfield tour" with JM, April 27, 2016.

41 **1,150 Georgia soldiers:** Carman, *Maryland Campaign*, vol. 2, 53.

42 **"The volley made them stagger":** *Under the Southern Cross: Soldier Life with Gordon Bradwell and the Army of Northern Virginia*, ed. Pharris Deloach Johnson (Macon, GA: Mercer University Press, 1999), 90.

42 **George Hartsuff:** Details about Brigadier General Hartsuff drawn from multiple sources including Col. Richard Coulter, *Official Report*, September 21, 1862, Antietam on the Web, http://antietam.aotw.org/exhibit.php?exhibit_id=378.

43 **Colonel William Christian:** Details about Christian drawn from multiple sources, including Jack Kunkel, *Showdown at Antietam: A Battlefield Tour of the Bloodiest Day in American History* (Middletown, DE: Pepper Publishing, 2013), 37.

43 **"forward, men, forward":** Paul Taylor, *Glory Was Not Their Companion: The Twenty-Sixth New York Volunteer Infantry in the Civil War* (Jefferson, NC: McFarland & Company, 2005), 85.

44 **Such reports ignore the chaos:** Duryee's men "broke in a disorderly mass toward the woods," wrote one observer, Bradwell, in *Under the Southern Cross*, 90.

44 **971 strong:** Carman, *Maryland Campaign*, vol. 2, 70.

45 **"A bullet passes into":** Rufus R. Dawes, *Service with the Sixth Wisconsin Volunteers* (Marietta, OH: E. R. Alderman & Sons, 1890), 88.

45 **"If all the stone":** Williams to "My Dear Daughters," September 22, 1862, *From the Cannon's Mouth*, 129.

46 **"a flock of birds":** Lieutenant Colonel W. W. Blackford, *War Years with Jeb Stuart* (New York: Charles Scribner's Sons, 1946), 151.

46 **Union choosing Elk Ridge:** J. Willard Brown, *The Signal Corps, U.S.A. in the War of the Rebellion* (Boston: U.S. Veteran Signal Corps Association, 1896), 331.

46 **Confederates setting up in the cupola:** *The Churches of Sharpsburg Walking Tour* (Sharpsburg, MD: Sharpsburg Historical Society, 2005), 2.

46 **using a simple code:** Details about which wigwag signal equals which alphabet letter from http://www.civilwarsignals.org.

48    **popularizing this folk hymn:** Florence Howe Hall, *The Story of the Battle Hymn of the Republic* (New York: Harper & Brothers, 1916), 59–60.

48    **Julia Ward Howe had heard soldiers:** Julia Ward Howe, *Reminiscences: 1819–1899* (Boston: Houghton, Mifflin and Company, 1900), 273–275.

48    **"the air seems full":** Lieutenant-Colonel Benjamin F. Cook, *History of the Twelfth Massachusetts Volunteers* (Boston: Twelfth [Webster] Regiment Association, 1882), 72.

48    **"wild beasts":** Carol Reardon and Tom Vossler, *A Field Guide to Antietam* (Chapel Hill: University of North Carolina Press, 2016), 76.

49    **lost 224 of 334 men:** Ted Alexander, *The Battle of Antietam: The Bloodiest Day* (Charleston, SC: History Press, 2011), 63.

49    **Tigers lost 60 percent:** Brigadier General Harry Hays, *Official Report*, 1862 (no month or day), Antietam on the Web, http://antietam.aotw.org/exhibit.php ?exhibit_id=180.

49    **"spin through the soft furrows":** Dawes, *Service with the Sixth Wisconsin*, 89.

49    **totaling 1,150 soldiers:** Carman, *Maryland Campaign*, vol. 2, 77.

50    **Captain Werner von Bachelle:** Biographical details about von Bachelle drawn from multiple sources, including Dawes, *Service with the Sixth Wisconsin*.

50    **Starke was also hit:** Alexander, *Antietam*, 66.

50    **50 percent more likely to be killed:** Dennis and Peter Gaffney, *The Civil War: Exploring History One Week at a Time* (New York: Hyperion Books, 2011), 326.

51    **2,300 soldiers:** George E. Otott, "Clash in the Cornfield: The 1st Texas Volunteer Infantry in the Maryland Campaign," *Civil War Regiments* 5, no. 3 (1997).

51    **"Caleenyuns":** Gould, *History of the First-Tenth-Twenty-Ninth Maine Regiment*, 252.

51    **men were making hoecakes:** Stephen W. Sears, *Landscape Turned Red: The Battle of Antietam* (Boston: Houghton Mifflin Company, 1983), 201.

52    **waging war in molasses:** Dawes, *Service with the Sixth Wisconsin*, 91.

52    **Texans were now 150 yards:** Susannah J. Ural, "Fighting 'Too Fast': The Texas Brigade Paid a High Price at Sharpsburg for Its Fighting Prowess," *Civil War Times* magazine, December 2017.

52    **9th, 11th, 12th, 7th, 4th, and 8th:** Otott, "Clash in the Cornfield."

53    **"the hottest place I ever saw":** "The Texans at Sharpsburg," *Confederate Veteran*, December 1914.

53    **45 had been killed, 141 wounded:** Otott, "Clash in the Cornfield."

53    **"The flags, the flags!":** Ibid.

53    **hand sewn by Charlotte Wigfall:** Carman, *Maryland Campaign*, vol. 2, 103.

54    **chunk of burning wood:** Kathleen A. Ernst, *Too Afraid to Cry: Maryland Civilians in the Antietam Campaign* (Mechanicsburg, PA: Stackpole Books, 1999), 131.

55    **"Genl Hooker wounded severely":** Sears, *Landscape Turned Red*, 215.

## CHAPTER 4. LITTLE MAC V. BOBBY LEE

56    **plump and luxurious armchair:** Charles Coffin, "Antietam Scenes," *Century Magazine*, June 1886.

57    **Greek Revival style:** Description of Pry House drawn from JM visit on June 9, 2017, and Keven Walker, *A Guide to the Antietam Farmsteads* (Sharpsburg, MD: Western Maryland Interpretive Association, 2010), 126.

57    **George Custer:** Kathleen Ernst, *Too Afraid to Cry: Maryland Civilians in the Antietam Campaign* (Mechanicsburg, PA: Stackpole Books, 1999), 121.

57    **field headquarters:** New research shows that the Pry house served as McClellan's field headquarters during the battle, while the headquarters for the Army of the Potomac was in nearby Keedysville, an important distinction. See Thomas G. Clemens, "In Search of McClellan's Headquarters," *Civil War Times*, June 2016.

57    **a number of McClellan's aides:** Peter S. Michie, *General McClellan* (New York: D. Appleton and Company, 1901), 7.

57    **Lee had awakened around 4:00 A.M.:** Time that Lee awakened on day of battle appears in multiple sources including James V. Murfin, *The Gleam of Bayonets: The Battle of Antietam and Robert E. Lee's Maryland Campaign* (Baton Rouge: Louisiana State University Press, 1965), 211.

58    **accident the general had recently suffered:** Douglas Freeman, *R. E. Lee*, vol. 2 (New York: Charles Scribner's Sons, 1934), 340.

58    **bounced along in an ambulance:** Charles Marshall to Ezra Carman, November 22, 1900, box 3, folder 1, Ezra A. Carman Papers, NYPL.

58    **required the help of an orderly:** Joseph L. Harsh, *Taken at the Flood: Robert E. Lee & Confederate Strategy in the Maryland Campaign of 1862* (Kent, OH: Kent State University Press, 1999), 377.

58    **At 5:30 A.M., Lee:** Ibid.

58    **general would monitor the battle:** Joseph L. Harsh, *Sounding the Shallows: A Confederate Companion for the Maryland Campaign of 1862* (Kent, OH: Kent State University Press, 2000), 200.

59    **claimed to stand five nine:** George B. McClellan, *McClellan's Own Story* (New York: Charles L. Webster & Company, 1887), 20.

59    **"I can do it all":** Carl Sandburg, *Abraham Lincoln: The War Years*, vol. 1 (New York: Harcourt, Brace & Company, 1939), 321.

59    **first to remove a diseased parotid:** W. Darrach, MD, *Memoir of George McClellan, M.D.* (Philadelphia: J. G. Auner, 1847), 22.

59    **eye lens extraction:** James F. Gayley, MD, *History of the Jefferson Medical College of Philadelphia* (Philadelphia: Joseph M. Wilson, 1858), 27.

59    **"obnoxious":** Ibid., 30.

59    **"impolitic":** Darrach, *Memoir of George McClellan*, 39.

60    **hailing from the lowlands of Galloway:** Michie, *General McClellan*, 2.

60    **"gallant and meritorious conduct":** Anonymous, *The Life, Campaigns, and Public Services of General McClellan* (Philadelphia: T. B. Peterson & Brothers, 1864), 20.

60    **source of the Red River:** Details About Red River Expedition drawn from Stephen W. Sears, *George B. McClellan: The Young Napoleon* (New York: Da Capo Press, 1999).

61    **earning $3,000 per year:** Ibid., 51.

62    **"!!Tuesday 22!!":** McClellan diary entry, May 22, 1860, reel 67, George Brinton McClellan Papers, Library of Congress.

62    **"some *very* blank verses":** William Starr Myers, *A Study in Personality: General George Brinton McClellan* (New York: D. Appleton-Century Company, 1934), 142.

62    **"A heart so pure":** McClellan to Mary Ellen Marcy, reel 5, extracts from 1859–60 letters, third letter, Library of Congress.

62    **"Glorious, isn't it!":** *New York Times*, July 20, 1861.

63    **put in eighteen-hour days:** Sears, *George McClellan*, 126.

64    the "slows": Montgomery Blair to George Curtis, January 21, 1880, printed in
      *McClellan's Last Service to the Republic*, by George Ticknor Curtis (New York: D.
      Appleton and Company, 1886), 96.
64    "idiot": George McClellan to Mary Ellen McClellan, August 16, 1861, printed
      in *The Civil War Papers of George B. McClellan*, ed. Stephen W. Sears (New York:
      Ticknor & Fields, 1989), 85.
64    "original gorrilla": George McClellan to Mary Ellen McClellan, November 17,
      1861, ibid., 135.
64    "Never mind; I will hold": Michael Burlingame, ed., *The Observations of John G.
      Nicolay and John Hay* (Carbondale, IL: Southern Illinois University Press, 2007),
      98.
64    "I beg to assure you": Abraham Lincoln to George McClellan, April 9, 1862,
      printed in *Collected Works of Abraham Lincoln*, vol. 5, ed. Roy Basler (Ann Arbor,
      MI: University of Michigan Digital Library Production Services, 2001), 185.
65    Everyone laughed: Benjamin Perley Poore, *Perley's Reminiscences of Sixty Years in
      the National Metropolis*, vol. 1 (Philadelphia: Hubbard Brothers, Publishers, 1886),
      120.
65    no shortage of candidates: William O. Stoddard, *Inside the White House in War
      Times* (New York: Charles L. Webster & Co., 1890), 26.
65    consider taking the field himself: James F. Simon, *Lincoln and Chief Justice
      Taney: Slavery, Secession, and the President's War Powers* (New York: Simon &
      Schuster, 2007), 211.
66    "Think On": Joseph Edmondson, *The Present Peerages: With Plates of Arms, and
      an Introduction to Heraldry* (London: J. Dodsely, 1785), 386.
66    he turned to Allan Pinkerton: Biographical details about Pinkerton drawn from
      multiple sources, including James Mackay, *Allan Pinkerton: The First Private Eye*
      (New York: John Wiley & Sons, 1996).
66    inflate the Rebel count by 5 percent: Sears, *George McClellan*, 109.
66    Magruder was an inventive: Details about Magruder drawn from multiple
      sources, including Thomas Settles, *John Bankhead Magruder: A Military Reap-
      praisal* (Baton Rouge: Louisiana State University Press, 2009).
68    "know that your General": Sears, *George McClellan*, 166.
68    "a perfect imbecile": Ibid., 103.
68    "the vilest man": George McClellan to Mary Ellen McClellan, May 18, 1862,
      printed in *The Civil War Papers of McClellan*, 269.
68    "a meddling, officious, incompetent": Sears, *George McClellan*, 131.
68    "every poor fellow": George McClellan to Mary Ellen McClellan, June 23, 1862,
      printed in *The Civil War Papers of McClellan*, 306.
68    reputedly, they were unusually flat: Douglas Freeman, *R. E. Lee*, vol. 1 (New
      York: Charles Scribner's Sons, 1934) 450.
68    "wonnut": William C. Davis, *Crucible of Command: Ulysses S. Grant and Robert E.
      Lee—The War They Fought, The Peace They Forged* (Boston: Da Capo Press, 2014), 145.
69    Lee had grown up in Alexandria: Details about Alexandria as Washington's
      hometown drawn from multiple sources, including Richard B. McCaslin, *Lee in
      the Shadow of Washington* (Baton Rouge: Louisiana State University Press, 2001).
69    Lee's father was Henry Lee III: Details about Henry Lee from multiple sources,
      including Freeman, *R. E. Lee*, vol. 1.
69    "first in war": Ibid., 9.

70   **trimming his hair a tiny bit every day:** Elizabeth Brown Pryor, *Reading the Man: A Portrait of Robert E. Lee Through His Letters* (New York: Viking, 2007), 198.

70   **bottle of whiskey:** Freeman, *R.E. Lee*, vol. 1, 302.

71   **"self-denial and self-control":** Paul C. Nagel, *The Lees of Virginia: Seven Generations of an American Family* (New York: Oxford University Press, 1990), 259.

71   **standard West Point cadet's room:** Freeman, *R. E. Lee*, vol. 1, 331.

71   **hide behind a log:** Ibid., 240.

71   **"It is well":** This quotation first appeared in John Esten Cooke, *A Life of Gen. Robert E. Lee* (New York: D. Appleton and Company, 1883), 184. Over time, the original has transformed into the now-familiar: "It is well that war is so terrible, otherwise we should grow too fond of it."

72   **"I John Brown":** Tony Horwitz, *Midnight Rising: John Brown and the Raid That Sparked the Civil War* (New York: Henry Holt, 2011), 256.

72   **Never mind that 300 men:** Freeman, *R.E. Lee*, vol. 1, 457.

72   **brigadier general for the Confederacy:** Ibid., 501.

72   **varying numbers of enslaved blacks:** Pryor, *Reading the Man*, 147.

73   **Custis's will provided for their disposition:** Ibid., 261.

73   **"I think it however":** R. E. Lee to Mary Custis Lee, December 27, 1856, appears in the Lee Family Digital Archive, https://leefamilyarchive.org/9-family-papers/339-robert-e-lee-to-mary-anna-randolph-custis-lee-1856-december-27.

73   **selling slaves to owners of distant plantations:** Pryor, *Reading the Man*, 145.

73   **biracial half sister named Maria Carter:** Arlington House exhibit, viewed by JM during tour on December 1, 2016.

73   **other such half siblings:** Letter from "A Citizen," *New-York Tribune*, June 24, 1859.

73   **"only child":** "Mr. Custis's Slaves," *Alexandria Gazette and Virginia Advertiser*, January 5, 1858.

73   **"painful discipline":** R. E. Lee to Mary Custis Lee, December 27, 1856, Lee Family Digital Archive.

74   **Wesley Norris:** While the controversial Lee-Norris whipping episode has long had its doubters, the supporting evidence is strong. Norris himself provided an account "Testimony of Wesley Norris," *National Anti-Slavery Standard*, April 14, 1866. Two other contemporaneous accounts, differing slightly in details, were also published: Letter from "A Citizen," and "Some Facts That Should Come to Light," both in the *New-York Tribune*, June 24, 1859. In *Reading the Man*, Pryor states that Norris's account "rings true," adding that "every detail of it can be verified," before providing a highly convincing point-by-point affirmation of the episode as recounted by Lee's slave (page 270).

74   **"the worst man I ever see":** Walter Creigh Preston, *Lee: West Point and Lexington* (Yellow Springs, OH: Antioch Press, 1934), 76.

74   **involved Lee's wife:** Details about Mary Lee and McClellan drawn from multiple sources, including Michael Korda, *Clouds of Glory: The Life and Legend of Robert E. Lee* (New York: HarperCollins, 2014), 316.

76   **"Here is a paper":** John Gibbon, *Personal Recollections of the Civil War* (New York: G. P. Putnam's Sons, 1928), 73.

76   **McClellan responded with uncharacteristic alacrity:** Typically, Antietam accounts assert that McClellan tarried for eighteen hours after he received Special Order 191, the famous Lost Order. Recent scholarship suggests otherwise. See

Gene Thorpe, "Defending McClellan: In Depth," *Washington Post*, September 8, 2012. While researching, JM also came across a letter that supports the notion that McClellan moved quickly upon receiving the order. "The results, the immediate movement of the army," wrote S. E. Pittman to Ezra A. Carman, June 2, 1886, box 2, folder 4, Ezra A. Carman Papers, NYPL.

## CHAPTER 5. GEORGIA BOYS AND GENERAL CHAOS

78  **numbered 12,500:** Ezra A. Carman, *The Maryland Campaign of September 1862*, vol. 2, ed. Thomas G. Clemens (Eldorado Hills, CA: Savas Beatie, 2012), 582. Carman's count was 12,693; JM rounded down to 12,500.

78  **treacherously steep:** Description of the terrain near the Burnside (née Rohrbach) Bridge drawn from multiple sources, including Martin Pritchett, Antietam guide, tour with JM, February 20, 2017.

78  **The goal was the Rohrbach Bridge:** Description of Rohrbach Ridge drawn from multiple sources, including Carman, *Maryland Campaign*, vol. 2, 404.

79  **fox grape, Virginia creeper:** Interview JM with Joe Calzarette, Antietam natural resources manager, August 10, 2016.

79  **formidable natural stronghold:** Stephen W. Sears, *Landscape Turned Red: The Battle of Antietam* (Boston: Houghton Mifflin Company, 1983), 260–261.

79  **climbed elms and sycamores:** Helen Ashe Hays, *The Antietam and Its Bridges* (New York: Knickerbocker Press, 1910), 88.

80  **Shortly after 8:00 A.M.:** How early on the morning of September 17, McClellan began sending attack orders to Burnside remains an issue of enduring historical debate. While McClellan maintained that he sent the first order at 8:00 A.M., Burnside would insist he didn't receive such an order until 10:00 A.M. Both generals had reason to stick to their stories. McClellan appears decisive if he issued his first attack order at 8:00 A.M., while Burnside is exonerated for the delays if the order didn't arrive until 10:00 A.M. The most authoritative account of the matter is Maurice D'Aoust, "Unraveling the Myths of the Burnside Bridge," *Civil War Times*, September 2007. D'Aoust convincingly argues that McClellan's first order reached Burnside "shortly after 8 A.M."

80  **Burnside was yet another general:** Biographical details about Burnside drawn from multiple sources, including William Marvel, *Burnside* (Chapel Hill: University of North Carolina Press, 1991).

81  **inspiration for the term *sideburns*:** "Ambrose Burnside," Biography.com, https://www.biography.com/people/ambrose-burnside-9232219.

81  **"Of all men I have known":** William Starr Myers, *A Study in Personality: General George Brinton McClellan* (New York: D. Appleton-Century Company, 1934), 153.

82  **personally supervised the placement of troops:** George B. McClellan, *McClellan's Own Story* (New York: Charles L. Webster & Company, 1887), 588–589.

82  **"the commanding general cannot":** Carman, *Maryland Campaign*, vol. 2, 399.

82  **"What is Burnside about?":** A Virginian [David Strother], "Personal Recollections of the War," *Harper's New Monthly Magazine*, February 1868.

82  **He dispatched another aide:** Between 8:00 and 9:00 A.M., McClellan dispatched another aide to check on Burnside; the man informed McClellan that little progress had been made. See D'Aoust, "Unraveling the Myths of the Burnside Bridge," *Civil War Times*, September 2007.

82    **Robert Toombs was a vigorous, hulking man:** Biographical details about Toombs drawn from multiple sources, including William Y. Thompson, *Robert Toombs of Georgia* (Baton Rouge: Louisiana State University Press, 1966).

83    **"Defend yourselves!":** Pleasant A. Stovall, *Robert Toombs: Statesman, Speaker, Soldier, Sage* (New York: Cassell Publishing Company, 1892), 174.

83    **Toombs's name was at the top of the list:** Ibid., 216.

83    **But he got stinking drunk:** Thompson, *Robert Toombs of Georgia*, 162. Alexander Stephens, vice president of the CSA, blamed "drinking to excess" for ruining the presidential chances of Toombs, his close friend and political ally.

83    **"swaggering braggarts and cunning poltroons":** William C. Davis, *The Union That Shaped the Confederacy: Robert Toombs & Alexander H. Stephens* (Lawrence: University Press of Kansas, 2001), 64.

84    **morning mail call:** Charles Walcott, *History of the Twenty-First Regiment Massachusetts Volunteers in the War for the Preservation of the Union, 1861–1865* (Boston: Houghton, Mifflin and Company, 1882), 198.

85    **Hill was one of Lee's most trusted generals:** Biographical details about A. P. Hill drawn from multiple sources, including William W. Hassler, *A. P. Hill: Lee's Forgotten General* (Chapel Hill: University of North Carolina Press, 1995).

85    **"Tell A. P. Hill he must come up":** Wilmer L. Jones, *Generals in Blue and Gray*, vol. 2: *Davis's Generals* (Westport, CT: Praeger Publishers, 2004), 273.

85    **contracted gonorrhea:** John G. Waugh, *The Class of 1846: From West Point to Appomattox: Stonewall Jackson, George McClellan and Their Brothers* (New York: Warner Books, 1994), 166.

85    **went on a whispering rampage:** Ibid., 169.

86    **"My God, Nelly":** Henry Kyd Douglas, *I Rode with Stonewall* (Chapel Hill: University of North Carolina Press, 1940), 178.

86    **There were roughly 450:** Troop numbers are notoriously difficult to pin down. According to Carman, *Maryland Campaign*, vol. 2, 404n, "400–500 seems a reasonable number for the bridge's defenders."

## Chapter 6. Instrument of Providence

87    **assigned a security detail:** Matthew Pinsker, *Lincoln's Sanctuary: Abraham Lincoln and the Soldiers' Home* (New York: Oxford University Press, 2003), 56.

87    **sprained his wrist:** Earl Schenck Miers, ed., *Lincoln Day by Day: A Chronology, 1809–1865*, vol. 3 (Washington, DC: Lincoln Sesquicentennial Commission, 1960), 139.

88    **spotted in the window:** Harold Holzer, "Abraham Lincoln's Refuge," *American History*, June 28, 2012.

88    **Lincoln followed pretty much the same route:** Commute route based on exhibit at President Lincoln's Cottage at the Soldiers' Home, viewed by JM during visit on December 2, 2016.

88    **5,000 Union soldiers:** Pinsker, *Lincoln's Sanctuary*, 32.

90    **"the power of making me miserable":** Stephen B. Oates, *With Malice Toward None: A Biography of Abraham Lincoln* (New York: Harper Perennial, 1994), 60.

90    **unusually integrated for a US city of its time:** Richard E. Hart, "Springfield's African Americans as a Part of the Lincoln Community," *Journal of the Abraham Lincoln Association* (Winter 1999).

90  **Lincoln befriended William de Fleurville:** Biographical details about Fleurville drawn from multiple sources including "William Fleurville," *History of Sangamon County, Illinois,* http://sangamoncountyhistory.org/wp/?p=2233.

91  **"This place was Lincoln's second home":** John E. Washington, *They Knew Lincoln* (New York: E .P. Dutton & Co., 1942), 190.

91  **On at least two occasions:** Allen C. Guelzo, *Lincoln's Emancipation Proclamation: The End of Slavery in America* (New York: Simon & Schuster, 2004), 24.

91  **representing a Kentuckian:** David Herbert Donald, *Lincoln* (New York: Simon & Schuster, 1995), 103.

92  **"You say A is white":** "On Slavery" a Lincoln note fragment believed to be dated July 1, 1854, printed in *Abraham Lincoln: Complete Works,* vol. 1, ed. John G. Nicolay and John Hay (New York: Century Co., 1894), 179.

94  **a private railcar:** Stephen W. Sears, *George B. McClellan: The Young Napoleon* (New York: Da Capo Press, 1999), 59.

94  **"strong Democrat of the Stephen A. Douglas School":** William Starr Myers, *A Study in Personality: General George Brinton McClellan* (New York: D. Appleton-Century Company, 1934), 118.

94  **a man named Songo:** Sears, *George B. McClellan,* 14.

94  **"Just think for one moment":** George McClellan to Mary Ellen McClellan, November 1861 (no day), printed in *McClellan's Own Story,* by George B. McClellan (New York: Charles L. Webster & Company, 1887), 175.

95  **"declaration of radical views":** George McClellan to Abraham Lincoln, July 7, 1862, printed in *The Civil War Papers of George B. McClellan,* ed. Stephen W. Sears (New York: Ticknor & Fields, 1989), 345.

95  **voluntary colonization:** Discussion of Lincoln's ideas about voluntary colonization drawn from multiple sources including Michael Vorenberg, "Abraham Lincoln and the Politics of Black Colonization," *Journal of the Abraham Lincoln Association* (Summer 1993).

96  **"Our minds are made up":** Frederick Douglass, *The North Star,* January 26, 1849, reprinted in *The Life and Writings of Frederick Douglass,* ed. Philip S. Foner (Chicago: Lawrence Hill Books, 1999), 126.

96  **gradual compensated emancipation:** Discussion of Lincoln's ideas about gradual compensated emancipation drawn from multiple sources, including Guelzo, *Lincoln's Emancipation Proclamation.*

97  **estimated at 1,800:** Eugene H. Berwanger, "Lincoln's Constitutional Dilemma: Emancipation and Black Suffrage," *Journal of the Abraham Lincoln Association* 5, no. 1 (1983).

97  **treasury $2 million per day:** Stephen W. Sears, *Landscape Turned Red: The Battle of Antietam* (Boston: Houghton Mifflin Company, 1983), 76.

97  **"Well, Mr. Sumner":** Ida M. Tarbell, *The Life of Abraham Lincoln: Drawn from the Original Sources and Containing Many Speeches, Letters, and Telegrams Hitherto Unpublished* (New York: Macmillan, 1928), 158.

98  **Camp Barker:** While some accounts claim Camp Barker was founded in 1863, it most certainly existed at the time of Antietam in 1862. (It can be difficult to pin down the inception date for something as transient as a Civil War era contraband camp.) Fortunately, the residents of Camp Barker produced a newspaper, *The Dragoon*—first issue dated March 5, 1862. For further support that the camp was

founded in 1862, see Ira Berlin et al., eds., *Freedom: The Wartime Genesis of Free Labor*, vol. 2, series 1 (Cambridge: Cambridge University Press, 1993), 31n.

98   **recently hired Mary Dines:** John E. Washington, *They Knew Lincoln* (New York: E. P. Dutton & Co., 1942), 83.

98   **standard toast and egg:** John Hay to William Herndon, September 5, 1866, printed in *Herndon's Informants: Letters, Interviews, and Statements About Abraham Lincoln*, ed. Douglas L. Wilson and Rodney O. Davis (Urbana: University of Illinois Press, 1998), 331.

98   **Lincoln picked up Vermont Avenue:** Commute route based on exhibit at President Lincoln's Cottage at the Soldiers' Home, viewed by JM during visit December 2, 2016.

98   **never felt at ease:** "Mr. Lincoln's White House," Gilder Lehrman Institute of American History, accessed online.

99   **spending $6,800 on fussy French wallpaper:** Jerrold M. Packard, *The Lincolns in the White House* (New York: St. Martin's Press, 2005), 54.

99   **$2,500:** Ibid., 53.

99   **The mansion had virtually no security:** *Lincoln Observed: Civil War Dispatches of Noah Brooks*, ed. Michael Burlingame (Baltimore: Johns Hopkins University Press, 1998), 80.

99   **They also took souvenirs:** Details of visitors' cutting keepsakes from the Lincoln White House rugs and curtains drawn from multiple sources including ibid., 82.

100  **lined up in front of Lincoln's office:** Harold Holzer, "Abraham Lincoln's White House," White House Historical Association, https://www.whitehousehistory.org/abraham-lincolns-white-house.

101  **She dressed exclusively in mourning now:** Pinsker, *Lincoln's Sanctuary*, 12.

101  **Mary had barred the two boys:** Harold Holzer, *Father Abraham: Lincoln and His Sons* (Honesdale, PA: Calkins Creek, 2011), 132.

101  **"I want to give Tad":** Ibid., 142.

101  **"Papa day":** Ferdinand Cowle Iglehart, "The Human Side of Lincoln," *Success* magazine, February 1905.

101  **"an instrument of providence":** Oates, *With Malice Toward None*, 293.

102  **Lincoln raised the topic repeatedly:** *Diary of Gideon Welles*, vol. 1 (Boston: Houghton Mifflin, 1911), 70.

103  **John Quincy Adams:** John T. Morse Jr., *John Quincy Adams: American Statesman* (Boston: Houghton, Mifflin and Company, 1882), 261.

103  **Lincoln had carefully studied Adams's arguments:** Guelzo, *Lincoln's Emancipation Proclamation*, 126.

104  **"our last shriek on the retreat":** Frederic Bancroft, *The Life of William H. Seward*, vol. 2 (New York: Harper & Brothers Publishers, 1900), 334.

104  **slipped a two-page handwritten draft:** William O. Stoddard, *Inside the White House in War Times* (New York: Charles L. Webster & Co., 1890), 167–168.

## CHAPTER 7. MERCY FOLLOWS A MASSACRE

105  **McClellan puffed on a cigar:** *A Virginia Yankee in the Civil War: The Diaries of David Hunter Strother*, ed. Cecil D. Eby Jr. (Chapel Hill: University of North Carolina Press, 1961), 110.

105  **one member of the staff was:** Ibid.

105  **passing within a half mile of McClellan's:** *History of the First Regiment Minnesota Volunteer Infantry, 1861–1864* (Stillwater, MN: Easton & Masterman, 1916), 198.

106  **column by the flank:** Marion V. Armstrong Jr., *Unfurl Those Colors!: McClellan, Sumner & the Second Army Corps in the Antietam Campaign* (Tuscaloosa: University of Alabama Press, 2008), 169.

106  **5,400 soldiers:** Ezra A. Carman, *The Maryland Campaign of September 1862*, vol. 2, ed. Thomas G. Clemens (Eldorado Hills, CA: Savas Beatie, 2012), app. 2, 576. Carman counted 5,437 infantry in Sedgwick's Division of II Corps.

106  **Edwin Vose Sumner:** Biographical details about Sumner drawn from multiple sources, including Marion V. Armstrong, *Disaster in the West Woods* (Sharpsburg, MD: Western Maryland Interpretive Association, 1996).

107  **open stretch of pasture:** Armstrong, *Unfurl Those Colors!,* 179.

107  **each nearly 500 yards wide:** Stephen W. Sears, *Landscape Turned Red: The Battle of Antietam* (Boston: Houghton Mifflin Company, 1983), 222.

107  **thirteen different Federal regiments:** D. Scott Hartwig, *To Antietam Creek: The Maryland Campaign of September 1862* (Baltimore, MD: Johns Hopkins University Press, 2012), 660.

107  **first state to offer soldiers:** *History of the First Regiment Minnesota,* 1.

107  **"treason":** Ibid., 2.

107  **collectively the Philadelphia Brigade:** Francis A. Walker, *History of the Second Army Corps in the Army of the Potomac* (New York: Charles Scribner's Sons, 1886), 102.

107  **Oliver Otis Howard:** Biographical details about Howard drawn from multiple sources including ibid.

108  **"our men and Secesh":** Corporal Edward A. Walker to George Knight, October 5, 1862, letter in 1st Minnesota regiment file, Antietam National Battlefield library.

108  **draw their first cannon fire:** Lieutenant Henry Ropes to father, September 20, 1862, from the *Letters of Lt. Henry Ropes, 20th Massachusetts* (Boston: manuscript, 1888), Boston Public Library, Rare Books and Manuscript Dept.

109  **a tricky piece of terrain:** James Buchanan, Antietam guide, tour with JM, May 23, 2017.

109  **The 34th New York got separated:** Carman, *Maryland Campaign*, vol. 2, 191.

109  **met with a barrage:** Ibid., 194.

110  **8,200 in total:** Ibid., 170n.

110  **managed to slip in behind:** Walker, *History of the Second Army Corps*, 106.

111  **"Back boys, for God's sake":** Joseph R. C. Ward, *History of the One Hundred and Sixth Regiment Pennsylvania Volunteers* (Philadelphia: F. McManus Jr. & Co., 1906), 104.

111  **the old general pantomimed:** Brigadier General Oliver O. Howard, *Official Report*, September 20, 1862, Antietam on the Web, http://antietam.aotw.org/exhibit .php?exhibit_id=53.

111  **"fool":** Stephen W. Sears, ed., *The Civil War Papers of George B. McClellan* (New York: Ticknor & Fields, 1989), 257.

112  **Some men simply lay down:** Armstrong, *Unfurl Those Colors!,* 187.

112  **Oliver Wendell Holmes Jr.:** Catherine Drinker Bowen, *Yankee from Olympus: Justice Holmes and His Family* (Boston: Little, Brown, 1944), 168.

113   **59th New York (frantic, confused:** Andrew E. Ford, *The Story of the Fifteenth Regiment Massachusetts Volunteer Infantry in the Civil War 1861–1864* (Clinton, MA: W. J. Coulter, 1898), 195–196.

113   **"prospects are bright":** Capt. Richard C. Derby, *The Young Captain* (Boston: Degen, Estes, & Co., 1865), 168.

113   **Captain Derby lay sprawled:** Ford, *Story of the Fifteenth Regiment Massachusetts*, 204.

113   **"No God Damned Southerner":** Roland E. Bowen to Friend Ainsworth, September 28, 1862, printed in *From Ball's Bluff to Gettysburg . . . and Beyond: The Civil War Letters of Private Roland E. Bowen, 15th Massachusetts Infantry 1861–1864*, ed. Gregory A. Coco (Gettysburg, PA: Thomas Publications, 1994), 135.

113   **McClellan suspected that something:** *A Virginia Yankee in the Civil War*, ed. Eby, 110.

114   **"Things look blue":** Sears, *Landscape Turned Red*, 230.

114   **2,200 men:** "Antietam Battlefield—West Woods," National Park Service, https://www.nps.gov/places/antietam-battlefield-west-woods.htm.

114   **lost 330:** While accounts of the 15th Massachusetts generally agree that the regiment lost more than 300 men during the battle, the numbers vary. Casualties of 330 is taken from the 15th Massachusetts monument at Antietam National Battlefield, JM visit on May 23, 2017.

115   **"Battle Oh horrid battle":** Jonathan Stowe, diary entry, September 17, 1862, printed in *Civil War Times Illustrated*, August 1972.

115   **at a rate of nearly one every second:** The battle can be conveniently broken into three four-hour time phases, with the first phase (5:45 A.M.–9:45 A.M.) as the most dangerous, producing 13,860 casualties or nearly one every second according to the Antietam Battlefield Board. Fewer soldiers were involved in the subsequent two phases of battle, and the casualty rate dropped accordingly.

115   **systems were in place:** National Museum of Civil War Medicine, Frederick, Maryland, JM visit on June 8, 2017.

115   **dressing station:** Details about dressing stations drawn largely from Gordon Dammann, Antietam guide, tour with JM, June 9, 2017.

117   **Edward Revere:** *Letters of Lt. Henry Ropes, 20th Massachusetts*, Boston Public Library, Rare Books and Manuscript Dept.

117   **farmhouse in the vicinity:** Tradition holds that Clara Barton was at the Joseph Poffenberger farm during the battle. However, various details in her account have led to the conclusion that she was likely at a different farm, perhaps Samuel Poffenberger's. See Maggie MacLean, "Poffenberger Farms of Antietam," July 4, 2015, *Civil War Women*, https://www.civilwarwomenblog.com/poffenberger-farms-of-antietam/. Such confusion is natural, given that four different Poffenbergers owned farms in close proximity to one another: Joseph, Samuel, Alfred, and John. Because of the uncertainty, JM has chosen to simply place Barton at a "farmhouse."

117   **Barton:** Biographical details about Barton drawn from multiple sources, including Elizabeth Brown Pryor, *Clara Barton: Professional Angel* (Philadelphia: University of Pennsylvania Press, 1987).

118   **minie ball from a soldier's cheek:** William E. Barton, *The Life of Clara Barton: Founder of the American Red Cross*, vol. 1 (Boston: Houghton Mifflin Company, 1922), 202.

118 **"I lisped these often difficult"**: Clara Barton, *The Story of My Childhood* (New York: Baker & Taylor Co., 1907), 21.

119 **"My little hands"**: Ibid., 82.

119 **Dolly remained in a rocking chair**: Donna Joly, Clara Barton Birthplace Museum, North Oxford, Massachusetts, interview with JM, February 21, 2018.

119 **"so bright, so scholarly"**: Clara Barton to Hiram Moffitt, August 3, 1879, printed in *Clara Barton and Dansville: Together with Supplementary Materials* (Dansville, NY: F. A. Owen Publishing Company, 1966), 110.

120 **$250 a year versus $600**: Pryor, *Clara Barton*, 52.

120 **Patent Office clerk, that paid $1,400**: Barton, *Life of Clara Barton*, 89.

120 **"folly and wickedness"**: Stephen B. Oates, *A Woman of Valor: Clara Barton and the Civil War* (New York: Free Press, 1994), 78.

120 **"my own army"**: Barton, *Life of Clara Barton*, 237.

121 **four days too late**: Brown, *Professional Angel*, 89.

121 **"Harper's Ferry, *not a moment*"**: Barton, *Life of Clara Barton*, 194.

121 **near the Rohrbach Bridge**: Oates, *A Woman of Valor*, 82.

121 **She awoke at 3:00 A.M.**: Ibid., 83.

121 **"Follow the cannon"**: Barton, *Life of Clara Barton*, 197.

121 **A bullet clipped her sleeve**: Ibid., 201.

122 **chose to never mend the bullet hole**: Ibid.

## CHAPTER 8. THE BLOODY LANE

123 **fully 10,000 soldiers**: Ezra A. Carman, *The Maryland Campaign of September 1862*, vol. 2, ed. Thomas G. Clemens (Eldorado Hills, CA: Savas Beatie, 2012), 297.

123 **unpaved and meandering country lane**: Description of sunken road drawn from multiple sources, including William Sagle, Antietam guide, tour with JM, October 11, 2016.

124 **(roughly 5,700 strong)**: Carman, *Maryland Campaign*, vol. 2, 297.

124 **"make a vigorous attack"**: Paper read on January 2, 1917, by retired Major General Samuel Sumner, printed in *Papers of the Military Historical Society of Massachusetts*, vol. 14 (Boston: Military Historical Society of Massachusetts, 1918), 11.

125 **"A man in Cincinnati"**: Daniel Harvey Hill, *Elements of Algebra* (Philadelphia: J. B. Lippincott & Co, 1857), 321.

125 *gratifying*: Robert K. Krick, "It Appeared as Though Mutual Extermination Would Put a Stop to the Awful Carnage," printed in *The Antietam Campaign*, ed. Gary W. Gallagher (Chapel Hill: University of North Carolina Press, 1999), 226.

125 **ready source of wheat, rye**: Details about Roulette farm drawn from multiple sources, including Keven M. Walker, *Antietam Farmsteads* (Sharpsburg, MD: Western Maryland Interpretive Association, 2010), 63.

126 **"The banners above them"**: General John B. Gordon, *Reminiscences of the Civil War* (New York: Charles Scribner's Sons, 1903), 85.

126 **combat unit was one day old**: Carman, *Maryland Campaign*, vol. 2, 244.

126 **ordered to fix bayonets**: Leo Hanham to Ezra Carman, "The Fifth Maryland Infantry at Antietam," undated, Ezra A. Carman Papers, National Archives.

126 **locked them into position**: Matt Borders, Antietam National Battlefield employee, bayonet demonstration with JM, October 11, 2016.

127 **"Aim low! Give 'em hell!":** John Mead Gould, *History of the First–Tenth–Twenty-Ninth Maine Regiment* (Portland: Stephen Berry, 1871), 239.

127 **one quarter of the first line:** Carman, *Maryland Campaign*, vol. 2, 249.

128 **"Give it to 'em! Drive 'em!":** Kathleen A. Ernst, *Too Afraid to Cry: Maryland Civilians in the Antietam Campaign* (Mechanicsburg, PA: Stackpole Books, 1999), 143.

129 **"Troops didn't know":** Samuel Fiske, September 18, 1862 letter, printed in Samuel Fiske, *Mr. Dunn Browne's Experiences in the Army* (Boston: Nichols and Noyes, 1866), 47.

129 **"I hugged the ploughed ground":** Edward W. Spangler, *My Little War Experience* (York, PA: York Daily Publishing Company, 1904), 34.

130 **stopped on a promontory:** Details of the close call for Lee and his fellow generals drawn largely from James Longstreet, "The Invasion of Maryland," *Battles and Leaders of the Civil War*, vol. 2, ed. Robert Underwood Johnson and Clarence Clough Buel (New York: Century Co., 1887), 671.

130 **first visited at age four:** Matthew Penrod, ranger, National Park Service, Arlington House tour with JM on December 1, 2016.

131 **almost like a museum:** Ibid.

131 **"been to me all a father Could":** Robert E. Lee to Martha Custis Williams Carter, January 2, 1854, Lee Family Digital Archive, https://leefamilyarchive.org/family-papers/letters/letters-1851-1860/9-family-papers/1174-robert-e-lee-to-martha-custis-williams-carter-1854-january-2.

131 **Six of Lee's seven children:** "Arlington House: The Robert E. Lee Memorial," National Park Service, https://www.nps.gov/arho/learn/historyculture/robert-lee.htm.

132 **pilfering a punchbowl:** Elizabeth Brown Pryor, *Reading the Man: A Portrait of Robert E. Lee Through His Letters* (New York: Viking, 2007), 306.

132 **cut down the old-growth trees:** Richard B. McCaslin, *Lee in the Shadow of Washington* (Baton Rouge: Louisiana State University Press, 2001), 83.

132 **Fragments of Society of Cincinnati china:** Penrod, Arlington House tour with JM on December 1, 2016.

132 **blanket that had covered Washington:** Pryor, *Reading the Man*, 307.

132 **"the enemy":** Douglas Freeman, *R. E. Lee*, vol. 1 (New York: Charles Scribner's Sons, 1934), 620.

132 **"Your old home":** Ibid., 619.

132 **McClellan had issued a secret order:** Murray H. Nelligan, *Arlington House: The Story of the Lee Mansion Historical Monument* (Burke, VA: Chatelaine Press, 2001), 416.

133 **"pretty boys":** Frederick L. Hitchcock, *War from the Inside: The Story of the 132nd Regiment Pennsylvania Volunteer Infantry in the War for the Suppression of the Rebellion* (Philadelphia: J. B. Lippincott Company, 1904), 65.

133 **"the rapid pouring of shot":** Ibid., 57.

133 **Rebel cannonball came skipping:** Stephen W. Sears, *Landscape Turned Red: The Battle of Antietam* (Boston: Houghton Mifflin Company, 1983), 239.

133 **Hiram Hummel, Jacob Long:** Names of 132nd Pennsylvania soldiers killed from Antietam on the Web, http://antietam.aotw.org/officers.php?officer_id=all.

134  **Another 114 were wounded:** Dead, wounded, and missing numbers from battle are taken from the 132nd Pennsylvania monument at Antietam National Battlefield, JM visit on October 11, 2016.

134  **survivors adopted a new tactic:** Discussion of change in tactics drawn from multiple sources including Hitchcock, *War from the Inside*, 59.

134  **particular success picking off Confederate officers:** Carman, *Maryland Campaign*, vol. 2, 262.

135  **every single officer in the 4th North Carolina:** Brigadier General D. H. Hill, *Official Report* (no month or day), 1862, Antietam on the Web, http://antietam.aotw .org/exhibit.php?exhibit_id=32.

135  **bullet also found George B. Anderson:** Krick, *Antietam Campaign*, 236.

135  **chain-of-command crisis:** Details drawn from multiple sources including Carman, *Maryland Campaign*, vol. 2, 262.

135  **dislodged both his eyeballs:** Krick, *Antietam Campaign*, 237.

135  **A 3,400-man Confederate division:** "Major General Richard Heron Anderson," Antietam on the Web, http://antietam.aotw.org/officers.php?officer_id=3&from =results.

136  **4,300 men:** Carman, *Maryland Campaign*, vol. 2, 297.

136  **In the vanguard:** Ezra A. Carman and E. B. Cope, Antietam battlefield, 10:30 A.M. map, *Atlas of the Battlefield of Antietam* (Washington, DC: Secretary of War, 1908), 9.

136  **Brigadier General Thomas Francis Meagher:** Biographical details about Thomas Meagher drawn from multiple sources, including Timothy Egan, *The Immortal Irishman: The Irish Revolutionary Who Became an American Hero* (Boston: Houghton Mifflin Harcourt, 2016).

137  **leading 1,100 men:** Carman, *Maryland Campaign*, vol. 2, 273n.

137  **"coldly, in a pinched":** Daniel M. Callaghan, *Thomas Francis Meagher and the Irish Brigade in the Civil War* (Jefferson, NC: McFarland & Company, 2006), 77.

137  **"Boys, raise the colors":** Capt. D. P. Conyngham, *The Irish Brigade and Its Campaigns* (New York: William McSorley & Co., 1867), 305.

138  **"that Fighting 69th":** 69th NYSV Historical Association, http://www.69thnysv. org/traditions-customs.htm.

138  **a chaplain on horseback:** Very Reverend W. Corby CSC, *Memoirs of Chaplain Life* (Chicago: La Monte, O'Donnell & Co., 1893), 112.

138  **"a big muscular woman":** Mike Pride and Mark Travis, *My Brave Boys: To War with Colonel Cross & the Fighting Fifth* (Lebanon, NH: University Press of New England, 2001), 134.

138  **sunken road at an angle:** William Sagle, Antietam guide, tour with JM, October 11, 2016.

138  **"Bring them colors":** Carman, *Maryland Campaign*, vol. 2, 271.

138  **The 29th Massachusetts joined the action:** Description of this regiment's charge drawn largely from William H. Osborne, *The History of the Twenty-Ninth Regiment of Massachusetts Volunteer Infantry* (Boston: Albert J. Wright, 1877).

139  **Roughly half of Meagher's men:** Brigadier General Thomas F. Meagher, *Official Report*, September 30, 1862, Antietam on the Web, http://antietam.aotw.org/ exhibit.php?exhibit_id=29.

139  **"They could do us little harm":** Charles A. Fuller, *Personal Recollections of the War of 1861* (Sherburne, NY: News Job Printing House, 1906), 59.

140  **300 prisoners:** Brigadier General John C. Caldwell, *Official Report*, September 24, 1862, Antietam on the Web, http://antietam.aotw.org/exhibit.php ?exhibit_id=273.

140  **James Lightfoot:** Details of Lightfoot's botched maneuver drawn from multiple sources including Carman, *Maryland Campaign*, vol. 2, 278.

140  **"It is the most beautiful":** *A Virginia Yankee in the Civil War: The Dairies of David Hunter Strother*. ed. Cecil D. Eby (Chapel Hill: University of North Carolina Press, 1961), 110.

140  **"the end of the Confederacy":** E. P. Alexander, *Military Memoirs of a Confederate: A Critical Narrative* (New York: Charles Scribner's Sons, 1907), 262.

141  **took up a musket himself:** Brigadier General D. H. Hill, *Official Report*, 1862, Antietam on the Web, http://antietam.aotw.org/exhibit.php?exhibit_id=32.

141  **manned a pair of abandoned cannons:** James Longstreet, *From Manassas to Appomattox* (Philadelphia: J. B. Lippincott Company, 1896), 250.

142  **knee raised stiffly:** Alexander Gardner, "Confederate Dead in Bloody Lane," stereo #553, September 19, 1862, Library of Congress.

## CHAPTER 9. DOWN TO RAISINS

143  **Lincoln had a regular habit:** Details about the president's routine of visiting the telegraph office drawn from multiple sources, including David Homer Bates, *Lincoln in the Telegraph Office* (New York: Century Co., 1907).

143  **"my persecutors":** "The War Effort: Telegraph Office," the Gilder Lehrman Institute of American History, http://www.mrlincolnswhitehouse.org/washington/the-war-effort/war-effort-telegraph-office/.

144  **White House hadn't been outfitted with a telegraph:** Tom Wheeler, *Mr. Lincoln's T-Mails: How Abraham Lincoln Used the Telegraph to Win the Civil War* (New York: Collins, 2006), 38.

144  **Washington's central telegraph office:** Tom Wheeler, "The First Wired President," *New York Times*, May 24, 2012.

144  **Arsenal, Navy Yard, and War Department:** Bates, *Lincoln in the Telegraph Office*, 35.

144  **1858 event:** Wheeler, *Mr. Lincoln's T-Mails*, 5.

144  **only president to hold a patent:** Jason Emerson, *Lincoln, the Inventor* (Carbondale, IL: Southern Illinois University Press, 2009), xi.

144  **"Discoveries and Inventions":** Wheeler, *Mr. Lincoln's T-Mails*, 7.

145  **During Bull Run:** Tom Wheeler, "In the Original Situation Room—Abraham Lincoln and the Telegraph," *Smithsonian Associates Civil War E-Mail Newsletter*, vol. 8, no. 8.

145  **"Well, boys, I am down to raisins":** Bates, *Lincoln in the Telegraph Office*, 41.

145  **"So," concluded Lincoln, "when I":** Ibid.

146  **among the first to make use of an encrypted:** William R. Plum, *The Military Telegraph During the Civil War in the United States* (Chicago: Jansen, McClurg & Company, Publishers, 1882), 44.

146  **"Mecca," "Nimrod":** Ibid., 45.

146  **three successive days, changing battle plans:** Wheeler, *Mr. Lincoln's T-Mails*, 5.

146  **Just such an incident:** Bates, *Lincoln in the Telegraph Office*, 94–95.

147  **"I will inform you":** George McClellan to Abraham Lincoln, September 8, 1862 telegram, printed in *The War of the Rebellion: A Compilation of the Official Records*

*of the Union and Confederate Armies, Part 2,* prepared by Lieutenant Colonel Robert N. Scott (Washington: Government Printing Office, 1887), 210.

147  **nothing of consequence:** The most recent telegram between General McClellan and Washington, DC, would be to Henry Halleck, dateline Sharpsburg, 7:00 A.M., September 16, reprinted in *The Civil War Papers of George B. McClellan: Selected Correspondence, 1860–65,* ed. Stephen W. Sears (New York: Ticknor & Fields, 1989), 465.

## CHAPTER 10. CAN 12,500 SOLDIERS TAKE ONE STONE BRIDGE?

149  **The Union opened with a fierce cannonade:** Ezra A. Carman, *The Maryland Campaign of September 1862,* vol. 2, ed. Thomas G. Clemens (Eldorado Hills, CA: Savas Beatie, 2012), 411.

149  **a diversionary tactic:** Scott D. Hann, "Take Care of the Men," *Save Historic Antietam Foundation Newsletter,* April 2008.

149  **artillery attack proved virtually impotent:** Discussion of why Federal artillery attack on Georgians was ineffective drawn from multiple sources, including Martin Pritchett, Antietam guide, tour with JM, February 20, 2017.

150  **weren't in one of the era's tight battle formations:** According to Carman, *Maryland Campaign of September 1862,* vol. 2, 411, the 11th Connecticut was in "skirmishing order" and even this loose formation would have been difficult to maintain given the terrain.

150  **Captain John Griswold:** W. A. Croffut and John M. Morris, *The Military and Civil History of Connecticut During the War of 1861–65* (New York: Ledyard Bill, 1868), 266.

150  **(he would die the next day):** The date of Griswold's death varies from account to account. His gravestone in the Griswold Cemetery in Old Lyme, Connecticut, dates his death to September 18, 1862.

150  **duty had fallen to the 28th Ohio:** Carman, *Maryland Campaign of September 1862,* vol. 2, 412.

151  **"The General wishes you":** *General George Crook: His Autobiography,* ed. Martin F. Schmitt (Norman: University of Oklahoma Press, 1946), 97.

151  **traveled in a complete circle:** Carman, *Maryland Campaign of September 1862,* vol. 2, 412.

151  **pinned behind a low sandy ridge:** Ibid.

151  **Colonel Henry Kingsbury:** Biographical details about Kingsbury drawn from multiple sources including "Antietam Panoramas: September Morning at Burnside Bridge," October 9, 2014, *John Banks' Civil War Blog,* http://john-banks.blog spot.com/2014/10/antietam-panoramas-september-morning-at.html.

152  **"delighted to listen to":** Croffut and Morris, *Military and Civil History of Connecticut During the War of 1861–65,* 278.

152  **a bullet struck him in the foot:** Accounting of where the four bullets struck Colonel Kingsbury drawn from ibid., 266–267.

152  **Isaac Peace Rodman:** Biographical details about Rodman drawn from multiple sources, including Robert E. Gough, *South Kingstown's Own: A Biographical Sketch of Isaac Peace Rodman, Brigadier General* (Bozeman, MT: self-published, 2011).

152    **leading 3,200 men:** Carman, *Maryland Campaign of September 1862*, vol. 2, 426.

153    **lugging naval howitzers:** Details about Rodman's men struggling with these heavy guns from Martin Pritchett, Antietam guide, tour with JM, February 21, 2017, and John Cannan, *Burnside's Bridge* (Conshohocken, PA: Combined Publishing, 2001), 77.

153    **1,650-yard front:** John M. Priest, *Antietam: The Soldiers' Battle* (Shippensburg, PA: White Mane Publishing Company, 1989), 218.

154    **totaling 300 men:** Carman, *Maryland Campaign of September 1862*, vol. 2, 415.

154    **sturdy chestnut fence:** Details about the fence and how it blocked the soldiers' progress drawn from Captain Lyman Jackman, *History of the Sixth New Hampshire Regiment in the War for the Union* (Concord, NH: Republican Press Association, 1891), 104.

154    **"peculiar-keyed voice":** Dr. Theodore Dimon, September 17–18 diary entry, printed in "A Federal Surgeon at Sharpsburg," ed. James I. Robinson Jr., *Civil War History* (June 1960).

155    **"McClellan appears to think":** Delos Sackett to George McClellan, February 20, 1876, printed in *McClellan's Own Story* (New York: Charles L. Webster & Co, 1887), 609.

155    **pair of knolls divided by a shallow cleft:** Description of this landscape feature based on Antietam tour, Martin Pritchett with JM, February 20, 2017.

155    **670 soldiers:** Carman, *Maryland Campaign of September 1862*, vol. 2, 417.

156    ***The Art of Dancing*:** Edward Ferrero, *The Art of Dancing* (New York: Dick & Fitzgerald, 1859). Such dances as Cheet and Virginia Reel appear on pages ix–xi.

156    **hard living off of it:** Examples of the 51st Pennsylvania's wild behavior drawn from Thomas H. Parker, *History of the 51st Regiment of P.V. and V.V.* (Philadelphia: King & Baird, Printers, 1869), 22.

156    **"Will you give us our whiskey?":** Ibid., 232.

156    **streamed downhill in two long lines:** Carman, *Maryland Campaign of September 1862*, vol. 2, 417.

156    **the soldiers veered off:** Ibid., 417–419.

157    **Rebel fire began to slow:** Ibid., 419.

157    **"military curiosities":** Carol Reardon and Tom Vossler, *A Field Guide to Antietam* (Chapel Hill: University of North Carolina Press, 2016), 229–230.

158    **A Rebel marksman:** Priest, *Antietam: The Soldiers' Battle*, 243.

158    **the crossing required twelve minutes:** Parker, *History of the 51st Regiment of P.V. and V.V.*, 235.

158    **It was roughly 1:00 P.M.:** A Virginian (David Strother), "Personal Recollections of the War," *Harper's New Monthly Magazine*, February 1868.

158    **attached pieces of newspaper:** Ibid.

158    **"hold the bridge":** *From New Bern to Fredericksburg: Captain James Wren's Diary*, ed. John M. Priest (Shippensburg, PA: White Mane Publishing Company, 1990), 91.

158    **among their number George Whitman:** George Whitman to his mother, September 21, 1862, printed in *Civil War Letters of George Washington Whitman*, ed. Jerome M. Loving (Durham, NC: Duke University Press, 1975), 67.

159    **Those unwieldy naval howitzers:** Carman, *Maryland Campaign of September 1862*, vol. 2, 426.

159   **slip into a curious lull:** Numerous accounts refer to the extended break in the battle action, often using the word *lull*; see A Virginian, "Personal Recollections of the War."

159   **temperature climbed to 75:** James V. Murfin, *The Gleam of Bayonets: The Battle of Antietam and Robert E. Lee's Maryland Campaign, September 1862* (Baton Rouge: Louisiana University Press, 1965), 212.

160   **skewering farmers' chickens:** Several examples of this found, including Edward W. Spangler, *My Little War Experience* (York, PA: York Daily Publishing Company, 1904), 38.

160   **portable chess sets:** William C. Davis and Russ A. Pritchard, *Fighting Men of the Civil War* (Norman: University of Oklahoma Press, 1998), 137. Also note: minie balls carved into chess pieces would later be found on Antietam battlefield, suggesting that the game was played there.

160   **chuck-a-luck:** Kathleen A. Ernst, *Too Afraid to Cry: Maryland Civilians in the Antietam Campaign* (Mechanicsburg, PA: Stackpole Books, 1999), 142.

160   **brag, a card game:** Rodney P. Carlisle, *Encyclopedia of Play in Today's Society*, vol. 1 (Thousand Oaks, CA: Sage Publications, 2009), 98.

160   **"The whirring of shells":** *History of the Thirty-Fifth Regiment Massachusetts Volunteers, 1862–1865* (Boston: Mills, Knight & Co., 1884), 44.

160   **broke out their tobacco:** National Museum of Civil War Medicine, Frederick, Maryland, JM visit on June 8, 2017.

160   **The 51st Pennsylvania, basking:** Parker, *History of the 51st Regiment of P.V. and V.V.*, 235.

160   **a pig and her litter:** Edward Oliver Lord, *History of the Ninth Regiment New Hampshire Volunteers in the War of the Rebellion* (Concord, NH: Republican Press Association, 1895), 129.

161   **flag of the 1st Texas:** Details of episode involving captured flag and prisoner drawn from F. B. Chilton, *Unveiling and Dedication of Monument to Hood's Texas Brigade* (Houston, TX: Rein & Sons Company, 1911), 108.

161   **McClellan conferred with two:** Details about the meeting between McClellan, Sumner, and Franklin drawn from multiple sources, including Stephen W. Sears, *Landscape Turned Red: The Battle of Antietam* (Boston: Houghton Mifflin Company, 1983), 272, which places the episode at 2:00 P.M.

162   **"great defeat" and "We are in the midst":** George McClellan telegram to Henry W. Halleck, September 17, 1862, 1:25 P.M., printed in *The Civil War Papers of George B. McClellan: Selected Correspondence 1860–1865*, ed. Stephen W. Sears (New York: Ticknor & Fields, 1989), 467.

162   **"I am well":** George McClellan telegram to "Mrs. McClellan," September 17, 1862, 1:45 P.M., printed in ibid., 468.

163   **"General are you going":** Captain Robert E. Lee (son), *Recollections and Letters of General Robert E. Lee* (New York: Doubleday, Page & Company, 1905), 78.

163   **Stonewall Jackson:** Episode involving Jackson gathering troops for a counterattack placed at 2:00 P.M. in Carman, *Maryland Campaign of September 1862*, vol. 2, 332.

163   **"Who-e-e! There are oceans":** Walter Clark, ed., *Histories of the Several Regiments and Battalions from North Carolina in the Great War 1861–'65*, vol. 5 (Goldsboro, NC: Nash Brothers, 1901), 78.

163   **"[W]hat a ghastly spectacle"**: Charles Coffin, "Antietam Scenes," *Century* magazine, June 1886.

164   **commandeer a horse**: Emmet Crozier, *Yankee Reporters, 1861–65* (New York: Oxford University Press, 1956), 266.

164   **"Who are you?"**: Louis M. Starr, *Bohemian Brigade: Civil War Newsmen in Action* (Madison: University of Wisconsin Press, 1987), 141.

164   **begun the war with eight hundred papers**: Discussion of the state of Southern press drawn largely from J. Cutler Andrews, *The South Reports the Civil War* (Princeton, NJ: Princeton University Press, 1970).

165   **finest correspondents were present**: Ibid., 50.

165   **"special artists"**: Details about special artists drawn from multiple sources, including Harry Katz, "Civil War Battlefield Art," *National Geographic* magazine, May 2012.

165   **"I jumped aside"**: Frank H. Schell, "Sketching Under Fire at Antietam," *McClure's* magazine, February, 1904.

165   **An entire team**: Meg Groeling, "Drawing the War, Part 1: Alfred Waud," *Emerging Civil War*, March 12, 2012, https://emergingcivilwar.com/2012/03/12/drawing-the-war-part-1-alfred-waud/.

166   **near Keedysville**: The location of Gardner's mobile darkroom during the battle is informed speculation. Gardner was the official photographer of the Army of the Potomac, and it would have made sense for him to keep his wagon with the Federal supply train, which extended into Keedysville.

166   **Brady himself had tried**: Brady claimed that his Bull Run images were destroyed when his wagon overturned. As an inveterate self-promoter, however, surely he would have recognized the value of salvaging even a fragment of a glass-plate negative—an invaluable record of the battle. More likely, Brady got caught up in the chaos following Bull Run and failed to capture any images, as is convincingly argued in William A. Frassanito, *Antietam: The Photographic Legacy of America's Bloodiest Day* (Gettysburg, PA: Thomas Publications, 1978), 30–32.

167   **Roughly seventy-five frightened people**: Clifton Johnson, *Battleground Adventures: The Stories of Dwellers on the Scenes of Conflict in Some of the Most Notable Battles of the Civil War* (Cambridge, MA: Riverside Press, 1915), 120.

167   **"like sardines in a box"**: Ibid., 121.

167   **Thaddeus Sobieski Constantine Lowe**: Biographical details about Lowe drawn from multiple sources, including Gail Jarrow, *Lincoln's Flying Spies: Thaddeus Low and the Civil War Balloon Corps* (Honesdale, PA: Calkins Creek, 2010).

168   **an erotic dream**: T. J. Stiles, *Custer's Trials: A Life on the Frontier of a New America* (New York: Alfred A. Knopf, 2015), 63.

168   **balloons to this battle**: Detail that Lowe was supposed to be at Antietam drawn from *Memoirs of Thaddeus S.C. Lowe, Chief of the Aeronautic Corps of the Army of the United States During the Civil War*, ed. Michael Jaeger and Carol Lauritzen (Lewiston, NY: Edwin Mellen Press, 2004), 147–148.

168   **paying $12.62**: Earl Schenck Miers, ed., *Lincoln Day by Day: A Chronology, 1809–1865*, vol. 3 (Washington, DC: Lincoln Sesquicentennial Commission, 1960), 140.

168   **girl falling into the river**: *New London (CT) Weekly Chronicle*, September 18, 1862.

168   **The steamer *Ida May***: *Louisville Daily Democrat*, September 18, 1862.

168   **horse show in Rockville, Connecticut**: *Hartford Daily Courant*, September 18, 1862.

168    **horticultural exhibition in Boston:** *Boston Herald*, September 18, 1862.

168    **Several "fancy drunks":** *Indianapolis Daily State Sentinel*, September 18, 1862.

168    **200 pounds of bologna sausage:** *Charleston Mercury*, September 16, 1862.

168    **harassed by late-season mosquitoes:** *Wilmington* (NC) *Journal*, September 18, 1862.

168    **a stray red and white heifer:** *Staunton (VA) Spectator*, December 2, 1862.

169    **Young Sarah Dawson:** September 17, 1862 diary entry, Sarah Morgan Dawson, *A Confederate Girl's Diary* (Boston: Houghton Mifflin, 1913), 228.

169    **14th Indiana, lay dying:** Richard Skidmore, ed., *The Alford Brothers: "We All Must Dye Sooner or Later"* (Hanover, IN: Nugget Publishers, 1995), 303, 328, 334.

169    **"Dearest Mother":** Wilder Dwight to mother, September 17, 1862, *Life and Letters of Wilder Dwight*, ed. Eliza Dwight (Boston: Ticknor and Fields, 1868), 293–294.

## Chapter 11. A Lurid Sunset

170    **It was 3:00 P.M.:** Maurice D'Aoust, "Unraveling the Myths of the Burnside Bridge," *Civil War Times*, September 2007.

170    **"the most terrible battle":** George McClellan telegram to Henry W. Halleck, September 17, 1862, 1:25 P.M., printed in *The Civil War Papers of George B. McClellan: Selected Correspondence 1860–1865*, ed. Stephen W. Sears (New York: Ticknor & Fields, 1989), 467.

170    **twenty-nine regiments:** Ezra A. Carman, *The Maryland Campaign of September 1862*, vol. 2, ed. Thomas G. Clemens (Eldorado Hills, CA: Savas Beatie, 2012), 579–580.

171    **3,000 Confederates:** Ibid., 437.

171    **forty malevolent cannons:** Ibid., 435.

172    **79th New York:** Details about the Highlanders drawn from multiple sources, including Tony Mandara, "Thank God Lincoln had only one 79th Highlander Regiment," *Crossfire*, December 2001.

172    **out-and-out mutiny:** William Todd, *The Seventy-Ninth Highlanders New York Volunteers in the War of Rebellion* (Albany, NY: Press of Brandow, Barton & Co, 1886), 61–63.

172    **"Thank God Lincoln":** Mandara, *Crossfire*, December 2001.

172    **under a hellish cannonade:** Colonel Benjamin C. Christ, *Official Report*, September 21, 1862, Antietam on the Web, http://antietam.aotw.org/exhibit.php?exhibit_id=306.

173    **navigate the grounds of a farm:** Details about the Sherrick farm drawn from Keven M. Walker, *A Guide to the Antietam Farmsteads* (Sharpsburg. MD: Western Maryland Interpretive Association, 2010), 92, and JM visit to house on February 21, 2017.

173    **Presently, two Union batteries:** Carman, *Maryland Campaign of September 1862*, vol. 2, 435.

174    **9th was a quirky collection:** Details about the 9th New York regiment, a.k.a. the Red Caps, drawn from multiple sources, including Lieutenant Matthew J. Graham, *The Ninth Regiment New York Volunteers (Hawkins' Zouaves)* (New York: self-published, 1900).

174    **The regiment's very first injury:** J. H. E. Whitney, *The Hawkins Zouaves: Their Battles and Marches* (New York: self-published, 1866), 14.

175 **"I noticed one of them":** Charles F. Johnson, *The Long Roll: One of the Hawkins Zouaves* (East Aurora, NY: Roycrofters, 1911), 192.

175 **A bullet clipped a Red Cap:** David L. Thompson, "With Burnside at Antietam," *Battles and Leaders of the Civil War*, vol. 2, ed. Robert Underwood Johnson and Clarence Clough Buel (New York: Century Company, 1887), 662.

175 **fatal hair parting:** Ibid., 661.

175 **"[We] lost men":** Graham, *The Ninth Regiment New York Volunteers*, 294.

175 **filled the gaps by crawling:** Thompson, "With Burnside at Antietam," 661.

176 **gristmill owned by Solomon Lumm:** Walker, *A Guide to the Antietam Farmsteads*, 93.

176 **sunken road transporting grain:** Martin Pritchett, Antietam guide, tour with JM, February 21, 2017.

176 **8th Connecticut, rapidly pulling ahead:** W. A. Croffut and John M. Morris, *The Military and Civil History of Connecticut During the War of 1861–65* (New York: Ledyard Bill, 1868), 270.

176 **even raised $40:** Ibid., 124.

176 **16th Connecticut, was unusually inexperienced:** Carman, *Maryland Campaign of September 1862*, vol. 2, 466.

177 **heavy fire from a pair of Confederate brigades:** Stephen W. Sears, *Landscape Turned Red: The Battle of Antietam* (Boston: Houghton Mifflin Company, 1983), 283.

177 **Some gunners introduced a devious twist:** Thompson, "With Burnside at Antietam," 661.

177 **"Zoo! Zoo! Zoo!":** Whitney, *Hawkins Zouaves*, 144.

178 **tore his head from his body:** Graham, *Ninth Regiment New York Volunteers*, 318.

178 **"the lower portion of his jaw":** Whitney, *Hawkins Zouaves*, 145.

178 **picking off the 9th New York's color guard:** Graham, *Ninth Regiment New York Volunteers*, 296.

178 **"scene of the wildest confusion":** Whitney, *Hawkins Zouaves*, 147.

179 **resorted to those gruesome bayonets:** In diaries and letters from soldiers involved in this portion of the battle, JM could find no references to bayonet use. That's not surprising. Bayonets were so gory, using them on fellow humans so taboo, that soldiers could be expected to leave such details out of their personal accounts. All that can reasonably be stated is that "perhaps" soldiers "resorted" to using them in this instance.

179 **"Oh, how I ran!":** *John Dooley Confederate Soldier: His War Journal*, ed. Joseph T. Durkin (Washington, DC: Georgetown University Press, 1945), 46.

179 **45th Pennsylvania, crested the hilltop:** Several other Federal regiments claimed to reach the plateau on which Sharpsburg sat, including the 45th Pennsylvania; see Carol Reardon and Tom Vossler, *A Field Guide to Antietam* (Chapel Hill: University of North Carolina Press, 2016), 241.

179 **"I thought it was the prettiest":** Clifton Johnson, *Battleground Adventures: The Stories of Dwellers on the Scenes of Conflict in Some of the Most Notable Battles of the Civil War* (Boston: Houghton Mifflin Company, 1915), 122.

179 **Savilla Miller:** Henry Kyd Douglas, *I Rode with Stonewall* (Chapel Hill: University of North Carolina Press, 1940), 170. Douglas recounts meeting Miller in the morning but adds that "she remained at her post all day."

180  **Lee was on the scene:** Carman, *Maryland Campaign of September 1862*, vol. 2, 456.

180  **"What troops are those?":** Walter Clark, ed., *Histories of Several Regiments from North Carolina in the Great War 1861–'65*, vol. 1 (Raleigh, NC: E. M. Uzzell, Printer and Binder, 1901), 575.

180  **He'd driven his men relentlessly:** William Woods Hassler, *A. P. Hill: Lee's Forgotten General* (Richmond, VA: Garrett & Massie, 1957), 104.

180  **trousers were soaking wet:** *Berry Benson's Civil War Book*, ed. Susan Williams Benson (Athens, GA: University of Georgia Press, 1992), 27.

180  **"Look well to your left":** J. Willard Brown, *The Signal Corps, U.S.A. in the War of the Rebellion* (Boston: U.S. Veteran Signal Corps Association, 1896), 333.

181  **"Commence firing, men":** Kathleen A. Ernst, *Too Afraid to Cry: Maryland Civilians in the Antietam Campaign* (Mechanicsburg, PA: Stackpole Books, 1999), 152.

181  **"In a moment we were riddled with shot":** Corporal B. F. Blakeslee diary, quoted in Croffut and Morris, *Military and Civil History of Connecticut During the War of 1861–65*, 271.

181  **believe they spotted a Union flag:** Carman, *Maryland Campaign of September 1862*, vol. 2, 466.

181  **particular episode would become notorious:** According to many contemporary accounts, the Confederates donned Federal uniforms, even flew the US flag. See, for example, "Our Connecticut Regiments," *Hartford Daily Courant*, September 22, 1862, which asserts that the Rebels "treacherously displayed the U.S. colors, until ready to grapple with the foe."

182  **pierced his left lung:** Robert E. Gough, *South Kingstown's Own: A Biographical Sketch of Isaac Peace Rodman, Brigadier General* (Bozeman, MT: self-published, 2011), 79.

183  **"John McCall falls bleeding":** Croffut and Morris, *Military and Civil History of Connecticut During the War of 1861–65*, 272.

183  **a regiment sprang into action:** Details about 7th Maine drawn from multiple sources, including T. Jeff Driscoll, "Battle of Antietam: 7th Maine's Senseless Charge on the Piper Farm," *American Civil War* magazine, September 2006.

184  **"Are you afraid to go":** Thomas W. Hyde, *Following the Greek Cross or, Memories of the Sixth Army Corps* (Boston: Houghton, Mifflin and Company, 1894), 100.

184  **"inspiration of John Barleycorn":** Ibid., 104.

184  **he seemed nearly possessed:** *John Dooley Confederate Soldier*, 47.

184  **drive the Federals into the Antietam:** Carman, *Maryland Campaign of September 1862*, vol. 2, 477.

185  **"Tell General Burnside":** John S. C. Abbott, *The History of the Civil War in America* (New York: Henry Bill, 1867), 159.

185  **Lawrence Branch, a general:** Carman, *Maryland Campaign of September 1862*, vol. 2, 479.

185  **"Meserve, I'm hit":** John M. Priest, *Antietam: The Soldiers' Battle* (Shippensburg, PA: White Mane Publishing Company, 1989), 285.

186  **"as quiet as a Quaker village":** *Savannah Republican*, October 1, 1862, http://savnewspapers.galileo.usg.edu/savnewspapers-j2k/view?docId=bookreader/svr/svr1862/svr1862-0115.mets.xml#page/1/mode/1up.

186  **"Both parties fought with a desperation":** Roland Bowen to uncle, October 8, 1862, printed in *From Ball's Bluff to Gettysburg . . . and Beyond: The Civil War Letters*

*of Private Roland E. Bowen, 15th Massachusetts Infantry 1861–1864*, ed. Gregory A. Coco (Gettysburg, PA: Thomas Publications, 1994), 135.

186   **boiled beef contained in a barrel:** *History of the Thirty-Fifth Regiment Massachusetts Volunteers, 1862–1865* (Boston: Mills, Knight & Co, 1884), 50.

187   **nineteen-year-old commissary sergeant:** While many accounts place McKinley's coffee run earlier in the battle, always authoritative Carman places it around sunset when the fighting had ended, which makes sense. See Carman, *Maryland Campaign of September 1862*, vol. 2, 488.

187   **Private Almon Reed:** Priest, *Antietam: Soldiers' Battle*, 302.

187   **Corn cribs and store houses:** Emmet Crozier, *Yankee Reporters, 1861–65* (New York: Oxford University Press, 1956), 270.

187   **"Half of Lee's army":** Douglas, *I Rode with Stonewall*, 174.

188   **four journalists from the *New-York Tribune*:** Crozier, *Yankee Reporters, 1861–65*, 267–268.

188   **Lee met with his generals:** While tradition holds that on the evening following the battle Lee met with his generals at the Jacob Grove house in Sharpsburg, there's convincing evidence that the meeting was held in a field near the Confederate commander's tent headquarters. See Joseph L. Harsh, *Sounding the Shallows: A Confederate Companion for the Maryland Campaign of 1862* (Kent, OH: Kent State University Press, 2000), 208.

188   **McClellan was also planning:** Carman, *Maryland Campaign of September 1862*, vol. 2, 501.

188   **"troubled by a dream":** Johnson, *Long Roll*, 198.

## CHAPTER 12. THURSDAY'S RECKONING

190   **just 174 were able:** While the 15th Massachusetts entered the battle 606-men strong and suffered 330 casualties, 174 represents the number of men who answered the morning call as opposed to the number of uninjured soldiers. This, according to Andrew E. Ford, *The Story of the Fifteenth Regiment Massachusetts Volunteer Infantry in the Civil War, 1861–1864* (Clinton, MA: Press of W. J. Coulter, 1898), 199.

190   **"faithful few":** Walter Clark, ed., *Histories of the Several Regiments and Battalions from North Carolina in the Great War 1861–'65*, vol. 1 (Goldsboro, NC: Nash Brothers, 1901), 167.

190   **muskets as crutches:** *Dear Belle: Letters from a Cadet & Officer to His Sweetheart, 1858–1865*, ed. Catherine S. Crary (Middletown, CT: Wesleyan, 1965), 156.

191   **bugle signal, calling cavalrymen:** Charles W. Reed, *Hardtack and Coffee, or The Unwritten Story of Army Life* (Boston: George M. Smith & Co., 1887), 176.

191   **familiar morning commute:** Commute route based on exhibit at President Lincoln's Cottage at the Soldiers' Home, viewed by JM during visit on December 2, 2016.

191   **"I used to see Mr. Lincoln":** Matthew Pinsker, *Lincoln's Sanctuary: Abraham Lincoln and the Soldiers' Home* (New York: Oxford University Press, 2003), 66.

192   **lifted the cover from the boy's face:** Elizabeth Keckley, *Behind the Scenes, or, Thirty Years a Slave, and Four Years in the White House* (New York: G. W. Carleton & Co., 1868), chap. 6.

192  **Lincoln had marked Thursdays:** Harold Holzer, *Father Abraham: Lincoln and His Sons* (Honesdale, PA: Calkins Creek, 2011), 130.

192  **"ever since my little boy died":** Reverend William Ives Budington, sermon, in *Our Martyr President, Abraham Lincoln: Voices from the Pulpit of New York and Brooklyn* (New York: Tibbals & Whiting, 1865), 135.

192  **fitted with pipes:** Jean H. Baker, *Mary Todd Lincoln: A Biography* (New York: W. W. Norton & Company, 2008), 208.

192  **complained about the foul odor:** Ibid., 209.

192  **staffers fetched them cups:** Daniel Mark Epstein, *The Lincolns: Portrait of a Marriage* (New York: Ballantine Books, 2008), 357.

192  **She barred the Marine Band:** Baker, *Mary Todd Lincoln*, 216.

193  **president had paid McClellan a visit:** "Our boys were at Genl McClellan's House today with the Lincoln boys," appears in the January 8, 1862 entry, *The Diary of Horatio Nelson Taft, 1861–1865*, vol. 1, Library of Congress, https://www.loc.gov/resource/mtaft.mtaft1/?sp=130.

193  **"Our anxiety is intense":** Gideon Welles, *Diary of Gideon Welles*, vol. 1 (Boston: Houghton Mifflin Company, 1911), 140.

193  **"The time is come":** Lord Russell to Lord Palmerston, September 17, 1862, printed in *The Life of Lord John Russell*, vol. 2, by Spencer Walpole (London: Longmans, Green, and Co., 1889), 349.

193  **refrain from initiating hostilities:** James V. Murfin, *The Gleam of Bayonets: The Battle of Antietam and Robert E. Lee's Maryland Campaign* (Baton Rouge: Louisiana State University Press, 1965), 295.

194  **until reinforcements arrived:** Size of Union and Confederate forces available to fight on the morning of September 18 based on several discussions in February and March 2018, via e-mail, between JM and Daniel J. Vermilya, author of *"Perceptions, not Realities . . .": The Army of the Potomac in the Maryland Campaign* (Sharpsburg, MD: Save Historic Antietam Foundation, 2012).

194  **"the national cause could afford":** *Report of Maj.-Gen. George B. McClellan, August 4, 1863* (New York: Sheldon and Company, 1864), 401.

194  **he became physically ill:** George McClellan to Mary Ellen McClellan, September 20, 1862, printed in *McClellan's Own Story* (New York: Charles I. Webster & Company, 1887), 613.

195  **The Confederates had won a decisive victory:** Confederate diary, author unknown, September 18, 1862 entry, Ezra A. Carman Papers, National Archives.

195  **Tommy Meagher of the Irish:** *A Virginian Yankee in the Civil War: The Diaries of David Hunter Strother*, ed. Cecil D. Eby Jr. (Chapel Hill: University of North Carolina Press, 1961), 113.

195  **Longstreet was dead:** J. Cutler Andrews, *The South Reports the Civil War* (Princeton, NJ: Princeton University Press, 1970), 213.

195  **What they saw was astonishing:** Details of devastation witnessed by soldiers drawn from multiple sources including Samuel Fiske, *Mr. Dunn Browne's Experiences in the Army* (Boston: Nichols and Noyes, 1866), 49–51.

195  **"thick as grasshoppers":** September 18, 1862, entry in *The Civil War Journals of John Mead Gould, 1861–1865*, ed. William B. Jordan Jr. (Baltimore: Butternut and Blue, 1997), 198.

195  **musket barrel had filled with blood:** Frederick L. Hitchcock, *War from the Inside: The Story of the 132nd Regiment Pennsylvania Volunteer Infantry in the*

*War for the Suppression of the Rebellion* (Philadelphia: J. B. Lippincott Company, 1904), 71.

195  **"We hope and pray":** Charles Coffin, "Antietam Scenes," *Battles and Leaders of the Civil War*, vol. 2, ed. Robert Underwood Johnson and Clarence Clough Buel (New York: Century Company, 1887), 685.

196  **Twenty-eight bullets were counted:** John Hayes, formerly of the 130th Pennsylvania to Ezra Carman, October 29, 1894, box 2, folder 2, Ezra A. Carman Papers, NYPL.

196  **tallied 358 bodies:** *Dear Belle: Letters from a Cadet & Officer to His Sweetheart, 1858–1865*, ed. Catherine S. Crary (Middletown, CT: Wesleyan, 1965), 156.

196  **mass in a makeshift hut:** Very Reverend W. Corby, CSC, *Memoirs of Chaplain Life* (Chicago: La Monte, O'Donnell & Co., Printers, 1893), 113.

196  **"I have lived through":** *Soldiers' Letters, from Camp, Battle-Field and Prison*, ed. Lydia Minturn Post (New York: Bunce & Huntington, Publishers, 1865), 160–161.

196  **"It gives me intensest pain":** Bell Irvin Wiley, *The Life of Johnny Reb: The Common Soldier of the Confederacy* (Indianapolis, IN: Bobbs-Merrill, 1943), 213.

196  **"Those in whose judgment":** McClellan to Mary Ellen McClellan, September 18, 1862, printed in *McClellan's Own Story*, 612.

196  **dispatch was rushed to the White House:** George M. Smalley, "Chapters in Journalism," *Harper's New Monthly* magazine, August 1894.

197  **"greatest fight since Waterloo":** "The Contest in Maryland," *New-York Tribune*, September 20, 1862.

197  **Baltimore operator was quite aware of the suspense:** Louis M. Starr, *Bohemian Brigade: Civil War Newsmen in Action* (Madison: University of Wisconsin Press, 1987), 145.

197  **"If not wholly a victory":** Smalley's celebrated full-length account of the battle ran in the *New-York Tribune*, September 20, 1862, but his telegraph dispatch that reached Lincoln was considerably shorter. For the text of that dispatch, see James Glen Stovall, "George Smalley Reports the Battle of Antietam," June 13, 2016, Knoxville Civil War Roundtable site, https://kcwrtorg.wordpress.com /2016/06/13/george-smalley-reports-the-battle-of-antietam/.

198  **lying stiff, his teeth firmly fastened:** W. A. Croffut and John M. Morris, *The Military and Civil History of Connecticut During the War of 1861–65* (New York: Ledyard Bill, 1868), 275.

198  **"And from a *teacup* too":** Ibid.

198  **white canvas stretcher:** William H. Osborne, *The History of the Twenty-Ninth Regiment of Massachusetts Volunteer Infantry* (Boston: Albert J. Wright, Printers, 1877), 191.

198  **A light rain began to fall:** Peter Alexander, "Account of Lee's Retreat from Sharpsburg," *Savannah Republican*, October 1, 1862, reprinted in *The Greenwood Library of American War Reporting*, vol. 3, ed. David A. Copeland (Westport, CT: Greenwood Press, 2005), 406.

199  **an uneventful day:** only two items listed for September 18, 1862, in Earl Schenck Miers, ed., *Lincoln Day by Day: A Chronology, 1809–1865*, vol. 3 (Washington, DC: Lincoln Sesquicentennial Commission, 1960), 140.

199  **White House as an usher:** Natalie Sweet, "A Representative 'of Our People': The Agency of William Slade, Leader in the African American Community and Usher to Abraham Lincoln," *Journal of the Abraham Lincoln Association* (Summer 2013).

199   **Slade dutifully gathered up these scraps:** John E. Washington, *They Knew Lincoln* (New York: E. P. Dutton & Co., 1942), 111.

199   **"make a horse laugh":** Ibid., 108.

199   **kept Lincoln company when the president suffered from insomnia:** Ibid., 110.

200   **Slade enjoyed great prominence:** Details of his various roles in African American community of Washington, DC, drawn from Sweet, "A Representative 'of Our People.'"

200   **subject often turned to slavery:** Washington, *They Knew Lincoln*, 111.

200   **"The trees and overhanging cliffs":** Peter Alexander, "Account of Lee's Retreat from Sharpsburg," *Savannah Republican*, October 1, 1862, reprinted in *The Greenwood Library of American War Reporting*, vol. 3, 406.

201   **middle of the Potomac, astride Traveller:** John H. Lewis, *Recollections from 1860 to 1865* (Washington, DC: Peake & Company, Publishers, 1895), 44.

201   **Twelve of the South Carolinians yoked themselves:** H. B. McClellan, *The Life and Campaigns of Major-General J. E. B. Stuart* (Boston: Houghton, Mifflin and Company, 1885), 133.

201   **"Thank god":** General John Walker, "Sharpsburg," *Battles and Leaders of the Civil War*, vol. 2, ed. Robert Underwood Johnson and Clarence Clough Buel (New York: Century Company, 1887), 682.

201   **traveled in an ambulance drawn by four gray horses:** *A Virginian Yankee in the Civil War: The Diaries of David Hunter Strother*, 113.

## CHAPTER 13. SURGICAL PROCEDURES, LINCOLN'S PRESCRIPTION

203   **His back ached:** Jonathan D. Sarna and Benjamin Shapell, *Lincoln and the Jews: A History* (New York: St. Martin's Press, 2015), 132.

203   **sharp pains coursed through his wrist:** Earl Schenck Miers, ed., *Lincoln Day by Day: A Chronology 1809–1865* (Washington, DC: Lincoln Sesquicentennial Commission, 1960), 139.

203   **the corns on his feet:** Abraham Lincoln, Testimonial for Isachar Zacharie, September 22, 1862, printed in *The Collected Works of Abraham Lincoln*, vol. 5, ed. Roy P. Basler (New Brunswick, NJ: Rutgers University Press, 1953), 436.

203   **no reliable word on the battle's final result:** "The battle of Antietam was fought Wednesday, and until Saturday I could not find out whether we had gained a victory or lost a battle," said Lincoln, quoted in John G. Nicolay and John Hay, *Abraham Lincoln: A History*, vol. 6 (New York: Century Co., 1886), 165.

203   **"We are still left entirely in the dark":** Henry W. Halleck to George McClellan, telegram, September 20, 1862, printed in *The Civil War Papers of George B. McClellan*, ed. Stephen W. Sears (New York: Ticknor & Fields, 1989), 475n.

204   **more than 17,000:** Antietam Battlefield Board.

204   **even a bowling alley:** Terry Reimer, *One Vast Hospital: The Civil War Sites in Frederick, Maryland, After Antietam* (Frederick, MD: National Museum of Civil War Medicine, 2001), 15.

204   **Letterman selected the Pry house:** Gordon Dammann, Antietam guide, tour with JM, June 9, 2017.

205   **graduate of Jefferson Medical College:** James Phalen, "The Life of Jonathan

Letterman," *Records of the American Catholic Historical Society of Philadelphia*, June 1947.

205 **Letterman—a gaunt, blunt-spoken man:** Biographical details about Jonathan Letterman drawn from multiple sources, including Scott McGaugh, *Surgeon in Blue: Jonathan Letterman, the Civil War Doctor Who Pioneered Battlefield Care* (New York: Arcade Publishing, 2013).

205 **Letterman had cased the surrounding countryside:** Jonathan Letterman, *Official Report*, March 1, 1863, Antietam on the Web, http://antietam.aotw.org/exhibit.php ?exhibit_id=73.

205 **credit for refining the three-tiered battlefield evacuation system:** Chuck Gordon, "Antietam: Forging the Modern Military Medicine System," July 24, 2009, army.mil, https://www.army.mil/article/24859/antietam_forging_the_modern_military_medicine_system.

205 **a dedicated military ambulance corps:** Jonathan Letterman, Special Orders, No. 147, August 2, 1862, printed in Jonathan Letterman, *Medical Recollections of the Army of the Potomac* (New York: D. Appleton and Company, 1866), 24.

205 **regimental musicians and civilian:** Gordon Dammann, Antietam guide, tour with JM, June 9, 2017.

205 **After Shiloh, thousands of wounded:** Winston Groom, "Why Shiloh Matters," *New York Times*, April 6, 2012.

205 **After Bull Run, some injured soldiers:** McGaugh, *Surgeon in Blue*, 47.

206 **The Rosecrans wagon:** Details about Rosecrans wagon from multiple sources including Joseph K. Barnes, *The Medical and Surgical History of the War of the Rebellion*, part 3, vol. 2 (Washington, DC: Government Printing Office, 1883), 949–950.

206 **"Gutbusters":** Glenna R. Schroeder-Lein, *The Encyclopedia of Civil War Medicine* (Armonk, NY: M. E. Sharpe), 14.

206 **a set of elliptical springs:** Duffy Neubauer, curator, Starkville Civil War Arsenal, interview with JM, November 21, 2016.

206 **Letterman had two hundred Rosecrans:** Letterman, *Medical Recollections*, 34.

206 **Within forty-eight hours:** Unpublished essay on Letterman by Gordon Dammann, provided to JM courtesy of Dammann.

206 **The Rebels had left roughly 2,000 wounded:** Schroeder-Lein, *Encyclopedia of Civil War Medicine*, 25.

206 **"Humanity teaches us":** Jonathan Letterman, *Official Report*, March 1, 1863.

206 **pioneer, helping to clarify triage:** Exhibit, National Museum of Civil War Medicine, Frederick, Maryland, JM visit, June 8, 2017.

207 **"father of battlefield medicine":** Ibid.

207 **dilapidated old factory:** Mary Bedinger Mitchell, "A Woman's Recollections of Antietam," *Battles and Leaders of the Civil War*, vol. 2, ed. Robert Underwood Johnson and Clarence Clough Buel (New York: Century Company, 1887), 691.

207 **"After every available space":** Thomas A. McGrath, *Shepherdstown: Last Clash of the Antietam Campaign September 19–20, 1862* (Lynchburg, VA: Schroeder Publications, 2016), 45.

207 **amputations accounted for three out of four battlefield operations:** Exhibit, National Museum of Civil War Medicine, JM visit, June 8, 2017.

207 **"The minnie ball striking":** Theodore Dimon to wife, September 25, 1862, quoted in "A Federal Surgeon at Sharpsburg," ed. James I. Robertson Jr., *Civil War History* (June 1960).

208 **Anesthesia was almost always used:** National Museum of Civil War Medicine, JM visit June 8, 2017.

208 **two common agents:** Dammann, Antietam guide, tour with JM, June 9, 2017.

208 **Survival rates varied by type of amputation:** Exhibit, National Museum of Civil War Medicine, JM visit June 8, 2017.

208 **two thirds of all soldier deaths:** Schroeder-Lein, *Encyclopedia Civil War Medicine*, xiii.

208 **"nostalgia":** Ibid., 250.

209 **"Old Mother Pendleton":** McGrath, *Shepherdstown*, 50.

209 **arranged the forty-four pieces:** David A. Norris, "Battle of Shepherdstown," Civil War Trust, https://www.civilwar.org/learn/articles/battle-shepherdstown.

209 **roughly 600 soldiers:** Peter S. Carmichael, "'We Don't Know What on Earth to Do with Him': William Nelson Pendleton and the Affair at Shepherdstown," essay in *The Antietam Campaign*, ed. Gary Gallagher (Chapel Hill: University of North Carolina Press, 1999), 266.

209 **morning of September 19:** McGrath, *Shepherdstown*, 61.

210 **irregular collection of guns:** Norris, "Battle of Shepherdstown," Civil War Trust.

210 **Roughly three hours passed:** McGrath, *Shepherdstown*, 86.

210 **"All?":** Carmichael, "'We Don't Know What on Earth to Do with Him.'"

210 **the general was visibly shaken:** Ibid.

211 **Fresh troops:** McGrath, *Shepherdstown*, 61.

211 **"Corn Exchange Regiment":** Details about the 118th Pennsylvania drawn from multiple sources, including ibid.

211 **repossessed another:** Norris, "Battle of Shepherdstown," Civil War Trust.

211 **"I do not receive orders":** Ibid.

211 **Enfields were defective:** McGrath, *Shepherdstown*, 143.

212 **Confederacy's *northern frontier*:** Stephen W. Sears, *Landscape Turned Red* (Boston: Houghton Mifflin Company, 1983), 307.

212 **Potomac crossing at Williamsport:** Robert E. Lee to Jefferson Davis, September 20, 1862, Lee Family Digital Archive, https://leefamilyarchive.org/9-family-papers/737-robert-e-lee-to-jefferson-davis-1862-september-2.

213 **"I am, therefore":** Robert E. Lee to Jefferson Davis, September 25, 1862, letter printed in, *Memoirs of Robert E. Lee*, by A. L. Long and Marcus J. Wright (London: Sampson Low, Marston, Searle, and Rivington, 1886), 540.

213 **sufficient to convince the president:** By Saturday, September 20, Lincoln had read enough press accounts to become convinced that the Union had "gained a victory," Nicolay and Hay, *Abraham Lincoln: A History*, vol. 6, 165.

213 **Battle of Meyer's Spring:** Frederick L. Hitchcock, *War from the Inside* (Philadelphia: J. B. Lippincott, 1904), 79.

213 **chance to grow more comfortable:** Louis P. Masur, "How the Emancipation Proclamation Came to Be Signed," *Smithsonian* magazine, January 2013.

213 **possibility of gradual compensated emancipation:** "tendering pecuniary aid to the free acceptance or rejection of all slave States, so called, the people whereof may not then be in rebellion against the United States and which States may

then have voluntarily adopted, or thereafter may voluntarily adopt, immediate or gradual abolishment of slavery within their respective limits," preliminary Emancipation Proclamation, September 22, 1862, National Archives, https://www .archives.gov/exhibits/american_originals_iv/sections/transcript_preliminary_ emancipation.html.

214 **mention of voluntary colonization:** "the effort to colonize persons of African descent, with their consent, upon this continent, or elsewhere, with the previously obtained consent of the Governments existing there, will be continued," ibid.

214 **"thereof," six times, "hereby" thrice:** Ibid.

214 **"the trite summonses":** Harold Holzer, *Emancipating Lincoln: The Proclamation in Text, Context, and Memory* (Cambridge, MA: Harvard University Press, 2012), 83.

214 **Over the weekend of September 20 and 21:** Lincoln worked on the proclamation over this weekend, and thanks to comments he made, it's even possible to identify where he worked on it. From Francis B. Carpenter, *Six Months at the White House: The Story of a Picture* (New York: Hurd and Houghton, 1867), 23: "I was then staying at the Soldiers' Home . . . Here I finished writing the second draft of the preliminary proclamation; came up on a Saturday [to the White House]." From Nicolay and Hay, *Abraham Lincoln*, vol. 6, 165: "I fixed it up a little Sunday, and Monday I let them have it." To recap, Lincoln finished his second draft of the preliminary proclamation at Soldiers' Home in the days immediately following Antietam before traveling to the White House on Saturday, September 20, where he continued to tinker over the weekend, before issuing it on Monday, September 22, 1862.

214 **"T. Warner, Co. G, in jaw":** "Update on Antietam Wounded," *Hartford Daily Courant*, September 22, 1862.

215 **news of the death of their loved one:** Rufus R. Dawes, *Service with the Sixth Wisconsin Volunteers* (Marietta, OH: E. R. Alderman & Sons, 1890), 99.

215 **A German-speaking mother:** *The Letters of Horace Howard Furness*, vol. 1, ed. Harold Howard Furness Jr. (Boston: Houghton Mifflin Company, 1922), 115.

215 **"Metzger Charles 4th":** Ibid., 116.

215 **"mein sohn":** Ibid., 117.

216 **"She obeyed the doctors":** General John B. Gordon, *Reminiscences of the Civil War* (New York: Charles Scribner's Sons, 1903), 91.

216 **"Oh my god":** Sergeant Jonathan P. Stowe, "Life with the 15th Mass.," *Civil War Times Illustrated*, August 1972.

216 **"Use more water":** Ibid.

216 **care of Dr. Issachar Zacharie:** Sarna and Shapell, *Lincoln and the Jews*, 132.

217 **"Gentlemen, why don't you laugh":** War Secretary Stanton's account of meeting, printed in Wayne Whipple, *The Story-Life of Lincoln* (Philadelphia: John C. Winston Company, 1908), 482.

217 **"Presdt's late Proclamation":** George McClellan to Mary Ellen McClellan, September 25, 1862, printed in *The Civil War Papers of George B. McClellan*, ed. Stephen W. Sears (New York: Ticknor & Fields, 1989), 481.

218 **"The remedy for political error":** George McClellan to Abraham Lincoln, telegram, October 7, 1862, ibid., 494.

218 **"Everyone can understand":** Dean B. Mahin, *One War at a Time: The International Dimensions of the American Civil War* (Washington, DC: Brassey's, 1999), 139.

218 **surprising level of awareness:** Allen C. Guelzo, *Lincoln's Emancipation Procla-mation: The End of Slavery in America* (New York: Simon & Schuster, 2004), 16.

219 **Slade was familiar with every last word:** John E. Washington, *They Knew Lincoln* (New York: E. P. Dutton & Co., 1942), 111.

## CHAPTER 14. THE DEAD OF ANTIETAM

220 **The space was well defined:** This episode describes the creation of Alexander Gardner's "Confederate dead in Bloody Lane," stereo #553, September 19, 1862, Library of Congress. As a stereographic image, the dimensions of the glass plate would have been "well-defined," ten inches wide by four inches tall. Details about the creation of this landmark image also provided by Todd Harrington, "Gardner at Antietam," tour with JM, September 2, 2017.

221 **3,650 soldiers had been killed:** Antietam Battlefield Board.

221 **highest for any day American history:** Detail drawn from multiple sources, including "Antietam: A Savage Day in American History," NPR *Morning Edition*, September 17, 2012 broadcast, https://www.npr.org/2012/09/17/161248814/antietam-a-savage-day-in-american-history.

221 **pull the blanket-with-body:** Kathleen A. Ernst, *Too Afraid to Cry: Maryland Civilians in the Antietam Campaign* (Mechanicsburg, PA: Stackpole Books, 1999), 163.

221 **bayonet, bend it into a hook:** Steven R. Stotelmyer, *The Bivouacs of the Dead: The Story of Those Who Died at Antietam and South Mountain* (Baltimore: Toomey Press, 1992), 4.

222 **"most disagreeable duty":** Kristilyn Baldwin, "The Visual Documentation of Antietam: Peaceful Settings, Morbid Curiosity, and a Profitable Business," *Gettysburg Journal of the Civil War Era* 1 (2010).

222 **The body of Captain Werner von Bachelle:** Details about von Bachelle's burial from multiple sources, including Rufus R. Dawes, *Service with the Sixth Wisconsin Volunteers* (Marietta, OH: E. R. Alderman & Sons, 1890), 93.

222 **"80 Rebels are buried":** Oliver Wendell Holmes, "Doings of the Sunbeam," *Atlantic Monthly*, July 1863.

222 **Between September 19 and 22:** William A. Frassanito, *Antietam: A Photographic Legacy of America's Bloodiest Day* (Gettysburg, PA: Thomas Publications, 1978), 52.

222 **Gardner was something of a polymath:** Biographical details about Gardner drawn from multiple sources including Joseph M. Wilson, *A Eulogy on the Life and Character of Alexander Gardner* (Washington, DC: R. Beresford, Printer, 1883).

223 **a new photographic process:** Discussion of collodion wet-plate process drawn from multiple sources, including Richard S. Lowry, *The Photographer and the President: Abraham Lincoln, Alexander Gardner, & the Images That Made a Presidency* (New York: Rizzoli, 2015), 30–31.

223 **long-lost portraits of officers:** Frassanito, *Antietam: A Photographic Legacy*, 19.

223 **Fenton confine his work to undistressing fare:** Lucian Ciupei, "Censorship in the Crimean War Photography: A Case Study: Carol Pop de Szathmari and Roger Fenton," *Journal of Media Research* 1, no. 12 (2012).

224  **designated official photographer:** Josephine Cobb, "Mathew B. Brady's Photographic Gallery in Washington," speech delivered before the Columbia Historical Society, February 18, 1953, 52.

224  **pour on the collodion:** Discussion of Gardner's process drawn from multiple sources including Mark Osterman, historian, George Eastman House International Museum of Photography and Film, Rochester, New York, interview with JM, August 29, 2017.

226  **The 51st Pennsylvania got their whiskey:** Thomas H. Parker, *History of the 51st Regiment of P.V. and V.V.* (Philadelphia: King & Baird, Printers, 1869), 242, 244–245.

226  **The 35th Massachusetts:** *History of the Thirty-Fifth Regiment Massachusetts Volunteers, 1862–1865* (Boston: Mills, Knight & Co., 1884), 58.

226  **9th New York were thrilled by an account:** J. H. E. Whitney, *The Hawkins Zouaves: Their Battles and Marches* (New York: self-published, 1866), 155.

226  **boxes marked "Yorktown":** *The Road to Richmond: The Civil War Memoirs of Maj. Abner R. Small of the 16th Maine Vols.; With His Diary as a Prisoner of War*, ed. Harold Adams Small (Berkeley: University of California Press, 1959), 51.

226  **"Worms eat hearty":** Ibid.

227  **"the atmosphere of the whole neighborhood":** J. Franklin Dyer, October 1, 1862, diary entry, printed in *The Journal of a Civil War Surgeon*, ed. Michael B. Chesson (Lincoln: University of Nebraska Press, 2003), 42.

227  **slang lexicon related to lice:** J. F. J. Caldwell, *The History of a Brigade of South Carolinians, Known First as "Gregg's"* (Philadelphia: King & Baird, Printers, 1866), 54.

227  **"melancholy spectacle":** Cornelia Peak McDonald, November 30, 1862 diary entry, printed in *A Woman's Civil War: A Diary, with Reminiscences of the War, from March 1862*, ed. Minrose C. Gwin. (Madison: University of Wisconsin Press, 1992), 95.

227  **"Our victory was complete":** McClellan to Henry W. Halleck, telegram, September 19, 1862, printed in *The Civil War Papers of George B. McClellan: Selected Correspondence, 1860–1865*, ed. Stephen W. Sears (New York: Ticknor & Fields, 1989), 470.

227  **"Not yet even have I":** McClellan to Mary Ellen McClellan, September 29, 1862, ibid., 486.

228  **roughly 2,000 more:** Glenna R. Schroeder-Lein, *The Encyclopedia of Civil War Medicine* (Armonk, NY: M. E. Sharpe), 24.

228  **Charley King:** Biographical details about the drummer boy drawn from multiple sources, including "Charles 'Charley' King" entry, *PA Civil War 150*, July 16, 2015, http://pacivilwar150.com/ThroughPeople/Children/CharlesCharleyKing.html.

228  **George B. Anderson:** Kevin R. Pawlak, *Shepherdstown in the Civil War: One Vast Confederate Hospital* (Charleston, SC: History Press, 2015), 104.

228  **Israel Richardson:** Jack C. Mason, *Until Antietam: The Life and Letters of Major General Israel B. Richardson* (Carbondale, IL: Southern Illinois University Press, 2009), 196.

229  **major generals killed by the battle rose to six:** "Six Generals Killed at Antietam," National Park Service, https://www.nps.gov/anti/learn/historyculture/6generals.htm.

229  **"Mr. Ainsworth":** Roland Bowen to Friend Ainsworth, September 28, 1862, printed in *From Ball's Bluff to Gettysburg . . . and Beyond: The Civil War Letters*

*of Private Roland E. Bowen, 15th Massachusetts Infantry 1861–64*, ed. Gregory A. Coco (Gettysburg, PA: Thomas Publications, 1994), 128.

229 **proper burial in a Millbury cemetery:** There is a gravestone for Henry Ainsworth in the Central Cemetery in Millbury, Massachusetts. However, it's possible that this is a cenotaph, and that his remains were never recovered from the Antietam battlefield.

230 **For a fee, enterprising locals:** Ernst, *Too Afraid to Cry*, 180.

230 **Coffins cost around $5:** Details about embalming drawn from multiple sources, including Lindsey Fitzharris, "The Embalming Craze During the Civil War," February 20, 2016, posted on National Museum of Civil War Medicine website, http://www.civilwarmed.org/embalming1/.

230 **$25 for a private and $50:** Kimberly Largent-Christopher, "Embalming Comes in Vogue During Civil War," *Washington Times*, April 2, 2009.

230 **two dead Rebels in the kitchen:** Oliver Reilly, *The Battlefield of Antietam* (Hagerstown, MD: Hagerstown Bookbinding and Printing Company, 1906), 24.

230 **exploded in front of his house:** Ibid., 30.

230 **Aaron Fry:** Ibid., 26.

231 **The Lutheran Church:** *The Churches of Sharpsburg Walking Tour* (Sharpsburg, MD: Sharpsburg Historical Society, 2005), 2.

231 **"The only thing my wife":** Ernst, *Too Afraid to Cry*, 196.

231 **Farmer Otto submitted a claim for $2,350.60:** John Nelson, "Battle of Antietam: Union Surgeons and Civilian Volunteers Help the Wounded," *America's Civil War* magazine, September 2007.

231 **property's damage at $2,459:** Pry House, JM visit on March 11, 2018.

231 **William Roulette counted seven hundred graves:** "Antietam Battlefield—Roulette Farm," Antietam National Battlefield, https://www.nps.gov/places/antietam -battlefield-roulette-farm.htm.

231 **Confederate cemetery established in Hagerstown:** Rose Hill Cemetery, Hagerstown, Maryland, JM visit, September 3, 2017.

232 **"The Dead of Antietam":** Details about Brady exhibit drawn largely from "Brady's Photographs," *New York Times*, October 20, 1862.

232 **peer into one of the stereoscopes:** Visitors to Brady's gallery are described as "bending down to look in the pale faces of the dead," a certain giveaway that stereoscopes had been set up for viewing, as opposed to prints of the images being displayed on the walls. See "Brady's Photographs," *New York Times*, October 20, 1862.

233 **"These wrecks of manhood":** Oliver Wendell Holmes, "Doings of the Sunbeam," *Atlantic Monthly*, July 1863.

233 **Gardner took the step of copyrighting:** Mark Katz, *Witness to an Era: The Life and Photographs of Alexander Gardner* (Nashville: Rutledge Hill Press, 1991), 47.

233 **he would soon end his association with Brady:** Frassanito, *Antietam: A Photographic Legacy*, 54.

## CHAPTER 15. BY PROCLAMATION

234 **On October 2, Lincoln arrived at Antietam:** Although Lincoln arrived in Harpers Ferry on October 1, 1862, he didn't tour the battlefield until October 2. See John W. Schildt, *Four Days in October* (self-published, 1978), 59.

234 **traveling party of five:** Ibid., 6–9.

235 **"—Let us go":** *A Diary of Battle: The Personal Journals of Colonel Charles S. Wainwright, 1861–1865*, ed. Allan Nevins (Boston: Da Capo Press, 1998), 110.

235 **two parties became separated:** On the question of whether Lincoln and McClellan toured the field together, Schildt, an authoritative source, indicates that they did not. See *Four Days in October*, 24–25.

235 **"Here lies the bodies":** Michael Burlingame, *Abraham Lincoln: A Life*, vol. 2 (Baltimore: Johns Hopkins University Press, 2008), 426.

236 **Dunker Church:** Lincoln visited the church according to some accounts such as Jacob Dolson Cox, *Military Reminiscences of the Civil War*, vol. 1 (New York: Charles Scribner's Sons, 1900), 364.

236 **"Mr. Lincoln was manifestly touched":** Rufus R. Dawes, *Service with the Sixth Wisconsin Volunteers* (Marietta, OH: E. R. Alderman & Sons, 1890), 100.

236 **soapstone and emery paper:** Edward G. Longacre, *Joshua Chamberlain: The Soldier and the Man* (Boston: Da Capo Press, 1999), 81.

236 **"We could see the deep sadness":** Joshua Chamberlain's speech, February 12, 1909, printed in *Ceremonies in Commemoration of the One Hundredth Anniversary of the Birth of Abraham Lincoln* (Philadelphia, 1909), 23.

237 **shaking the hands of wounded Confederates:** John W. Schildt, *Mount Airy: The Grove Homestead* (Chewsville, MD: Antietam Publication, 1992), 40.

237 **Lincoln requested that Ward Lamon:** Ward Hill Lamon, *Recollections of Abraham Lincoln, 1847–1865* (Washington, DC: self-published, 1911), 149.

237 **"I visited the old churchyard":** Ibid., 150.

238 **"I went up to the field":** William Roscoe Thayer, *The Life and Letters of John Hay*, vol. 1 (Boston: Houghton Mifflin Company, 1915), 132.

238 **"Western officer":** George McClellan to Mary Ellen McClellan, October 2, 1862 printed in *The Civil War Papers of George B. McClellan: Selected Correspondence, 1860–1865*, ed. Stephen W. Sears (New York: Ticknor & Fields, 1989), 488.

238 **"I urged him to follow":** George B. McClellan, *McClellan's Own Story* (New York: Charles L. Webster & Company, 1887), 627.

238 **the general received a telegram:** From Henry Halleck, the text read: "The President directs that you cross the Potomac and give battle to the enemy or drive him south. Your army must move now while the roads are good," *Civil War Papers of George B. McClellan*, 491n.

239 **J. E. B. Stuart:** Details of Stuart's raid drawn from multiple sources, including "The Chambersburg Raid," John Pelham Historical Association, http://www.gallantpelham.org/articles/showart.cfm?id_art=21.

240 **The fear that Braxton Bragg:** *Civil War Papers of George B. McClellan*, 510n.

240 **settle his army into winter quarters:** Stephen W. Sears, *George B. McClellan: The Young Napoleon* (New York: Da Capo, 1999), 336.

240 **envisioned a fresh attack:** Ibid.

240 **Hannibal Hamlin:** Earl Schenck Miers, *Lincoln Day by Day: A Chronology 1809–1865* (Washington, DC: Lincoln Sesquicentennial Commission, 1960), 145.

240 **"You remember my speaking":** Lincoln to McClellan, October 13, 1862, printed in *The Collected Works of Abraham Lincoln*, vol. 5, ed. Roy P. Basler (New Brunswick, NJ: Rutgers University Press, 1953), 460–461.

241 **swelled to 130,000:** John C. Waugh, *Lincoln and McClellan: The Troubled Partnership Between a President and His General* (New York: Palgrave Macmillan, 2010), 174.

241 **a full week:** On October 27, 1862, McClellan sent a telegram to Lincoln that included, "I commenced crossing the Army into Virginia yesterday," i.e., October 26, *Civil War Papers of George B. McClellan*, 512. On November 1, he sent another telegram to the president: "I have the honor to inform you that all the Corps of this Army have crossed the Potomac except Franklin's which comes up this morning," ibid., 517. Hence, a seven-day crossing, October 26 to November 1.

241 **"We moved with McClellan rapidity":** *Sergt. Austin C. Kearns: Three Years with Company K*, ed. Arthur A. Kent (London: Associated University Press, 1976), 138.

241 **no gradual emancipation, no compensation:** Text of Emancipation Proclamation, January 1, 1863, National Archives, https://www.archives.gov/exhibits/featured -documents/emancipation-proclamation/transcript.html.

241 **strike the reference to voluntary colonization:** Ibid.

241 **black men would be invited to enlist in the army:** In the Emancipation Proclamation, Lincoln included the following about African Americans joining the Union armed forces: "And I further declare and make known, that such persons of suitable condition, will be received into the armed service of the United States to garrison forts, positions, stations, and other places, and to man vessels of all sorts in said service," ibid.

242 **"The colored population":** Abraham Lincoln to Andrew Johnson, March 26, 1863, printed in *The Collected Works of Abraham Lincoln*, vol. 6, ed. Roy P. Basler (New Brunswick, NJ: Rutgers University Press, 1953), 149.

242 **Roughly 180,000 African Americans:** "Black Soldiers in the U.S. Military During the Civil War," National Archives, https://www.archives.gov/education/ lessons/blacks-civil-war.

242 **court order related to the Arlington:** Elizabeth Brown Pryor, *Reading the Man: A Portrait of Robert E. Lee Through His Private Letters* (New York: Viking, 2007), 274.

242 **set free would be Perry Parks:** Robert E. Lee manumission letter, January 2, 1863, collection of the Museum of the Confederacy, Richmond, VA, accessed online.

242 **freedman's village:** Robert M. Poole, *On Hallowed Ground: The Story of Arlington National Cemetery* (New York: Bloomsbury, 2009), 51–53.

243 **meant as a taunt:** Ibid., 60.

243 **On November 7:** The Comte de Paris, *History of the Civil War in America*, vol. 2 (Philadelphia: Porter & Coates, 1876), 555.

243 **blinding snowstorm:** Waugh, *Lincoln and McClellan*, 181.

243 **Burnside raised a series of vehement objections:** Drawn from multiple sources, including William Marvel, *Burnside* (Chapel Hill: University of North Carolina Press, 1991), 159.

244 **"Of course I was much surprised":** McClellan to Mary Ellen McClellan, November 7, 1862, printed in *Civil War Papers of George B. McClellan*, 520.

245 **"In parting from you":** McClellan bulletin, "To the Army of the Potomac," ibid., 521.

245 **Some men dropped their muskets:** James V. Murfin, *The Gleam of Bayonets: The Battle of Antietam and Robert E. Lee's Maryland Campaign* (Baton Rouge: Louisiana State University Press, 1965), 320.

245 **standard bearers threw down their emerald flags:** Brooks D. Simpson, "General McClellan's Bodyguard," essay in *The Antietam Campaign*, ed. Gary W. Gallagher (Chapel Hill: University of North Carolina Press, 1999), 66.

245  **uncoupled his railcar:** Stephen W. Sears, *Landscape Turned Red: The Battle of Antietam* (Boston: Houghton Mifflin Company, 1983), 344.

246  **"Good bye, lads":** Ibid., 345.

246  **run against Lincoln:** That McClellan ran against Lincoln for president in 1864 serves as the ultimate refutation of the oft-repeated claim that he was willing to seize power by means of a coup. Yes, it's true that certain Army of the Potomac officers entertained such schemes, but there's no good evidence that McClellan was a party. Meanwhile, the contrary evidence is extensive: McClellan furnished Lincoln with a protective cavalry escort and circulated a bulletin among the soldiers urging those who differed with the president over the Emancipation Proclamation to register their dissent democratically, at the polls. Significantly, when McClellan was fired, he didn't stir up his loyal army and march on Washington. He followed orders and turned over command. Yet, the myth persists; even recently there have been books featuring McClellan the would-be military dictator, eager to seize power by coup. The notion that this notoriously cautious general would even consider such a flagrant assault on the American political system is patently absurd.

246  **abolitionists had visited the White House:** Allen C. Guelzo, *Lincoln's Emancipation Proclamation* (New York: Simon & Schuster, 2004), 200–201.

246  **"Will Uncle Abe Lincoln":** George Templeton Strong, December 27, 1862, entry in *Diary of the Civil War, 1860–1865,* ed. Allan Nevins (New York: Macmillan Company, 1962), 282.

246  **The previous night, Lincoln hadn't slept:** Robert Todd Lincoln's account, printed in *Christian Science Monitor,* September 22, 1937.

247  **The levee:** Account of this event drawn from multiple sources, including "New Year's Day in Washington," *Baltimore Sun,* January 2, 1863.

247  **"The press was tremendous":** *Lincoln Observed: Civil War Dispatches of Noah Brooks,* ed. Michael Burlingame (Baltimore: Johns Hopkins University Press, 1998), 15.

247  **"how much we have passed through":** Ruth Painter Randall, *Mary Lincoln: Biography of a Marriage* (Boston: Little, Brown and Company, 1953), 320.

248  **"Heartbreak Day":** David Williams, *I Freed Myself: African American Self-Emancipation in the Civil War Era* (New York: Cambridge University Press, 2004), 115.

248  **more than three hundred former slaves:** *Baltimore Sun,* January 2, 1863.

248  **In Brooklyn, an all-day vigil:** Alan Singer, "The Grand Emancipation Jubilee," History News Network, December 31, 2012, https://historynewsnetwork.org/article/149938.

248  **relay system had even been put in place:** Frederick Douglass, *Life and Times of Frederick Douglass* (Hartford, CT: Park Publishing, 1882), 428.

248  **"Every moment of waiting":** Ibid.

249  **War Department had even granted secret permission:** Matthew Pinsker, "Emancipation Among Black Troops in South Carolina," Emancipation Digital Classroom, posted November 6, 2012, http://housedivided.dickinson.edu/sites/emancipation/2012/11/06/emancipation-among-black-troops-in-south-carolina/.

249  **1st South Carolina was throwing a levee:** Account of this event drawn from Thomas Wentworth Higginson, January 1, 1863, diary entry printed in his book *Army Life in a Black Regiment* (Boston: Fields, Osgood, & Co., 1870).

250   **promised to abolitionist senator:** Guelzo, *Lincoln's Emancipation Proclamation*, 206.

250   **result of being gnawed:** Benjamin Perley Poore, in *Reminiscences of Abraham Lincoln*, ed. Allen Thorndike Rice (Edinburgh: William Blackwood and Sons, 1886), 230.

250   **His arm felt stiff and numb:** Detail drawn from multiple sources, including Frederick W. Seward, *Seward at Washington as Senator and Secretary of State* (New York: Derby and Miller, 1891), 151.

250   **"some compunctions":** Ibid.

250   **"That will do":** Francis B. Carpenter, *Six Months at the White House: The Story of a Picture* (New York: Hurd and Houghton, 1867), 270.

# ACKNOWLEDGMENTS

For this book, once again, it was a pleasure to work with the team at Da Capo Press. From the big picture down to the smallest detail, this book benefitted from an easy collaboration with Robert Pigeon, my editor, who brought wisdom, enthusiasm, and a deep knowledge of the Civil War. Props to Alex Camlin for the bold, eye-catching cover (yes, Lincoln lived in a full-color world).

What a luxury to work a fifth straight time with Lissa Warren, a consummate pro who knows how to get books their due. I'm pleased to have the benefit yet again of Kevin Hanover and his talented marketing team. Merloyd Lawrence, the editor of my previous three books, got this project rolling—thanks Merloyd!

Christine Marra moves a book through production with the efficiency of a field general. Kudos to her team: Iris Bass (copy editing), Josephine Mariea Moore (proofreading), and Donna Riggs (indexing). The elegant interior design is courtesy of Jane Raese.

To understand Antietam, it's essential to visit the battlefield and surrounding area. I had the good fortune to accompany a number of excellent guides for tours of Antietam National Battlefield. Walking the Cornfield and Bloody Lane with Bill Sagle was revelatory, akin to time traveling back to September 17, 1862. Jim Buchanan devoted four hours to minutely detailing the West Woods action (a portion of the battle that only lasted about half an hour in real time) and in the process brought it vividly to life. Marty Pritchett, who served with the Coast Guard, lent a discerning, real-world perspective to the fighting at the Burnside Bridge and beyond (that final, fateful hillside). These three guides read portions of my manuscript, and were generous and thoughtful throughout the project in fielding my many questions.

Other guides helped me by illuminating other facets of the battle. To gain an understanding of the vast medical emergency that followed Antietam, I had the pleasure of a tour with Dr. Gordon Dammann. Dammann is founder of the superb National Museum of Civil War Medicine in Frederick, Maryland. I accompanied eminent historian John Schildt for a powerful "Footsteps of Lincoln" tour. Todd Harrington, a photographer skilled with circa-1862 equipment, took me on an enlightening (pun intended) "Footsteps of Alexander Gardner" tour. Vernell Doyle, president of the Sharpsburg Historical Society, led me on a memorable walk through the town, which still retains so much from that September day. When this book was just a grain of an idea, Gary Rohrer got me started with an excellent overview tour of the battlefield.

Thanks as well to park ranger Matt Penrod for the captivating tour of Arlington, Robert E. Lee's mansion, and to Erin Carlson Mast and Joan Cummins for showing me around Lincoln's cottage at the Soldiers' Home, a deeply poignant place.

I wish to thank Emma Winter Zeig, my research assistant, for chasing down some fascinating, difficult-to-find details. Greg Bresiger, my neighbor, provided research help and valuable insight regarding Lord Palmerston, Copperheads, and European interference during the Civil War (This is stuff he just happens to know about, the way other people know about the Mets or microbrews.) I appreciate the support of Biographers International and my local offshoot of this organization, the Gotham Biographers Group.

Thanks to Sylvia Charlesworth and Jerry Kressman for their unwavering belief in me. Thanks Mom and Dad, who went above and beyond their parental duties (unconditional love and all) to read my manuscript and offer helpful suggestions. And first, last, always, boundless appreciation to my wife, Liza Charlesworth, and my twin sons, Dash and Theo.

# INDEX